MILLIE SNYDER'S Lean & Luscious

3RD EDITION

Over 375 delicious, easy and good-for-you recipes enjoyed by families for over 25 years.

MILLIE SNYDER

The popular cookbook series that sold over one million copies is back!

Headline Books, Inc.
Terra Alta, WV

Lean & Luscious

by Millie Snyder

This book has been adapted from the *Lean & Luscious* series, originally co-authored by Bobbie Hinman and Millie Snyder.

The recipe the children are enjoying on the cover is the Italian Veggie Bake on page 164.

To order additional copies of this book or to contact the author:

Headline Books, Inc.
P O Box 52
Terra Alta, WV 26764
www.HeadlineBooks.com
800-570-5951

www.LeanAndLuscious.com

ISBN-13: 978-0-938467-73-1

Library of Congress Control Number: 2013938675

Snyder, Millie
Lean & luscious 3rd edition by Millie Snyder
p.cm.
Includes index
ISBN 978-0-938467-73-1
1. Low fat recipes. 2. Quick and easy cooking. 3. Reducing diets—Recipes. 4. Weight loss.

PRINTED IN THE UNITED STATES OF AMERICA

This book is dedicated to all of the wonderful people who are striving for a healthier lifestyle. Thanks for making my books a part of your life.

Enjoy and be healthy!

Special Thanks

There are so many people I want to thank for their support in getting this edition of Lean & Luscious off the ground and back into the hands of loyal fans and new readers alike.

Thank you to all of my wonderful grandchildren—Allison, Jackson, Holden, Aubrey and Hunter—for the pure happiness, endless laughter and unconditional love you bring into my life every day; it's for you and your generation that I hope my message of health and happiness shines through the brightest.

Thank you to all my former Weight Watchers colleagues and those members in West Virginia, Ohio, Kentucky, and Tennessee, for embracing a delicious and healthy approach to weight loss and for giving me the opportunity to thrive as a businesswoman and agent of change.

Thank you to Barbra Streisand, for being my inspiration for so many years and for showing me dreams can come true if you work hard and believe in yourself.

Thank you to all those at The Weinstein Organization—Janelle, Mark, Ashley, Corrie, Kelly, and Alexa—for embracing my vision and helping me breathe new life into the *Lean & Luscious* brand.

Finally, thank you to my readers – for all the people who have enjoyed the books over the years, and all the people who are buying the book for the first time. I'm so happy to share with you this new and updated edition! You will love the recipes. And I am so overjoyed that I can contribute to this quality of eating more healthfully.

Important

This book is not intended as a promotion or recommendation for any specific diet, nor as a substitute for your physician's advice. Its purpose is to show you how you and your family can follow a healthy balanced diet and still enjoy tasty meals.

Contents

Foreword

Obesity has become a serious health problem in most developed countries. Such an increase in weight gain in many people has probably been caused by reduced levels of physical activity and by changes in the patterns of food intake.

While the relevance of nutrition to the occurrence of cancer and heart disease is evident, important issues remain to be solved and further studies are needed. However, it is clear that eating a diet that is high in calories, fat, and sugars and being overweight can be harmful for one's general health. A poor diet appears to play a role in increasing the risk of cancer, heart disease, and diabetes. In addition, a poor diet may lead to importance and increased problems with arthritis. Thus, there is ample reason to live a healthy lifestyle by controlling one's weight and fat intake.

Millie Snyder has updated her wonderful book entitled *Lean & Luscious*. In addition to providing introductory tips on lowering calories, fats, and cholesterol, the recipes in this book are delicious and easy to prepare. Each recipe gives the number of calories and the content of sodium, cholesterol, proteins, carbohydrates, and fats. This is important because it makes compliance with a diet easier. The recipes provided in this book are not only therapeutic and healthful but also cost-effective and perfect for busy families.

Steven J. Jubelirer, M.D.
Senior Scientist, Charleston
Area Medical Center (CAMC)
Education and Research Institute
Clinical Professor of Medicine/Oncology
West Virginia University, Charleston Division

To My Dear Readers,

In May of 2010 I was a guest speaker for Women's Empowerment in Beckley, West Virginia. I was talking about following your dreams and the importance of not letting anyone talk you out of them. When I mentioned I was the author of *Lean & Luscious*, one woman in the audience let out a delightful little scream. After my presentation, I had the opportunity to talk with the woman who cheered the words "lean and luscious." She told me she had each book in the series and they were her favorite cookbooks. It reminded me why I wrote *Lean & Luscious* in the first place: I love to help people take control of their lives.

Forty-seven years ago I made what was a painful lifestyle and personal commitment to change the way I used and abused food in my life. Though I was full of fear and doubt, I decided that there was only one person in this world who could help me. And that person was me. I joined Weight Watchers in Baltimore, MD.

My eventual victory over self-destructive eating habits made me determined to help other people make positive changes in their own lives. I was the Area Director for Weight Watchers in West Virginia for 44 years, and I was able to help thousands of people every year do just that.

Each one of my delicious, easy-to-prepare, *Lean & Luscious* recipes provides a roadmap, showing you the way back to your own kitchen. Using readily available and affordable ingredients, this book will teach you how to economically cook the foods you love with care and simplicity. You'll see for yourself how easy and enjoyable it is to live healthier while eating the food you and your family love.

That's why I'm thrilled to bring *Lean & Luscious* back!

I am also very excited that you and I are both helping to make a change in this world together. I've been given so much in life, so I want to give back.

1. Love and respect yourself
2. Eat smart
3. Be kind to everyone

(Mix well and serve generously!)

Warm Regards,
Millie

Introduction: About My Book

Lean & Luscious was originally created in 1985 as a collection of recipes designed to allow you to enjoy your favorite foods without adding unnecessary calories or fat. As so often happens, times and ideas change and knowledge is gained. Huge strides have been made in the fields of health and nutrition. In order to keep up with the many scientific breakthroughs, I have adapted my cooking styles, making use of the latest information on health and diet.

I am very excited about this 3rd Edition. My recipes are in-line with what we know about food today. The ingredients I use support a diet that emphasizes cooking with foods in their most natural form. I wholly support the use of organic foods, meats from free-range animal farms and shopping at local markets whenever possible, because the quality of your meal is directly affected by the quality of the ingredients you use.

All my recipes use readily available, affordable ingredients that can be found at anyone's local grocery store. Organic and free-range ingredients have come down in price because demand for them has dramatically increased. Eating quality food is actually an economical approach, because by improving your health you can potentially lower costly healthcare expenses.

It is my wish that using these recipes will help you to create a new, healthful way of cooking and eating. My quick, easy-to-prepare dishes will transform ordinary meals into culinary delights, while teaching you and your family new and healthier eating habits.

For each recipe, I have included calorie counts, as well as updated, complete nutritional breakdown. I hope that you will use this information to prepare satisfying meals that are good for you and your family. In transforming and creating my recipes, I have always tried to keep in mind the fact that foods have their own built-in flavors. I have used spices to enhance, not hide, these flavors. I have attempted to bring out the best in food by eliminating the use of excess sugar, salt, and fats and replacing them with unique, flavorful combinations of extracts and spices. My goal is to make foods taste so good that this enlightened way of eating can easily become a way of life.

The Elimination of Obesogenic

This edition of *Lean & Luscious* is dedicated to eradicating the word obesogenic. Defined by The Merriam-Webster Dictionary as *promoting excessive weight gain; producing obesity*, it's a relatively new word in the dictionary, referring to conditions that lead people to become excessively fat, including eating too much of the wrong things and not getting enough exercise.

The word lives in the shadows cast by the nation's obesity epidemic, a terrifying public health crisis affecting adults and children of all ages, in every income bracket, and in every community. We simply can't afford to have this word in our vocabulary – we can't allow anything obesogenic to thrive in our households, communities, and country, especially when there's so much we can do to keep obesity and all of its related health risks at bay.

Our environments make it tremendously difficult to make the right choices. Each day we have to travel through an obstacle course around the temptation that surrounds us. When you fill up your car with gas, you can easily enter the service station to fill up on frozen sodas and gigantic candy bars. It's tough to decline the donuts and bagel trays at the office, not to mention the three o'clock cookie break. Even our children have come to expect fast food and sugary snacks when under the care of their friends' parents or babysitters.

We have the power to change so that we don't need a word like obesogenic to describe the choices we make!

This book is a tool to combat the obesity epidemic, and I hope it inspires you to take your health into your hands—and heart. By embracing all that it means to lead a Lean & Luscious lifestyle, you can become a force to remove the word obesogenic from our vocabulary. By learning how to prepare and enjoy healthy, delicious foods – and managing your weight naturally – you won't need a word like obesogenic to describe your way of life. And by loving and taking care of yourself and your family, you're taking responsibility for your little corner of the world and ensuring the word obesogenic doesn't describe it.

Remember, as individuals we can fix what we can and get to the bottom of what it means to nourish ourselves from the inside out so we're living the vibrant lives I believe we're all meant to live; together, we can fight against all things obesogenic and improve the quality of our lives for generations to come!

What Is a Balanced Diet?

Throughout this book I refer to a "balanced diet." This term has changed over the years and now has come to mean a diet low in calories and high in food quality. Health professionals feel that our diet should be rich in fruits and vegetables, whole grains, lean proteins and Omega-3 fatty acids such as those found in salmon or olive oil.

Health professionals generally recommend that we reduce or eliminate foods containing saturated and trans fats, cholesterol (no more than 300 mg/day), processed sugars and added salt. Typically these are found in fried foods, commercial baked goods and processed foods. The more "shelf stable" a food is, the more overly-processed it tends to be.

One of the newer components of maintaining a balanced diet is addressing the total amount of calories in our diet. There is no single guideline for caloric intake that applies to everyone. To maintain body weight in a healthy range you need to balance calories from foods and beverages with calories expended. If you lead a sedentary lifestyle you will require fewer calories from your diet than someone else who is very active. To prevent gradual weight gain over time, make small decreases in food and beverage calories and increase your physical activity.

Carbohydrates were demonized in recent history, but the type of carbs we eat can make all the difference. Choose fiber-rich fruits, vegetables and whole grains often. These high-fiber foods are also relatively low in calories, so if you plan your diet around fresh fruits and vegetables, along with whole grains and beans, and use smaller portions of meats and dairy products, it becomes easy to eat fewer calories. Isn't it nice that most of the foods that are low in fat are high in fiber and also low in calories?

Sugar is high in calories and low in nutrients and should therefore be used sparingly. In all of my recipes I have kept the use of sugar to a minimum. I have found that you can greatly reduce the amount of sugar in a recipe and, by increasing the vanilla extract, still achieve delicious, sweet results. (There is controversy surrounding the safety of artificial sweeteners, and, wanting my recipes to be as wholesome as possible, I have chosen not to use any artificial sweeteners in these recipes.)

Although sodium is a mineral that occurs naturally in many foods, most of the sodium in the American diet comes from table salt and from sodium that is added to processed foods and beverages. Although some sodium is essential to our health, the recommendation from many health professionals is that we limit our daily sodium intake to less than 2,300 milligrams, or about 1 teaspoon of salt. In my recipes, I have used herbs and spices in place of most of the salt, and I always recommend tasting the finished product and then adding salt only if necessary. I also choose low-sodium or salt-free canned foods whenever available and recommend rinsing canned beans to remove excess salt.

Can Food *Really* Be Both *Lean & Luscious*?

Growing up in typical American homes, I always thought that meats had to be smothered with sauce or gravy in order to taste good. I thought that desserts had to be laden with butter and sugar if they were to have any flavor at all. And, like so many people, I thought that "low-fat" meant "low flavor." Faced with the awesome responsibility of changing my own and my family's eating habits, I was determined to keep the flavor while eliminating fat and calories.

The good news is that it works. Over the years, I have found 3 basic ways to accomplish this goal:

1. Choose healthful cooking methods: Eliminate deep-frying and sautéing in lots of butter and oil. Healthier cooking methods include steaming, broiling, grilling, poaching, and stir-frying.

2. Rely on herbs, spices, and extracts for flavor. Experiment with the vast selection of flavors that will enhance your food without adding fat.

3. Substitute high-fat ingredients with their low-fat counterparts.

Following are some basic substitutions to guide you.

BASIC SUBSTITUTIONS

Instead of	*Use*
Whole eggs	2 egg whites in place of each egg, or use egg substitutes
Whole milk	Skim milk or 1% milk (no higher)
Cream	Evaporated skim milk or plain nonfat yogurt
Sour cream	Fat-free sour cream or plain nonfat yogurt or plain Greek yogurt
Ice cream	Reduced-fat or nonfat ice cream or frozen yogurt
Whipped cream	Vanilla nonfat yogurt (as a dessert topping)
Cream cheese	Fat-free cream cheese or Neufchatel
Cheese	Reduced-fat or fat-free cheese
Mayonnaise	Reduced-calorie mayonnaise

Butter	Margarine that lists a liquid oil as the first ingredient, or vegetable oil (however, all are high in fat and should be used sparingly).
Vegetable oil	An oil with a high amount of monounsaturated fat, such as olive oil or canola oil Nonstick cooking spray for greasing pans
Salad dressings with lots of oil	Replace half the oil with water or fruit juice
High-fat marinades	Nonfat or low-fat salad dressings
Sugar	Use half the amount called for (this works in most recipes except cookies)
White rice	Brown rice or other whole grains like Bulgur, Quinoa, and whole wheat couscous
All-purpose flour	Replace half with whole wheat flour
French fries	Baked potatoes (with a low-fat topping such as plain Greek yogurt or nonfat yogurt and chopped chives)
Meat in casseroles	Replace *half* with beans, trim visible fat, remove poultry skin

How to Use the Nutritional Information Found in This Book

Nutritional facts help us make more informed choices about the foods we eat. No single meal can give you a complete daily nutritional balance, and eating the same menu each week will make you bored and frustrated. Food should be a celebration of life, not a regiment!

This information allows you to plan your meals more effectively so you don't get too much or too little of anything, and enables you to eat a variety of tastes and textures without trepidation.

After each recipe, you will find the nutritional information for that particular recipe.

Here's an example:

1. Calories 250

2. Total Fat 12g
   Cholesterol 30mg
   Sodium 470mg

3. Total Carbohydrate 31g
   Dietary Fiber 0g

4. Protein 5g

1. Calories: Calories provide the measure of how much energy you get from a serving of this food. A general guideline to calories per serving:
   - 40 calories is low
   - 100 calories is moderate
   - 400 calories or more is high

2. Fat, Cholesterol and Sodium: These are the nutrients you want to limit, however remember to make a distinction between "good" fats found in fish and soy products, and "bad" fats found in animal meat. Good fats can actually help lower your cholesterol, lower inflammation, and improve brain function in young children. High cholesterol and sodium may increase your risk of certain chronic diseases, some cancers, or high blood pressure.

3. Carbohydrates and Dietary Fiber: Most Americans don't get enough dietary fiber in their diets, but we get plenty of "empty carbs" (poor quality) from low-grain breads and processed sugar. A good measure of quality carbohydrates should be from higher amounts of dietary fiber. Diets rich in dietary fiber, particularly soluble fiber, have the added benefit of being "stomach slowers". This means that the food takes longer to breakdown and exit the stomach, which makes you feel fuller longer and helps you cut down on snacking in between meals. Soluble fiber also helps your body naturally regulate your blood sugar levels and can help reduce your risk for diabetes.

4. Protein: All the cells of your body contain protein and it is an essential nutrient. But the right type of protein can make all the difference in your health. Emphasize plant sources of protein such as beans, lentils, soy and unsalted nuts. Eat fish (fish with gills rather than shellfish) often. Meat, poultry and dairy products should be lean or low fat. Protein has 4 calories per gram, and you should get 10% to 35% of your daily calories from protein.

It is important to note that the nutritional analysis may vary slightly depending on the brands of food that are used. I hope that you will use this information to help you to select recipes and to balance your diet in a delicious and healthful way.

Butter Versus Margarine

While most of my recipes in this book recommend margarine, you can substitute butter for any of these based on your preference.

Not so long ago, many people used margarine instead of butter because it was thought to be more heart-healthy. That's why I included it in most of my recipes. We have come to learn that all fats and cholesterols are not created equal and they are not as unhealthy as we once believed. In fact, there is room for both saturated and unsaturated fats – and even cholesterol – in a healthy, balanced diet.

Here are some facts for you to consider:

Butter comes from animal fat, so it's naturally high in saturated fat and cholesterol. Most of us (including me!) think butter tastes better and when used in moderation it's a delicious addition to almost any meal! Plus, it usually yields superior results in baking because it's not as likely as oil-based fats to be damaged by heat and cooking.

Tip: To enjoy butter with less saturated fat and cholesterol, you might want to try using whipped butter or butter blended with canola or olive oil – just keep in mind you might not get the best results with baking.

Margarine is made with cholesterol-free vegetable oil and is higher in unsaturated, or "good," fats than butter. Yet today, we know that some margarines, particularly the more solid varieties you'll find in stick form, contain trans fats that have been shown to decrease HDL (the "good" cholesterol) and raise LDL (the "bad" cholesterol) in some people.

Tip: If you elect to cook or season your food with margarine, choose soft or liquid margarines – usually found stored in a tub – because these are typically free of trans fats.

Suggested Menus

Breakfast

South Sea Salad, page 23
Toasted Bagel with Jam
Orange Juice

Half Melon
15-Minute Muesli, page 145
Whole Wheat Toast

Cold Cereal with Sliced Banana
Skim Milk
Cinnamon Yogurt Muffin, page 191

Broiled Grapefruit Delight, page 207
Scrambled Eggs Florentine, page 40
Maple Bran Muffin, page 192

Orange Upside-Down French Toast, page 53
Fresh Fruit Cup

Lunch

"Pretend" Salmon Salad on whole wheat pita
with lettuce & tomato, page 63
Apricot-Almond Cranberry Sauce, page 204

French Onion Soup, page 12
Tuna Mousse, page 2
Crackers
Baked Pears, page 202

Tossed Salad with Fat-Free Dressing
Bean and Cheese Quesadillas, page 101
Fresh Fruit Salad

Barbecue Turkey Loaf on whole wheat bread
with lettuce and tomato, page 92
Fresh Fruit
Tossed Salad with Cheesy Herb Dressing, page 35

Spinach Frittata, page 42
Whole Wheat Bread
Half Melon

Dinner

Tossed Salad with Dijon Vinaigrette, page 35
Snapper Creole, page 61
Brown Rice
Golden Carrot Loaf, page 152
Apple Crisp, page 260

Sherried Mushroom Soup, page 16
Chinese Pepper Steak, page 119
Fried Rice, page 139
Steamed Green Beans
Baked Pineapple Tapioca, page 205

Tossed Salad with fat-free dressing
Bean Stroganoff, page 104
Yolk-Free Noodles
Steamed Green Beans
Company Fruit Compote, page 198

Cucumbers Dijon on bed of lettuce, page 29
Golden Crowned Chicken, page 79
Steamed Broccoli
Favorite Rice Casserole, page 140
Mixed Fruit Sherbet, page 229

Tossed Salad with Creamy Italian Dressing, page 36
Pacific Pasta Sauce with Salmon over Pasta, page 131
French Bread
Orange Fruit Cups, page 207

Notes:

Appetizers, Dips, and Spreads

Used as party foods, meal-starters, or delicious snacks, the selections in this chapter are meant to whet your appetite or simply offer some easy "munchies."

I've kept the fat content as low as possible by using only low-fat and nonfat dairy products. However, it's important to remember that dairy products contain no fiber. For that reason, I recommend using fresh fruits and vegetables as "dippers" and whole grain, low-fat crackers, or breads for my spreads. It's important to note that most packaged chips, often used for dipping, are usually fried and are very high in fat.

Also, remember that many salads and fruits make ideal appetizers, so be sure to check the other chapters.

Clams Casino

Entertaining is so elegant with this delectable appetizer. If you can get some real clam shells and scrub them well, you can serve this special dish right in the shells. There are also a variety of ceramic shells available in specialty shops.

Makes 8 servings

3 10-ounce cans minced clams, drained (This will yield about 16 ounces of clams.) (Reserve ½ cup of the clam juice.)
¾ cup dry breadcrumbs
2 tablespoons minced onion flakes
2 teaspoons dried parsley flakes
½ teaspoon dried oregano
¼ teaspoon garlic powder
¼ teaspoon salt
1 tablespoon plus 1 teaspoon grated Parmesan cheese
Lemon wedges

Preheat oven to 375°. Spray 8 clam shells (either real or ceramic) with nonstick cooking spray. In a medium bowl, combine all ingredients (including clam juice), except Parmesan cheese and lemon wedges. Mix well. Divide mixture evenly and spoon into prepared shells. Sprinkle with Parmesan cheese. Place shells on a baking sheet. Bake 25 minutes, until hot and bubbly. Serve with lemon wedges.

Per Serving: Calories 133, Total Fat 1.9g, Cholesterol 39mg, Sodium 345mg, Total Carbohydrate 11.5g, Dietary Fiber 0.3g, Protein 17.3g

Tuna Mousse

This elegant-looking mousse can also be made with salmon. It makes a beautiful and very tasty appetizer that is an ideal party centerpiece. I've also served it with crusty bread as a light lunch dish.

Makes 12 servings (2½ tablespoons each serving)

1 envelope unflavored gelatin
½ cup water
1 8-ounce can salt-free (or regular) tomato sauce
1 6 ½-ounce can tuna (packed in water), drained
2/3 cup low-fat (1%) cottage cheese
2 tablespoons reduced-calorie mayonnaise
1 tablespoon sugar
¼ teaspoon pepper
⅛ teaspoon salt
½ cup finely chopped celery
2 tablespoons finely chopped onion

Sprinkle gelatin over water in a small bowl and let soften a few minutes. In a small saucepan, over medium heat, heat tomato sauce to boiling. Reduce heat to low and stir in gelatin mixture. Heat, stirring, for 1 minute. In a blender, combine tuna, cottage cheese, mayonnaise, sugar, pepper, and salt. Add tomato sauce mixture. Blend until smooth. Stir in celery and onion. Pour mixture into a 3-cup mold. Chill until firm. Unmold to serve.

Per Serving: Calories 54, Total Fat 1.1g, Cholesterol 8mg, Sodium 156mg, Total Carbohydrate 3.5g, Dietary Fiber 0.4g, Protein 7.8g

Chesapeake Bay Crab Puffs

My unusual version of this normally deep-fried delicacy is actually a crab-filled muffin. It can be served alongside a tossed salad as an appetizer or a delicious light lunch.

Makes 4 muffins

½ cup liquid egg substitute
1 slice whole wheat bread (1-ounce slice), crumbled
⅓ cup nonfat dry milk
⅓ cup water
1 tablespoon plus 1 teaspoon all-purpose flour
1 tablespoon canola oil
1½ teaspoons Worcestershire sauce
1 teaspoon lemon juice
1 teaspoon baking powder
½ teaspoon baking soda
½ teaspoon seafood seasoning (such as Old Bay)
½ cup crabmeat (4 ounces)

Preheat oven to 350°. Spray 4 muffin cups with nonstick cooking spray. In a blender, combine all ingredients, except crabmeat. Blend until smooth. Combine half of this mixture with the crabmeat in a small bowl. Mix well. Divide crab mixture evenly into prepared muffin cups. Pour remaining batter evenly over crab mixture. Spray the tops of the muffins with nonstick cooking spray. Bake 12 to 15 minutes, or until firm and lightly browned. Cool in pan 5 minutes, then serve.

Per Serving: Calories 150, Total Fat 5.2g, Cholesterol 17mg, Sodium 832mg, Total Carbohydrate 11.5g, Dietary Fiber 0.6g, Protein 13.9g

Spinach Cheese Balls

Great for parties, these cheesy cornmeal balls can be made a day ahead and refrigerated until it's time to bake them.

Makes 12 serving (3 cheese balls each serving)

2 teaspoons canola oil
½ cup chopped onion
1 10-ounce package frozen chopped spinach, thawed and drained well
½ cup liquid egg substitute
1½ ounces shredded reduced-fat Cheddar cheese (⅓ cup)
¼ cup grated Parmesan cheese
¼ cup bottled fat-free Italian dressing
¼ teaspoon garlic powder
2 teaspoons baking powder
¾ cup yellow cornmeal (4½ ounces)

Heat oil in a large nonstick skillet over medium-high heat. Add onion and cook until golden, stirring frequently. Remove from heat. Stir in spinach. In a small bowl, combine egg substitute, both cheeses, Italian dressing and garlic powder. Mix well. Stir into spinach. Stir baking powder into cornmeal and add to spinach mixture, mixing thoroughly. Place mixture in a bowl and chill several hours or overnight.

Shape chilled mixture into balls, about 1½ inches in diameter. Preheat oven to 375°. Place cheese balls on a nonstick baking sheet. Bake 10 to 12 minutes, until bottoms are lightly browned. Serve hot.

Per Serving: Calories 72, Total Fat 2.2g, Cholesterol 3mg, Sodium 245mg, Total Carbohydrate 8.7g, Dietary Fiber 1.3g, Protein 4.4g

Onion Dip

A take-off on the ever-popular party dip, this version has all of the flavor with only a trace of the fat. I've replaced the sour cream with nonfat Greek yogurt, making a dip that's still as creamy and delicious as ever.

Makes 8 servings (3 tablespoons each serving)

1½ cups nonfat Greek yogurt
2 tablespoons minced onion flakes
2 packets low-sodium instant beef-flavored broth mix

In a small bowl, combine all ingredients, mixing well. Chill several hours to blend flavors. Serve with vegetable dippers.

Per Serving: Calories 31, Total Fat 0.1g, Cholesterol 1mg ,Sodium 55mg, Total Carbohydrate 4.5g, Dietary Fiber 0.1g, Protein 2.9g

Party Clam Dip

A favorite party dish goes low-fat and no one will ever guess! Garnished with chopped chives, either fresh or dried, and served with vegetables or melba toast rounds, this makes a wonderful party dish.

Makes 12 servings (2½ tablespoons each serving)

1½ cups plain nonfat yogurt*
1 10 ½ -ounce can minced clams, drained (This will yield about 6 ounces of clams.)
1½ tablespoons minced onion flakes
1½ teaspoons Worcestershire sauce
¼ teaspoon salt
¼ teaspoon pepper
⅛ teaspoon garlic powder

In a small bowl, combine all ingredients. Mix well. Chill several hours to blend flavors. Serve with vegetable dippers. **If desired, you can substitute nonfat sour cream for the yogurt.*

Per Serving: Calories 39, Total Fat 0.4g, Cholesterol 9mg, Sodium 95mg, Total Carbohydrate 3.7g, Dietary Fiber 0.1g, Protein 5.5g

Yogurt Cheese

This creamy, cream cheese-like spread can also be made with flavored yogurt, such as vanilla or lemon. It also works with yogurt containing fruit. Just stir the fruit into the yogurt first. You can use the cheese as is or in place of cream cheese in your favorite recipe. (This process will not work with yogurt that contains gelatin.)

Makes 8 servings (2 tablespoons each serving)

2 cups nonfat yogurt

Line a colander with several layers of cheesecloth (or you can use a coffee filter placed in a strainer). Fill with yogurt. Place colander in a pan to catch the drippings. Refrigerate 24 hours. Remove cheese and place in a small bowl. Refrigerate until needed.

Per Serving: Calories 34, Total Fat 0.1g, Cholesterol 1mg, Sodium 47mg, Total Carbohydrate 4.7g, Dietary Fiber 0g, Protein 3.5g

Crab and Cheese Ball

You can either use the yogurt cheese on page 5 or fat-free cream cheese in this wonderful spread that has a lively taste with a bit of a kick. It looks lovely garnished with fresh chives or parsley.

Makes 8 servings (3 tablespoons each serving)

1 cup yogurt cheese (see page 5)*
½ cup crabmeat (4 ounces)
1 tablespoon lemon juice
1 tablespoon prepared horseradish
2 teaspoons minced onion flakes
½ teaspoon dried chives
⅛ teaspoon salt
Dash of Worcestershire sauce

Combine all ingredients in a bowl. Blend well with a fork. Chill at least 1 hour, until firm. Shape mixture into a ball or log. Chill. To serve, spread on crackers or vegetable dippers. **If desired, you can substitute fat-free cream cheese for the yogurt cheese.*

Per Serving: Calories 35, Total Fat 1.1g, Cholesterol 8mg, Sodium 83mg, Total Carbohydrate 1.7g, Dietary Fiber 0.1g, Protein 4.5g

Three-Cheese Spread

A tantalizing blend of flavors awaits the cheese lover in this delicious spread.

Makes 8 servings (3 tablespoons each serving)

1 cup yogurt cheese (see page 5)*
½ cup reduced-fat Cheddar cheese (2 ounces)
⅓ cup blue cheese, crumbled (2 ounces)
⅛ teaspoon garlic powder
Few drops of bottled hot pepper sauce

Combine all ingredients in a bowl. Mix with a fork until well blended. Line a small bowl with plastic wrap. Spoon cheese into bowl and press down firmly. Chill. To serve, invert cheese onto a serving plate and remove plastic wrap. Spread cheese on crackers or celery stalks. **If desired, you can substitute fat-free cream cheese for the yogurt cheese.*

Per Serving: Calories 64, Total Fat 3.6g, Cholesterol 8mg, Sodium 169mg, Total Carbohydrate 1.4g, Dietary Fiber 0g, Protein 6.5g

Chili-Cheddar Cheese Spread

Spread on crackers or sliced veggies, this is a great Sunday afternoon football snack.

Makes 12 servings (2½ tablespoons each serving)

1 cup yogurt cheese (see page 5)*
4 ounces shredded reduced-fat Cheddar cheese (1 cup)
2 tablespoons very finely minced onion
2 tablespoons bottled chili sauce
1 teaspoon dry mustard
¼ teaspoon garlic powder

In a large bowl, combine all ingredients. Mix with a fork until well blended. Chill several hours to blend flavors. **If desired, you can substitute fat-free cream cheese for the yogurt cheese.*

Per Serving: Calories 38, Total Fat 1.5g, Cholesterol 3mg, Sodium 108mg, Total Carbohydrate 1.7g, Dietary Fiber 0.2g, Protein 4.5g

Mexican Pinto Spread

This spicy spread is not only delicious on crackers, but it also makes a wonderful sandwich. Either way, its flavor is enhanced by the addition of fresh, sliced tomatoes.

Makes 8 servings (3 tablespoons each serving)

¼ cup chopped onion
2 cloves garlic, coarsely chopped
1 1-pound can pinto beans, rinsed and drained (This will yield approximately 9 ounces of cooked beans.)
1 teaspoon vinegar
1 teaspoon chili powder
½ teaspoon ground cumin
½ teaspoon dried oregano

Place onion and garlic in a food processor. Process with a steel blade until finely chopped. Add beans, vinegar, and spices. Process until smooth. (A blender can be used, but you will need to blend the mixture in small batches and be careful not to let the mixture get soupy.) Spoon mixture into a bowl and chill thoroughly.

Per Serving: Calories 32, Total Fat 0.4g, Cholesterol 0mg, Sodium 97mg, Total Carbohydrate 5.9g, Dietary Fiber 1.7g, Protein 1.7g

Caraway Cheese Spread

An adaptation of an Eastern European recipe, this unusual dish can be spread on thin slices of dark party rye or on crackers, and it also makes a tasty stuffing for celery sticks.

Makes 8 servings (3 tablespoons each serving)

1½ cups nonfat ricotta cheese
1 tablespoon Dijon mustard
3 tablespoons very finely minced onion
2 teaspoons caraway seeds
2 teaspoons paprika

In a small bowl, combine all ingredients, mixing well. Chill several hours or overnight, to blend flavors.

Per Serving: Calories 44, Total Fat 0.6g, Cholesterol 8mg, Sodium 49mg, Total Carbohydrate 5.2g, Dietary Fiber 0.6g, Protein 4.3g

Salmon Paté

This elegant spread is delicious on crackers or on cucumber slices. For a pretty presentation, chill the paté in a bowl that is lined with plastic wrap, then invert it onto a serving plate and peel off the plastic.

Makes 8 servings (2 tablespoons each serving)

8 ounces drained canned salmon
2 teaspoons lemon juice
1 teaspoon dill weed
½ teaspoon dried tarragon
½ teaspoon onion powder
¼ teaspoon garlic powder
⅛ teaspoon pepper

Combine all ingredients in a food processor. With a steel blade, process until smooth. Spoon into a bowl. Chill several hours or overnight.

Per Serving: Calories 40, Total Fat 1.3g, Cholesterol 23mg, Sodium 113mg, Total Carbohydrate 0.5g, Dietary Fiber 0.2g, Protein 6.5g

Stuffed Figs with Orange-Cheese Filling

These pretty confections make such an attractive dish. They can be served as an appetizer, dessert, snack, or even breakfast fare.

Makes 12 servings (2 figs each serving)

24 large dried figs (¾-ounce each)
½ cup fat-free cream cheese
1 tablespoon sugar
¼ teaspoon orange extract
24 walnut pieces (about 1 ounce)
Ground cinnamon

Place figs in a large saucepan. Add water to cover and bring to a boil over medium heat. Cook, uncovered, 5 minutes, or until figs are just tender. Drain and cool. Then chill several hours. Combine cream cheese, sugar, and orange extract in a bowl. Mix until smooth. Chill several hours.

To assemble, slice the top (stem end) off of each fig and open each one up, using your finger or the back of a spoon. Spoon 1 teaspoon of cheese mixture into each fig, mounding it slightly. Top each one with a piece of walnut. Sprinkle very lightly with cinnamon. Serve right away or chill several hours, or overnight, until serving time.

Per Serving: Calories 149, Total Fat 2.1g, Cholesterol 1mg, Sodium 57mg, Total Carbohydrate 29.7g, Dietary Fiber 5.3g, Protein 3g

Chocolate Ricotta Spread

This unusual, sweet spread makes a great appetizer when served with thin apple or pear slices. It can also be served as a light, refreshing dessert.

Makes 4 servings (2 tablespoons each serving)

½ cup part-skim ricotta cheese
1 tablespoon sugar
2 teaspoons cocoa (unsweetened)
½ teaspoon vanilla extract
¼ teaspoon rum or almond extract

Combine all ingredients in a small bowl. Mix well. Serve right away or chill for later serving.

Per Serving: Calories 59, Total Fat 2.5g, Cholesterol 10mg, Sodium 38mg, Total Carbohydrate 5.3g, Dietary Fiber 0.3g, Protein 3.7g

Tofu, Peanut Butter, and Banana Spread

Kids love this sweet spread. It's delicious on toast or crackers and also tastes great on apple slices. You'll have to try this one to believe it!

Makes 4 servings (2¼ tablespoons each serving)

3 ounces silken (or soft) tofu (⅓ cup)
½ medium ripe banana, mashed
1 tablespoon peanut butter (Choose one without added sugar or fat.)
2 teaspoons sugar
1 teaspoon lemon juice
1 teaspoon honey
1 teaspoon vanilla extract
Ground cinnamon

In a small bowl, combine tofu and banana. Mash with a fork or potato masher. Add remaining ingredients, except cinnamon. Mix well, then beat vigorously with a fork or wire whisk until blended. (If a creamier spread is desired, place mixture in a blender and blend just until smooth, but do not let mixture get soupy.) Chill. Before serving, mix well, then sprinkle with cinnamon.

Per Serving: Calories 76, Total Fat 2.9g, Cholesterol 0mg, Sodium 27mg, Total Carbohydrate 9.4g, Dietary Fiber 0.8g, Protein 2.8g

Soups

There's nothing like a bowl of hot soup to warm your bones and cheer your feelings. Most soups are made from stock or broth, with several choices available to you. If you prefer to make a homemade stock, by simmering chicken and/or vegetables in water along with herbs, it's important to chill the stock before using it in a soup so that the fat can be easily skimmed off the top. If you prefer to use a canned broth, choose a low-sodium variety. Remember, you can always add salt if needed. Packets of low-sodium instant broth mix can also be used, and added to the soup with the specified amount of water.

As a meal starter or as the entrée itself, these soups will prove to be delicious and satisfying—without a lot of calories, fat, or fuss.

French Onion Soup

Instead of being covered with "gobs" of cheese, this version proves to be tasty with only a sprinkling of Parmesan. It's light, simple, and very elegant. Vive la France!

Makes 4 servings (1 cup each serving)

2 teaspoons canola oil
2 cups thinly sliced onion
4 cups low-sodium beef broth (or 4 cups of water and 4 packets low-sodium instant beef-flavored broth mix)
¼ cup dry red wine
1 bay leaf
Salt and pepper to taste
2 tablespoons grated Parmesan cheese

Heat oil in a medium saucepan over medium heat. Add onions and cook until golden, stirring frequently, and separating slices into rings. Add small amounts of water if necessary (a few teaspoons at a time), to prevent sticking. (A nonstick saucepan is ideal for making this soup.) Add broth, wine, and bay leaf. Bring soup to a boil. Reduce heat to medium-low, cover, and simmer 20 minutes, stirring occasionally. Add salt and pepper to taste. Remove and discard bay leaf. Spoon soup into serving bowls and sprinkle each serving with Parmesan cheese, using 1½ teaspoons for each serving.

Per Serving: Calories 79, Total Fat 3.3g, Cholesterol 7mg, Sodium 502mg, Total Carbohydrate 8.2g, Dietary Fiber 1.4g, Protein 4.2g

Manhattan Clam Chowder

With its exquisite blend of flavors, you'll see why this thick, chunky chowder is so popular.

Makes 6 servings (1⅓ cups each serving)

2 teaspoons canola oil
1 cup sliced onion
1 cup diced carrots
1 cup diced celery
1 1-pound can salt-free (or regular) tomatoes, chopped and drained (Reserve liquid.)
1 large, diced, cooked potato (12 ounces) (You can either bake, boil or microwave the potato.)
4 whole black peppercorns
1 bay leaf
1 tablespoon dried parsley flakes
1½ teaspoons dried thyme
¼ teaspoon dried basil
1 10 ½ ounce can clams, drained (Reserve liquid.) Yields approximately 6 ounces of clams.
Salt to taste

Heat oil in a medium saucepan over medium heat. Add onion, carrots, and celery. Cook 5 minutes, stirring frequently. Add small amounts of water as necessary (about a tablespoon at a time), to prevent sticking. Add tomatoes, potato, and spices.

In a 1-quart bowl or jar, combine reserved tomato liquid and clam liquid. Add water to make 1 quart. Pour liquid over vegetables and bring to a boil. Cover, reduce heat to medium-low, and simmer 45 minutes. Add clams. Simmer, covered, 15 minutes more. Remove and discard bay leaf before serving. Add salt to taste.

Per Serving: Calories 140, Total Fat 1.7g, Cholesterol 9mg, Sodium 316mg, Total Carbohydrate 24.8g, Dietary Fiber 3.8g, Protein 6.1g

Old-World Cabbage Soup

This delectable soup tastes just like Mom's, but it takes half the time to prepare. It tastes best when reheated, so I always plan to make it a day ahead.

Makes 8 servings (1¼ cups each serving)

2 1-pound cans salt-free (or regular) tomatoes, chopped and undrained
4 cups thinly shredded cabbage
½ cup finely chopped onion
⅓ cup lemon juice
1 cup low-sodium instant chicken- or vegetable-flavored broth (or 1 cup of water and 1 packet low-sodium instant chicken or vegetable broth mix)
2 teaspoons sugar
Salt and pepper to taste

Combine all ingredients in a large saucepan. Bring to a boil over medium heat. Reduce heat to medium-low, cover, and simmer 40 minutes, or until cabbage is tender. Add additional lemon juice or sugar to taste.

Per Serving: Calories 52, Total Fat 0.3g, Cholesterol 0mg, Sodium 32mg, Total Carbohydrate 10.3g, Dietary Fiber 2.3g, Protein 2.1g

Creamy Chicken Chowder

Cottage cheese and skim milk replace the cream in this rich-tasting chowder that's so thick and creamy, you won't believe it's so low in fat. And what a great use for leftover chicken.

Makes 4 servings (1¼ cups each serving)

1 cup sliced mushrooms
1 cup low-fat (1%) cottage cheese
1 cup skim milk
3 cups low-sodium chicken or vegetable broth (or 3 cups of water and 3 packets low-sodium instant chicken- or vegetable-flavored broth mix)
2 tablespoons dried chives
1 teaspoon paprika
⅛ teaspoon pepper
⅛ teaspoon ground nutmeg
6 ounces cooked chicken, cut into small cubes, skin discarded (1 ½ cups)

Place mushrooms in a medium saucepan over medium heat. Cook, stirring frequently, until tender, 3 to 5 minutes. Add small amounts of water if necessary (about a tablespoon at a time), to prevent sticking.

In a blender, combine cottage cheese and milk. Blend until smooth. Add to saucepan. Add remaining ingredients, except chicken. Heat over low heat, stirring constantly, until mixture just starts to boil. Add chicken. Cook, stirring, until heated through.

Per Serving: Calories 151, Total Fat 2.7g, Cholesterol 42mg, Sodium 373mg, Total Carbohydrate 6.3g, Dietary Fiber 0.3g, Protein 25.1g

Chicken Rice Soup

The dill adds a nice touch to this delicious soup that's not only warm and homey, but also easy to prepare. You can have comfort food in no time. If you store leftover cooked rice in the freezer, it's always ready for times like this.

Makes 4 servings (1¼ cups each serving)

2 teaspoons canola oil
¼ cup diced onion
½ cup diced celery
¼ cup diced carrots
4 cups low-sodium chicken broth (or 4 cups of water and 4 packets low-sodium instant chicken-flavored broth mix)
½ teaspoon poultry seasoning
¼ teaspoon dill weed
4 ounces cooked chicken, cubed, skin discarded (1 cup)
1 cup cooked rice
Salt and pepper to taste

Heat oil in a medium saucepan over medium heat. Add onion, celery, and carrots. Cook, stirring frequently, until tender, about 5 minutes. Add small amounts of water as necessary (a few teaspoons at a time), to prevent sticking. Add broth, poultry seasoning, and dill weed. Bring mixture to a boil, then reduce heat to medium-low, cover, and simmer 20 minutes. Add chicken and rice. Heat through. Add salt and pepper to taste.

Per Serving: Calories 144, Total Fat 3.8g, Cholesterol 28mg, Sodium 144mg, Total Carbohydrate 14.2g, Dietary Fiber 0.9g, Protein 13.2g

Creole Seafood Chowder

This colorful, tasty dish provides a delectable way to use leftover seafood, and it's hearty enough to be a meal in itself. It's party-perfect when garnished with fresh parsley and oyster crackers.

Makes 4 servings (1¼ cups each serving)

2 teaspoons canola oil
¼ cup each chopped onion, celery, and green bell pepper
⅔ cup low-fat (1%) cottage cheese
1 1-pound can salt-free (or regular) tomatoes, undrained
½ cup water
1 packet low-sodium instant chicken- or vegetable-flavored broth mix
½ teaspoon dried oregano
½ teaspoon dried parsley flakes
¼ teaspoon dried basil
⅛ teaspoon dried thyme
4 ounces cooked and diced fish, crab, or shrimp (or any combination of cooked seafood) (1½ cups)
Salt and pepper to taste
Dash of seafood seasoning (such as Old Bay)

Heat oil in a medium saucepan over medium heat. Add onion, celery, and green pepper. Cook, stirring frequently, until vegetables are tender, about 8 minutes. Add small amounts of water as necessary (about a tablespoon at a time) to prevent sticking.

In a blender, combine remaining ingredients, except seafood, salt, pepper, and seafood seasoning. Blend until smooth. Add to saucepan. Reduce heat to low and bring mixture to a simmer, stirring frequently. Add seafood and heat through, stirring. Add salt and pepper to taste and a dash of seafood seasoning.

Per Serving: Calories 112, Total Fat 3.1g, Cholesterol 19mg, Sodium 233mg, Total Carbohydrate 8.1g, Dietary Fiber 1.7g, Protein 13.1g

Cream of Carrot Soup

This version of a French favorite is quick and easy and much, much lower in fat than the original. Evaporated skim milk replaces the cream, and the result is still silky and rich.

Makes 6 servings (1 cup each serving)

2 teaspoons canola oil
3 cups chopped carrots
½ cup chopped onion
3½ cups low-sodium chicken or vegetable broth (or 3½ cups of water and 3 packets low-sodium instant chicken; or vegetable-flavored broth mix)
1 bay leaf
1½ cups evaporated skim milk
Salt and pepper to taste

Heat oil in a medium saucepan over medium heat. Add carrots and onion. Cook 5 minutes, stirring frequently. Add small amounts of water (about a tablespoon at a time), to prevent sticking. Add broth and bay leaf. Bring mixture to a boil, then cover, reduce heat to medium-low, and simmer 30 minutes, or until carrots are tender. Remove and discard bay leaf.

Place soup in a blender, reserving about ¼ cup of the carrot and onion. Blend until smooth. Return to saucepan and add reserved vegetables. Stir in milk. Heat through, but do not boil. Add salt and pepper to taste.

Per Serving: Calories 110, Total Fat 1.9g, Cholesterol 4mg, Sodium 158mg, Total Carbohydrate 15.4g, Dietary Fiber 2.1g, Protein 7.5g

Sherried Mushroom Soup

If your supermarket has different varieties of fresh mushrooms, you can really make an exotic-tasting soup. The splash of sherry at the end adds a wonderful, delicate flavor that really enhances this woodland vegetable.

Makes 6 servings (1 cup each serving)

2 teaspoons canola oil
1 pound fresh mushrooms, sliced
2 cups thinly sliced carrots
½ cup chopped onion
5 cups low-sodium chicken or vegetable broth (or 5 cups of water and 5 packets low-sodium instant chicken; or vegetable-flavored broth mix)
½ teaspoon dried thyme
⅛ teaspoon pepper
2 tablespoons dry sherry
Salt to taste

Heat oil in a large saucepan over medium heat. Add mushrooms, carrots, and onion. Cook, stirring frequently, 5 minutes. Add small amounts of water if necessary (about a tablespoon at a time), to prevent sticking. Add broth, thyme, and pepper. When mixture boils, reduce heat to medium-low, cover, and simmer 45 minutes, or until vegetables are tender. Remove from heat and stir in sherry and salt to taste.

Per Serving: Calories 80, Total Fat 2.3g, Cholesterol 3mg, Sodium 139mg, Total Carbohydrate 10g, Dietary Fiber 2.4g, Protein 4.7g

Garlic and White Bean Soup

Sounds exotic, doesn't it? No one will believe it only takes a few minutes to make this delectable soup. Keep canned beans on hand in the pantry and you'll be able to throw this together with only a moment's notice.

Makes 6 servings (1 cup each serving)

2 1-pound cans white kidney beans (cannellini), rinsed and drained (Yields 2 cups—¼ pounds—of cooked beans.)
3 cups low-sodium chicken or vegetable broth (or 3 cups of water and 3 packets low-sodium instant chicken- or vegetable-flavored broth mix)
2 cloves garlic, coarsely chopped
2 tablespoons dried parsley flakes
2 teaspoons dried basil
2 tablespoons grated Parmesan cheese
Salt and pepper to taste

In a blender, combine all ingredients, except salt and pepper. Blend until smooth. Pour mixture into a medium saucepan. Heat through and add salt and pepper to taste.

Per Serving: Calories 91, Total Fat 0.8g, Cholesterol 4mg, Sodium 394mg, Total Carbohydrate 13.3g, Dietary Fiber 3g, Protein 7.4g

Creamy Potato Soup

A delight served hot on a chilly day or served cold on a hot day, this versatile soup is a real taste treat. It has a thick, creamy texture that tastes a lot like real cream.

Makes 4 servings (1 cup each serving)

2 cups evaporated skim milk
1 pound cooked potatoes, peeled, diced (You can either bake, boil, or microwave the potatoes.)
2 tablespoons minced onion flakes
2 packets low-sodium instant chicken- or vegetable-flavored broth mix
¼ teaspoon celery salt
2 teaspoons margarine
Freshly ground black pepper to taste
1 teaspoon dried chives

In a medium saucepan, combine milk, potatoes, onion flakes, broth mix, and celery salt. Cook on low heat, stirring frequently, until mixture is hot. Do not boil. Remove soup from heat and stir in margarine. Spoon into serving bowls and sprinkle with pepper and dried chives.

Per Serving: Calories 236, Total Fat 2.3g, Cholesterol 4mg, Sodium 177mg, Total Carbohydrate 42g, Dietary Fiber 1.9g, Protein 12.1g

Tomato Butternut Soup

An exciting combination of flavors awaits you in this delicately spiced soup. The recipe calls for butternut squash, but any winter squash will do.

Makes 6 servings (1 cup each serving)

2 teaspoons canola oil
½ cup chopped onion
2 cloves garlic, finely chopped
2 cups butternut squash, peeled and cut into ½- to 1-inch cubes (about 9 ounces)
1 1-pound can salt-free (or regular) tomatoes, chopped and undrained
2½ cups low-sodium chicken or vegetable broth (or 2½ cups of water and 2½ packets low-sodium instant chicken- or vegetable-flavored broth mix)
2 tablespoons dried parsley flakes
1 teaspoon dried basil
⅛ teaspoon dried thyme
1 bay leaf
2 tablespoons dry sherry

Heat oil in a medium saucepan over medium heat. Add onion and garlic. Cook, stirring frequently, until onion is tender, 3 to 5 minutes. Add small amounts of water if necessary (a few teaspoons at a time) to prevent sticking. Add remaining ingredients, except sherry. Bring mixture to a boil. Reduce heat, cover, and simmer 30 minutes, or until squash is tender. Remove from heat and stir in sherry. Remove and discard bay leaf before serving.

(Optional: You can puree the soup if you want a creamier texture.)

Per Serving: Calories 77, Total Fat 1.8g, Cholesterol 2mg, Sodium 87mg, Total Carbohydrate 11.9g, Dietary Fiber 1.8g, Protein 3.1g

Notes:

Salads and Salad Dressings

Salads are so versatile. A salad can be an appetizer, a side dish, a snack, a main course, or even a dessert. Made with fruits and vegetables, salads are valuable sources of vitamins, minerals, and fiber.

To reduce the amount of fat in salads, I recommend using nonfat yogurt in place of sour cream and replacing part of the oil with fruit juice or water. The oils that I use in my recipes are monounsaturated oils, such as canola oil or olive oil. When mayonnaise is used, I specify reduced-calorie mayonnaise, which has been whipped with water to reduce the fat and calories.

It's important to note that even though some of the salads and dressings contain more than the recommended 30% of calories from fat, each serving contains only a few grams of fat. It's important to practice portion control and not smother your salads with dressing. As in restaurants, I suggest ordering dressing on the side—this can be practiced at home as well. Also, remember that the percentage of calories should be figured by the day, not the individual food, so if you eat a little more fat in one meal or one dish, you can compensate by eating less fat in the other meals or dishes. Ideally, you should evaluate your daily or weekly diet rather than single foods.

Enjoy my taste-tempting delights and delicious salads and dressings.

My Waldorf Salad

It's easy to lower the fat content of mayonnaise-based salads by doing what I've done here. I've replaced the mayonnaise with a combination of nonfat yogurt and reduced-calorie mayonnaise. It's still one of my favorite crunchy salads. (For a new taste, try tossing in a sliced banana.)

Makes 4 servings

½ cup plain nonfat yogurt
2 tablespoons reduced-calorie mayonnaise
1 teaspoon lemon juice
1 tablespoon sugar
4 small, sweet apples, unpeeled, chopped
1 cup chopped celery
2 tablespoons chopped walnuts (½ ounce)

In a medium bowl, combine yogurt, mayonnaise, lemon juice, and sugar. Mix well. Add remaining ingredients, mixing thoroughly. Chill several hours to blend flavors.

Per Serving: Calories 119, Total Fat 4g, Cholesterol 2mg, Sodium 86mg, Total Carbohydrate 18.1g, Dietary Fiber 2.4g, Protein 2.6g

Tropical Ambrosia Salad

I've replaced the usual sour cream with nonfat plain Greek yogurt and taken out most of the high-fat coconut. Yet, this cool, delicious salad retains the wonderful, refreshing flavors of the Caribbean.

Makes 4 servings

1 8-ounce can pineapple chunks or tidbits (packed in juice), drained
1 8-ounce can mandarin orange slices (packed in juice), drained
1 cup vanilla nonfat Greek yogurt
2 teaspoons shredded coconut (unsweetened)
1 teaspoon vanilla extract
¼ teaspoon coconut extract

Place pineapple and oranges in a medium bowl. In a small bowl, combine remaining ingredients, mixing well. Add to fruit, stirring until well blended. Chill.

Per Serving: Calories 118, Total Fat 1.5g, Cholesterol 2mg, Sodium 38mg, Total Carbohydrate 23g, Dietary Fiber 1.3g, Protein 3.1g

Carrot and Raisin Salad

You've probably met the high-fat cousin of this popular salad. It's offered at many salad bars and usually contains a lot more than the 2 grams of fat in each of my servings. Served alone or on a bed of greens, this is truly a tempting salad.

Makes 4 servings

2 cups finely shredded carrots
1 8-ounce can crushed pineapple (packed in juice), drained
¼ cup raisins
2 tablespoons plus 2 teaspoons reduced-calorie mayonnaise
1 tablespoon lemon juice
2 teaspoons sugar
¼ teaspoon coconut extract

Place carrots, pineapple, and raisins in a medium bowl. Toss to combine. In a small bowl or custard cup, stir together remaining ingredients. Add to carrot mixture, mixing well. Chill.

Per Serving: Calories 133, Total Fat 2g, Cholesterol 3mg, Sodium 73mg, Total Carbohydrate 27.6g, Dietary Fiber 2.8g, Protein 1.2g

South Sea Salad

This refreshing salad makes an ideal brunch dish. I like to serve it on a bed of greens, accompanied by a toasted bagel with jam. It's lovely to look at and oh-so delicious.

Makes 2 servings

1 cup low-fat (1%) cottage cheese
½ teaspoon vanilla extract
½ cup strawberries, sliced
¼ cup canned crushed pineapple (packed in juice), drained
1 teaspoon shredded coconut (unsweetened)

Combine all ingredients and mix well. Chill several hours to blend flavors.

Per Serving: Calories 126, Total Fat 2.4g, Cholesterol 5mg, Sodium 460mg, Total Carbohydrate 11.7g, Dietary Fiber 1.3g, Protein 14.5g

Cranberry Salad Mold

Not just for Thanksgiving, this colorful mold with its interesting texture provides a cool accompaniment to any dinner. Using fat free, sugar free gelatins in strawberry, cherry or whatever fruit you prefer, greatly reduces the number of calories normally found in gelatin molds.

Makes 4 servings

2 cups cranberries
1 small, sweet apple, unpeeled, chopped
½ cup canned crushed pineapple (packed in juice), drained (Reserve 2 tablespoons of the juice.)
⅓ cup sugar
1 cup water
1 6 ounce package fat free, sugar free strawberry or cherry gelatin
1 cup small ice cubes
½ cup finely chopped celery
1 teaspoon lemon extract
1 teaspoon orange extract

In a blender or food processor, combine cranberries, apple, pineapple, reserved pineapple juice, and sugar. Turn blender on and off a few times to finely chop the fruits. Follow the directions on the package of flavored gelatin and reduce ⅓ of the water used. Stir ice cubes into gelatin mixture. Stir until gelatin just begins to thicken. Remove and discard any remaining ice. Stir chopped fruit into gelatin. Add celery and extracts, mixing well. Pour mixture into a 3-cup mold. Chill until firm. Unmold to serve. (If you prefer, you can chill the mixture in a bowl and serve it right from the bowl.)

Per Serving: Calories 145, Total Fat 0.1g, Cholesterol 0mg, Sodium 17mg, Total Carbohydrate 31.8g, Dietary Fiber 3.1g, Protein 4.3g

Tangy Aspic Mold

A great lunch consists of a serving of this delicious mold alongside a scoop of low-fat cottage cheese, accompanied by a chunk of crusty French bread.

Makes 4 servings

2 tablespoons cold water
1 tablespoon lemon juice
1 envelope unflavored gelatin
2 cups tomato juice
2 tablespoons minced onion flakes
1 tablespoon firmly packed brown sugar
1 bay leaf
2 whole cloves
3 whole peppercorns
2 whole allspice
½ teaspoon celery seed
¼ teaspoon dried basil
¼ teaspoon salt
Bottled hot sauce to taste

In a small bowl, combine water and lemon juice. Sprinkle gelatin over this mixture and set aside for a few minutes to soften. In a medium saucepan, combine remaining ingredients, except hot sauce. Bring to a boil over medium heat. Reduce heat to medium-low and simmer 15 minutes. Remove from heat, strain, and discard spices. Add hot sauce to taste. Add gelatin mixture to tomato juice. Stir until gelatin is completely dissolved. Pour mixture into a small mold. Chill until firm. Unmold to serve.

Per Serving: Calories 60, Total Fat 0.2g, Cholesterol 0mg, Sodium 594mg, Total Carbohydrate 11.4g, Dietary Fiber 0.9g, Protein 3.2g

Marinated Artichoke Hearts

This tangy salad is a perfect addition to an antipasto. Just arrange a medley of fresh and pickled vegetables, along with an assortment of reduced-fat cheeses, on a bed of lettuce, pile these artichoke hearts in the middle, and serve it proudly at any gathering.

Makes 4 servings

1 1-pound can artichoke hearts, drained
2 tablespoons red wine vinegar
1 tablespoon water
1 tablespoon olive oil
1 teaspoon sugar
½ teaspoon dried oregano
¼ teaspoon dry mustard
¼ teaspoon garlic powder
¼ teaspoon salt
⅛ teaspoon pepper

Place artichoke hearts in a medium bowl. In a small bowl, combine remaining ingredients, mixing well. Pour over artichoke hearts and toss until evenly coated. Chill overnight to blend flavors. Stir occasionally while chilling.

Per Serving: Calories 63, Total Fat 3.7g, Cholesterol 0mg, Sodium 173mg, Total Carbohydrate 6.3g, Dietary Fiber 4.1g, Protein 1.3g

Easy Italian Green Bean Salad

Either fresh or frozen green beans will work in this easy salad, and the fat-free dressing allows you to add all of the flavor without adding fat. If the dressing you choose has a lot of herbs and spices, you may not even need to add the ones in the recipe.

Makes 4 servings

1 10-ounce package frozen cut green beans
1 cup sliced mushrooms
½ cup salt-free (or regular) tomato sauce
2 tablespoons bottled fat-free Italian dressing
¼ teaspoon dried oregano
¼ teaspoon dried basil
⅛ teaspoon garlic powder

Cook green beans according to package directions, adding mushrooms and cooking them along with the beans. Drain and place in a medium bowl. Combine remaining ingredients in a small bowl and mix well. Pour over green beans. Chill several hours or overnight.

Per Serving: Calories 46, Total Fat 0.1g, Cholesterol 0mg, Sodium 109mg, Total Carbohydrate 9.6g, Dietary Fiber 2.4g, Protein 1.6g

Gourmet Zucchini Salad

This salad is so simple, yet it tastes so elegant. It's at home with a family dinner or at a fancy dinner party.

Makes 4 servings

1½ cups zucchini, unpeeled and sliced crosswise into ⅛-inch slices
½ cup thinly sliced celery
¼ cup thinly sliced onion
¼ cup thinly sliced green pepper
¼ cup red wine vinegar
2 tablespoons sugar
1 tablespoon plus 1½ teaspoons olive oil
2 tablespoons water
½ teaspoon dried basil
¼ teaspoon salt
⅛ teaspoon pepper

Combine vegetables in a shallow bowl. Combine remaining ingredients in a small bowl, mixing well. Pour over vegetables. Chill overnight to blend flavors. Stir several times while chilling.

Per Serving: Calories 89, Total Fat 5.2g, Cholesterol 0mg, Sodium 162mg, Total Carbohydrate 9.7g, Dietary Fiber 1.4g, Protein 0.8g

Herbed Potato Salad

Plain nonfat Greek yogurt replaces the mayonnaise, and red onions add a splash of color in this sweet and tangy version of an all-American favorite.

Makes 6 servings

2 large potatoes (20 ounces total)
½ cup finely chopped red onion
½ cup finely chopped cucumber, peeled and seeded
½ cup plain nonfat Greek yogurt
1 tablespoon vinegar
2 teaspoons olive oil
2 teaspoons dried parsley flakes
1 teaspoon sugar
½ teaspoon dill weed
¼ teaspoon dried oregano
¼ teaspoon salt
⅛ teaspoon pepper

Place potatoes in 2 inches of boiling water in a medium saucepan. Cover and cook over medium heat 15 to 20 minutes, or until potatoes are tender. Do not let them get mushy. (Length of cooking time will depend on the variety of potatoes used.) Drain potatoes and let them sit until cool enough to handle. Remove skin and cut potatoes into 1-inch chunks. Place in a large bowl. Add onion and cucumber and mix well. In a small bowl, combine remaining ingredients. Mix well and add to potatoes. Toss until potatoes are evenly coated. Chill several hours to blend flavors.

Per Serving: Calories 120, Total Fat 1.6g, Cholesterol 0mg, Sodium 119mg, Total Carbohydrate 23g, Dietary Fiber 2g, Protein 3.3g

Best Cole Slaw

An old family standby for years, no backyard cookout is ever complete without it.

Makes 8 servings

1 small cabbage, thinly shredded (4 cups)
1 medium carrot, grated
3 tablespoons sugar
1 teaspoon celery seed
1 teaspoon salt
½ cup reduced-calorie mayonnaise
3 tablespoons plain nonfat yogurt
2 tablespoons vinegar
Freshly ground black pepper

Place cabbage and carrot in a large bowl. Sprinkle sugar, celery seed, and salt on top. Let stand for 5 minutes. In a small bowl, combine mayonnaise, yogurt, and vinegar, mixing well. Spoon over cabbage. Toss to blend. Add pepper to taste. Chill several hours or overnight. Mix occasionally while chilling.

Per Serving: Calories 77, Total Fat 3.1g, Cholesterol 4mg, Sodium 385mg, Total Carbohydrate 11.2g, Dietary Fiber 1.3g, Protein 1g

Cucumber and Onion Salad

This salad makes an excellent side dish for light summer meals and cookouts. It's also a great addition to a tossed salad and even tastes great on sandwiches.

Makes 4 servings

1½ cups cucumber, peeled and sliced paper-thin
½ cup onion, sliced paper-thin
⅓ cup vinegar
⅓ cup water
⅓ cup sugar
¼ teaspoon salt
Dash pepper

Layer cucumber and onion in a jar or bowl. Combine remaining ingredients and pour over vegetables. Chill overnight, stirring several times.

Per Serving: Calories 86, Total Fat 0.1g, Cholesterol 0mg, Sodium 150mg, Total Carbohydrate 20.8g, Dietary Fiber 0.7g, Protein 0.5g

Brown Rice and Vegetable Salad

Loaded with fiber and flavor, this hearty salad makes a tasty dinner accompaniment or a filling lunch. I like to serve it on a bed of fresh spinach, garnished with sliced tomato and cucumber.

Makes 4 servings

2 cups cooked brown rice
½ cup shredded carrots
½ cup shredded zucchini, unpeeled
2 tablespoons finely chopped onion
¼ cup lemon juice
1 tablespoon plus 1 teaspoon olive oil
1 tablespoon dried parsley flakes
½ teaspoon dried thyme
½ teaspoon garlic powder
½ teaspoon salt
Pepper to taste

In a medium bowl, combine rice, carrots, zucchini, and onion. Toss to combine. In a small bowl, combine remaining ingredients. Pour over rice mixture. Chill several hours. Mix before serving.

Per Serving: Calories 170, Total Fat 5.3g, Cholesterol 0mg, Sodium 303mg, Total Carbohydrate 27.3g, Dietary Fiber 2.9g, Protein 3.1g

Caesar Salad

This is a slimmed-down, easy version of an ever-popular salad. It makes a perfect beginning to almost any meal.

Makes 4 servings

2 slices (1 ounce each) whole wheat bread, cubed
2 tablespoons grated Parmesan cheese
1 small head romaine lettuce, chilled, torn into bite-size pieces (about 4 cups)
¼ cup red wine vinegar
2 tablespoons olive oil
2 tablespoons lemon juice
½ teaspoon Worcestershire sauce
½ teaspoon salt
¼ teaspoon dry mustard
¼ teaspoon garlic powder
Freshly ground black pepper to taste

To make croutons, spread bread cubes in a single layer on an ungreased baking sheet. Toast in a 300° oven until dry and light brown. Spray bread cubes lightly with nonstick cooking spray and sprinkle them with half of the Parmesan cheese. Place lettuce in a large bowl. In a small bowl, combine remaining ingredients except remaining Parmesan cheese and pepper. Mix well and pour over lettuce. Toss to coat lettuce evenly. Divide evenly onto 4 salad plates. Top each serving with remaining Parmesan cheese, freshly ground pepper, and croutons.

Per Serving: Calories 135, Total Fat 8.7g, Cholesterol 2mg, Sodium 451mg, Total Carbohydrate 10.4g, Dietary Fiber 2.3g, Protein 4.1g

Cucumbers Dijon

This super-quick salad has a nice "kick" and makes a great addition to any tossed salad. It's also delicious packed into pita bread with sliced turkey and tomato.

Makes 4 servings

¼ cup plain nonfat yogurt
1 tablespoon plus 1½ teaspoons Dijon mustard
2 cups cucumber, peeled, sliced very thin
2 teaspoons dried chives

In a medium bowl, combine yogurt and mustard. Stir in cucumber and chives. Chill several hours. (This salad tastes best when served the same day.)

Per Serving: Calories 24, Total Fat 0.4g, Cholesterol 0mg, Sodium 88mg, Total Carbohydrate 3.5g, Dietary Fiber 0.8g, Protein 1.6g

Italian Mushroom Salad

As an appetizer, salad, or side dish, this easy dish dresses any meal, and it's so easy to prepare.

Makes 4 servings

3 tablespoons bottled fat-free Italian dressing
1 tablespoon grated Parmesan cheese
2 cups mushrooms, thinly sliced

In a medium bowl, combine dressing and Parmesan cheese, mixing well. Stir in mushrooms. Chill several hours.

Per Serving: Calories 23, Total Fat 0.6g, Cholesterol 1mg, Sodium 176mg, Total Carbohydrate 3.2g, Dietary Fiber 0.4g, Protein 1.3g

Marinated Vegetable Salad

A colorful and tasty addition to any meal, this has become a family favorite in my house. If you like, you can eliminate one cup of the cauliflower and add one cup of broccoli in its place.

Makes 6 servings

2 cups cauliflower, cut into small flowerets
1 cup carrots, cut crosswise into ½-inch slices
1 cup celery, cut into 1-inch slices
1 medium, green bell pepper, cut into ½-inch strips
1 cup small mushrooms (or larger mushrooms cut into quarters)
½ cup chopped red onion
10 small stuffed green olives, cut in half crosswise
½ cup water
¼ cup vinegar
2 tablespoons olive oil
2 tablespoons plus 2 teaspoons sugar
1½ teaspoons dried oregano
¾ teaspoon salt
½ teaspoon pepper
¼ teaspoon garlic powder

Combine all ingredients in a large nonstick skillet. Bring to a boil over medium heat, stirring occasionally. Reduce heat to medium-low, cover, and simmer 5 minutes, or until vegetables are barely tender-crisp. Place salad in a bowl and chill overnight.

Per Serving: Calories 115, Total Fat 5.3g, Cholesterol 0mg, Sodium 406mg, Total Carbohydrate 14.7g, Dietary Fiber 2.8g, Protein 1.7g

Hot German Potato Salad

Who said salads have to be cold? This tangy, hot salad is high in flavor and surprisingly low in fat.

Makes 4 servings

15 ounces red-skinned potatoes
2 tablespoons very finely minced onion
1 tablespoon dried chives
2 teaspoons imitation bacon bits
1 teaspoon dry mustard
¼ teaspoon salt
Pepper to taste
Dash celery seed
¼ cup vinegar
2 tablespoons water
1 teaspoon sugar

Place potatoes in 2 inches of boiling water in a medium saucepan. Cover and cook over medium heat 10 to 15 minutes, or until potatoes are tender. Do not let them get mushy. (Length of cooking time will depend on the variety of potatoes used.) Drain potatoes and let them sit until cool enough to handle. Cut potatoes into 1-inch chunks. Place in a large bowl. Toss with onion, chives, and bacon bits. Sprinkle mustard, salt, pepper, and celery seed over potatoes. Mix well. In a small saucepan, heat vinegar, water, and sugar until hot, stirring to dissolve sugar. Pour over potatoes. Toss and serve.

Per Serving: Calories 113, Total Fat 0.8g, Cholesterol 0mg, Sodium 174mg, Total Carbohydrate 24.1g, Dietary Fiber 2.1g, Protein 2.3g

Carrot Slaw

This colorful, festive salad really comes to life when presented on a bed of greens and garnished with ripe, red tomato wedges.

Makes 4 servings

2 cups coarsely shredded carrots
½ cup finely chopped green bell pepper
¼ cup plus 2 tablespoons raisins
¼ cup finely chopped onion
1 small, sweet apple, unpeeled, coarsely shredded
2 tablespoons plus 1½ teaspoons vinegar
1 tablespoon plus 1 teaspoon olive oil
1 tablespoon water
1 tablespoon plus 1 teaspoon sugar
¼ teaspoon salt
¼ teaspoon celery seed
¼ teaspoon dry mustard

In a large bowl, combine carrots, green pepper, raisins, onion, and apple. Toss to combine. Add remaining ingredients and mix well. Chill overnight.

Per Serving: Calories 163, Total Fat 4.8g, Cholesterol 0mg, Sodium 171mg, Total Carbohydrate 28.1g, Dietary Fiber 3.4g, Protein 1.6g

Middle East Eggplant Salad

This delicious salad also makes a great sandwich when piled into a crusty roll and topped with a slice of reduced-fat cheese.

Makes 6 servings

1 tablespoon olive oil
3 cups eggplant, peeled and cut into small cubes
½ cup chopped onion
½ cup chopped green bell pepper
2 cloves garlic, crushed
½ cup chopped tomato
2 tablespoons red wine vinegar
1 tablespoon dried parsley flakes
Salt and pepper to taste

Heat oil in a large nonstick skillet over medium-high heat. Add eggplant, onion, green pepper, and garlic. Cook, stirring frequently, until eggplant is tender and begins to brown. Spoon eggplant mixture into a large bowl. Add remaining ingredients and mix well. Chill several hours or overnight.

Per Serving: Calories 46, Total Fat 2.3g, Cholesterol 0mg, Sodium 11mg, Total Carbohydrate 5.4g, Dietary Fiber 1.6g, Protein 0.8g

Italian Cauliflower Salad

Simple and delicious, this salad is a perfect way to start any Italian meal.

Makes 6 servings

3 cups cauliflower, cut into small flowerets
2 tablespoons finely chopped green bell pepper
2 tablespoons finely chopped onion
¼ cup water
3 tablespoons bottled fat-free Italian dressing
¼ teaspoon salt
⅛ teaspoon dried oregano
⅛ teaspoon dried basil
⅛ teaspoon garlic powder

Combine all ingredients in a medium saucepan. Cover and cook over medium heat, stirring occasionally, until cauliflower is tender-crisp, about 10 minutes. Chill thoroughly.

Per Serving: Calories 21, Total Fat 0.1g, Cholesterol 0mg, Sodium 211mg, Total Carbohydrate 4.1g, Dietary Fiber 1.4g, Protein 1g

Asparagus Vinaigrette

For years, this has been one of my favorite dinner party dishes. Someone always asks me for the recipe. It has just a few simple ingredients, yet the blend of flavors is exquisite.

Makes 4 servings

1 10-ounce package frozen asparagus spears
3 tablespoons red wine vinegar
1 teaspoon Dijon mustard
2 tablespoons plus 1½ teaspoons water
1 tablespoon plus 1 teaspoon olive oil
2 teaspoons dried chives
½ teaspoon dried parsley flakes
Salt and pepper to taste

Cook asparagus according to package directions. Drain and place in a shallow bowl. Stir vinegar into mustard in a small bowl until blended. Add water, oil, chives, parsley, salt, and pepper. Mix well. Spoon over asparagus. Chill several hours, turning asparagus occasionally. Spoon a little of the marinade over each serving.

Per Serving: Calories 68, Total Fat 4.9g, Cholesterol 0mg, Sodium 33mg, Total Carbohydrate 3.6g, Dietary Fiber 1.2g, Protein 2.2g

Dilly Beans

This is a great dish to make in the summer when tender, fresh green beans are plentiful. The tangy beans can be served anyplace you would ordinarily serve pickles.

Makes 6 servings

1 pound green beans, ends trimmed and strings removed
½ cup thinly sliced onion
½ cup vinegar
2 tablespoons canola oil
2 cloves garlic, cut into paper-thin slivers
1 teaspoon sugar
1 teaspoon dill weed
½ teaspoon dry mustard
¼ teaspoon salt
⅛ teaspoon pepper

Cook beans, covered, in 1 inch of boiling water until just tender-crisp, about 15 minutes. Drain, reserving cooking liquid. Place beans in a shallow bowl. Add water to reserved liquid to make 1 cup. Combine liquid with remaining ingredients in a small bowl. Pour over beans. Cover and chill 1 to 2 days.

Per Serving: Calories 88, Total Fat 4.8g, Cholesterol 0mg, Sodium 100mg, Total Carbohydrate 9.4g, Dietary Fiber 2.6g, Protein 1.7g

Pineapple Slaw

A refreshing change-of-pace salad, this easy slaw has the sweetness of pineapple and is laced with the exotic flavor of curry powder.

Makes 4 servings

2 cups finely shredded cabbage
½ cup canned crushed pineapple (packed in juice), drained
¼ cup finely chopped green bell pepper
2 tablespoons finely chopped onion
2 tablespoons reduced-calorie mayonnaise
1 teaspoon sugar
½ teaspoon curry powder
¼ teaspoon celery seed
¼ teaspoon salt
Pepper to taste

Combine cabbage, pineapple, green pepper, and onion in a large bowl. Toss to combine. Place mayonnaise in a small bowl. Stir in spices. Spoon over cabbage mixture. Mix well. Chill several hours or overnight. Mix well before serving.

Per Serving: Calories 61, Total Fat 1.5g, Cholesterol 2mg, Sodium 192mg, Total Carbohydrate 10.8g, Dietary Fiber 1.6g, Protein 0.9g

Herbed Yogurt Dressing

Nonfat yogurt makes a delicious, creamy base for salad dressings. Be creative and vary the herbs and spices, and you can create lots of different flavor combinations.

Makes 8 servings (2½ tablespoons each serving)

2 teaspoons canola oil
1 cup plain nonfat yogurt
2 tablespoons red wine vinegar
1 tablespoon minced onion flakes
½ teaspoon dried oregano
½ teaspoon dill weed
⅛ teaspoon garlic powder
Salt and pepper to taste

Stir oil into yogurt. Add remaining ingredients, mixing well. Chill several hours to blend flavors. Stir before serving.

Per Serving: Calories 30, Total Fat 1.2g, Cholesterol 0mg, Sodium 29mg, Total Carbohydrate 3g, Dietary Fiber 0.1g, Protein 1.9g

Dijon Vinaigrette

Try this tangy dressing on steamed broccoli or asparagus as well as on a tossed salad.

Makes 4 servings (2 tablespoons each serving)

3 tablespoons red wine vinegar
2 tablespoons water
1 tablespoon plus 1 teaspoon canola oil
1 tablespoon plus 1 teaspoon Dijon mustard
¼ teaspoon garlic powder

Combine all ingredients in a small bowl. Beat with a fork or wire whisk until blended. Chill several hours to blend flavors.

Per Serving: Calories 48, Total Fat 4.8g, Cholesterol 0mg, Sodium 68mg, Total Carbohydrate 0.6g, Dietary Fiber 0.3g, Protein 0.3g

Cheesy Herb Dressing

This thick, cheese-flavored dressing also doubles as a delicious sandwich spread.

Makes 6 servings (2 tablespoons each serving)

½ cup plain nonfat yogurt
1 tablespoon canola oil
1 tablespoon grated Parmesan cheese
1 tablespoon dried parsley flakes
1½ teaspoons lemon juice
¼ teaspoon garlic powder
¼ teaspoon dried basil

Combine all ingredients and mix well. Chill several hours to blend flavors.

Per Serving: Calories 37, Total Fat 2.6g, Cholesterol 1mg, Sodium 36mg, Total Carbohydrate 1.9g, Dietary Fiber 0.1g, Protein 1.6g

Creamy Italian Dressing

Turn an ordinary tossed salad into a gourmet delight with this creamy, herbed dressing.

Makes 8 servings (2 tablespoons each serving)

¾ cup plain nonfat Greek yogurt
¼ cup reduced-calorie mayonnaise
2 tablespoons skim milk
1 tablespoon red wine vinegar
½ teaspoon dried oregano
½ teaspoon dried basil
½ teaspoon sugar
⅛ teaspoon garlic powder
Salt and pepper to taste

In a large bowl, combine all ingredients, mixing well. Chill several hours to blend flavors.

Per Serving: Calories 33, Total Fat 1.4g, Cholesterol 2mg, Sodium 63mg, Total Carbohydrate 3.7g, Dietary Fiber 0g, Protein 1.4g

French Tomato Dressing

This tart and tangy dressing makes greens come alive. It's also a delicious dressing to spoon over a platter of sliced tomatoes and onions.

Makes 6 servings (2 tablespoons each serving)

½ cup tomato juice
2 tablespoons canola oil
2 tablespoons red wine vinegar
1 teaspoon Dijon mustard
1 teaspoon sugar
½ teaspoon Worcestershire sauce
½ teaspoon dried oregano
¼ teaspoon salt
¼ teaspoon dried basil
¼ teaspoon pepper

Combine all ingredients in a small jar and shake well. Chill to blend flavors.

Per Serving: Calories 50, Total Fat 4.5g, Cholesterol 0mg, Sodium 116mg, Total Carbohydrate 2g, Dietary Fiber 0.3g, Protein 0.2g

Cheesy Thousand Island Dressing

Low-fat cottage cheese replaces the mayonnaise in this creamy version of an all-time favorite dressing. It also makes a delicious spread for a sliced turkey and tomato sandwich.

Makes 12 servings (2 tablespoons each serving)

1 cup low-fat (1%) cottage cheese
¼ cup ketchup
1 tablespoon canola oil
1 teaspoon paprika
¼ teaspoon salt
⅛ teaspoon pepper
2 tablespoons finely minced celery
2 tablespoons finely minced green pepper
2 tablespoons finely minced onion
1 tablespoon sweet pickle relish

In a blender, combine cottage cheese, ketchup, oil, paprika, salt, and pepper. Blend until smooth. Stir in remaining ingredients. Chill several hours to blend flavors.

Per Serving: Calories 32, Total Fat 1.3g, Cholesterol 1mg, Sodium 192mg, Total Carbohydrate 2.5g, Dietary Fiber 0g, Protein 2.4g

Blue Cheese Dressing

The distinctive flavor of blue cheese plays to its full advantage in this creamy dressing, and "diluting" the cheese with low-fat cottage cheese really helps lower the total fat.

Makes 8 servings (2 tablespoons each serving)

⅔ cup low-fat (1%) cottage cheese
1½ ounces blue cheese, crumbled (¼ cup)
2 teaspoons olive oil
2 teaspoons red wine vinegar
1 teaspoon dry mustard
1 teaspoon minced onion flakes
Salt and pepper to taste

Combine all ingredients in a blender. Blend until smooth. Chill several hours to blend flavors.

Per Serving: Calories 45, Total Fat 2.9g, Cholesterol 5mg, Sodium 156mg, Total Carbohydrate 1g, Dietary Fiber 0.1g, Protein 3.5g

Creamy Orange Dressing

Spoon this delectable dressing over fresh fruit and create an appetizer or a light dessert with a delicious difference.

Makes 8 servings (2½ tablespoons each serving)

1 cup plain nonfat Greek yogurt
¼ cup frozen orange juice concentrate, thawed

In a small bowl, combine yogurt and juice concentrate. Mix well. Chill several hours.

Per Serving: Calories 31, Total Fat 0.1g, Cholesterol 0mg, Sodium 23mg, Total Carbohydrate 5.8g, Dietary Fiber 0.1g, Protein 2g

Eggs and Cheese

There are an endless number of recipes available for eggs and cheese. Both are versatile, tasty, and inexpensive. There's only one problem: Both eggs and cheese are high in fat and cholesterol. Fortunately, there are a few easy solutions to the problem.

The cholesterol in eggs is found entirely in the yolk. Although this is true, the egg has been vindicated as a "bad" choice. It is recommended to watch other saturated fats throughout the day. Still not convinced? The easiest way around this dilemma is to use either 2 egg whites to replace each whole egg or a liquid egg substitute. Either will work in baked goods and most recipes that call for eggs. In omelets, many people prefer the flavor and the ease of the egg substitutes.

Cheese is a perfect match for so many foods. There are reduced-fat and fat-free versions of most cheeses. Some of the fat-free cheeses seem to lack flavor and "meltability," so our choice is usually the reduced-fat versions. Some cheeses, such as feta and Parmesan, have a rich, distinctive taste that goes a long way, so by simply cutting back on the amount used, you can still enjoy their wonderful flavors.

I've made the adjustments for you and combined eggs and cheese with many other delicious ingredients, bringing you many scrumptious taste delights.

Scrambled Eggs Florentine

Spinach makes a colorful and nutritious addition to this favorite American breakfast. You can also turn this into a great sandwich by placing the cooked eggs between 2 slices of whole wheat toast, with a little ketchup or tomato sauce.

Makes 4 servings

2 cups liquid egg substitute
1 10-ounce package frozen chopped spinach, thawed and drained well
2 tablespoons minced onion flakes
2 tablespoons grated Parmesan cheese
1 tablespoon imitation bacon bits
½ teaspoon garlic powder
1/16 teaspoon ground nutmeg
Freshly ground black pepper to taste

In a large bowl, combine all ingredients. Mix well. Spray a large nonstick skillet or griddle with nonstick cooking spray. Heat over medium heat. Pour egg mixture into skillet. Cook, stirring frequently, until eggs are done to taste.

Per Serving: Calories 154, Total Fat 6g, Cholesterol 4mg, Sodium 365mg, Total Carbohydrate 6.2g, Dietary Fiber 2.4g, Protein 19g

Spanish Omelet

Easy and delicious, this omelet makes a perfect brunch dish or weekend treat.

Makes 4 servings

Omelet:
2 teaspoons canola oil
1 cup chopped onion
1 cup chopped green bell pepper
2 cups liquid egg substitute
¼ teaspoon garlic powder
⅛ teaspoon pepper
Salt to taste

Sauce:
1 8-ounce can salt-free (or regular) tomato sauce
¼ teaspoon *each* dried basil and oregano
⅛ teaspoon garlic powder

Heat oil in a large nonstick skillet over medium heat. Add onion and green pepper. Cook, stirring frequently, until lightly browned, about 10 minutes. While onion and pepper are browning, combine all sauce ingredients in a small saucepan. Heat until hot and bubbly. Place egg substitute in a large bowl and add garlic powder and pepper, mixing well. Add to skillet. Cook, stirring frequently, until eggs are done to taste. To serve, divide egg mixture onto 4 serving plates. Top with sauce.

Per Serving: Calories 165, Total Fat 6.7g, Cholesterol 2mg, Sodium 233mg, Total Carbohydrate 9.8g, Dietary Fiber 2.3g, Protein 16.8g

Mexican Tomato Omelet

Tomato slices add color and flavor to this upside-down omelet. Garnish it with fresh basil, serve it with salsa, and it really reflects the Mexican cuisine's use of color.

Makes 2 servings

2 teaspoons canola oil
1 cup liquid egg substitute
1 teaspoon dried basil
1 teaspoon ground cumin
¼ teaspoon garlic powder
Salt and pepper to taste
1 tablespoon grated Parmesan cheese
1 tablespoon skim milk
1 medium ripe tomato, sliced

Heat oil in an 8-inch nonstick skillet over medium heat. In a medium bowl, combine egg substitute with remaining ingredients, *except* tomato slices. Beat with a fork or wire whisk until blended. Pour into hot skillet. Reduce heat to medium-low, cover skillet, and cook 5 minutes. Arrange tomato slices over eggs and continue to cook, covered, 5 minutes more, or until eggs are set enough to invert without breaking. Slide omelet out of pan onto a plate. Then, invert into pan so that tomatoes are now on the bottom. Cook, uncovered, 1 minute, or until eggs are set. Invert onto serving plate tomato-side up.

Per Serving: Calories 188, Total Fat 10.1g, Cholesterol 4mg, Sodium 294mg, Total Carbohydrate 6.4g, Dietary Fiber 1.3g, Protein 17.8g

Spinach Frittata

This hearty dish is fit for any meal, from a Sunday brunch to a quick and inexpensive dinner. For variations, feel free to add any leftover cooked vegetables. I love this frittata!

Makes 8 servings

2 teaspoons olive oil
1 cup chopped onion
3 cups liquid egg substitute
2 10-ounce packages frozen chopped spinach, thawed and drained well
½ teaspoon garlic powder
¼ teaspoon ground nutmeg
Salt and pepper to taste
3 tablespoons grated Parmesan cheese

Preheat oven to 375°. Heat oil in a 10-inch heavy, ovenproof skillet over medium heat. Add onion. Cook, stirring frequently, until tender, about 5 minutes. Combine egg substitute, spinach, garlic powder, nutmeg, salt, pepper, and half of the Parmesan cheese. Mix well and pour into skillet. Sprinkle with remaining cheese. Cook for 2 minutes without stirring, then place skillet in oven. Bake, uncovered, until eggs are set and lightly browned. Cut into pie-shaped wedges to serve.

Per Serving: Calories 126, Total Fat 5.1g, Cholesterol 3mg, Sodium 264mg, Total Carbohydrate 5.3g, Dietary Fiber 2.5g, Protein 14.6g

Company Egg Cups

Similar to miniature quiches, these egg cups are fun to serve, but you don't really have to wait for company to try them.

Makes 4 servings

¼ cup *each* finely chopped mushrooms, onion, and green bell pepper
2 cloves garlic, finely chopped
½ teaspoon dried oregano
Salt and pepper to taste
2 teaspoons reduced-calorie margarine
4 slices thin-sliced whole wheat bread (½-ounce slices)
1 cup liquid egg substitute
4 teaspoons grated Parmesan cheese

Preheat oven to 375°. Heat a small nonstick skillet over medium heat. Add mushrooms, onion, green pepper, and garlic. Sprinkle with oregano, salt, and pepper. Cook, stirring frequently, until vegetables are tender, about 5 minutes. Add small amounts of water if necessary to prevent sticking. Spread ½ teaspoon of margarine on each slice of bread. Press each slice, margarine-side down, into the cup of a muffin pan, forming a cup. Divide vegetable mixture evenly into the crusts. Fill with egg substitute. Sprinkle 1 teaspoon of Parmesan cheese over the top of each cup. Bake, uncovered, 15 minutes, or until eggs are set.

Per Serving: Calories 118, Total Fat 4.1g, Cholesterol 3mg, Sodium 240mg, Total Carbohydrate 9.6g, Dietary Fiber 1.7g, Protein 10.3g

Fruittata

I've combined eggs with vegetables. Now, why not combine eggs with fruit? This unique omelet, topped with a creamy, rum-flavored sauce, makes a truly elegant brunch dish.

Makes 4 servings

Fruittata:
1 cup liquid egg substitute
1 tablespoon sugar
1 teaspoon vanilla extract
¼ teaspoon rum extract
¼ teaspoon orange or lemon extract
¼ teaspoon ground cinnamon
⅓ cup nonfat dry milk
⅓ cup water
2 teaspoons margarine
½ cup blueberries, fresh or frozen
⅓ cup canned crushed pineapple (packed in juice), drained
⅓ cup canned peaches (packed in juice), drained and cut into small chunks
Ground cinnamon

Vanilla-Rum Topping:
¾ cup vanilla nonfat yogurt
½ teaspoon rum extract

Preheat oven to 375°. In a medium bowl, combine egg substitute, sugar, extracts, cinnamon, dry milk, and water. Beat with a fork or wire whisk until blended. Melt margarine in a 7- or 8-inch ovenproof skillet or baking dish over medium heat. Add fruit, stirring to distribute evenly in pan. Pour egg mixture over fruit. Sprinkle lightly with additional cinnamon. Cook for 2 minutes without stirring, then place pan in oven. Bake, uncovered, 20 to 25 minutes, or until eggs are set. Combine yogurt and rum extract. Serve as a topping on hot fruittata.

Per Serving: Calories 184, Total Fat 4.2g, Cholesterol 4mg, Sodium 214mg, Total Carbohydrate 23.3g, Dietary Fiber 1.1g, Protein 13.1g

Banana Puff

If you were to cross an omelet with a soufflé, the result would be this delicious breakfast treat. Adding the maple syrup at the end really makes this dish taste wonderful.

Makes 4 servings

¼ cup liquid egg substitute
¾ cup vanilla nonfat yogurt
2 tablespoons sugar
1 teaspoon vanilla extract
¼ teaspoon rum extract
¾ cup all-purpose flour
2 teaspoons baking powder
1 teaspoon baking soda
¼ teaspoon ground cinnamon
3 egg whites (Do not use egg substitute.)
1 medium ripe banana, diced
4 teaspoons maple syrup

Preheat oven to 400°. Spray a 9-inch cake pan with nonstick cooking spray. Combine egg substitute, yogurt, sugar, and extracts in a large bowl. Beat on low speed of an electric mixer until blended. Continue to beat 1 minute more. In a small bowl, combine flour, baking powder, baking soda, and cinnamon, mixing well. Add to first mixture, beating on low speed until all ingredients are moistened. In a separate bowl, with clean, dry beaters, beat egg whites on high speed until stiff. Fold into batter, gently but thoroughly. Fold in banana. Spread batter in prepared cake pan. Sprinkle lightly with additional cinnamon. Bake 20 minutes, or until puffy and lightly browned. Drizzle each serving with 1 teaspoon of the maple syrup.

Per Serving: Calories 181, Total Fat 0.8g, Cholesterol 0mg, Sodium 561mg, Total Carbohydrate 36.5g, Dietary Fiber 1.4g, Protein 6.8g

Lemon Soufflé

As an elegant brunch dish or an inspired dessert, this popular dish is sure to please. It's usually made with whole eggs, which are separated and then beaten. I've replaced the yolks with egg substitute, and the taste is still divine. It will definitely impress!

Makes 4 servings

½ cup liquid egg substitute
3 tablespoons sugar
1 teaspoon lemon extract
½ teaspoon vanilla extract
½ teaspoon grated fresh lemon peel
4 egg whites (Do not use egg substitute.)
¼ teaspoon cream of tartar

Preheat oven to 350°. Spray a 1½ -quart soufflé dish or deep baking dish with nonstick cooking spray. In a large bowl, beat egg substitute on medium speed of an electric mixer for 1 minute. Add 2 tablespoons of the sugar, the extracts, and lemon peel. Beat on high speed for 2 minutes. In another bowl, using clean, dry beaters, beat egg whites and cream of tartar on high speed until soft peaks form. Add remaining sugar and beat until egg whites are stiff. Fold egg whites into first mixture, a third at a time, folding gently, until the two mixtures are just blended. Pour mixture into prepared dish. Place in a shallow baking pan and pour hot water into larger pan to a depth of 1 inch. Bake 30 minutes, or until soufflé has puffed and top is lightly browned. Serve right away.

Per Serving: Calories 77, Total Fat 1g, Cholesterol 0mg, Sodium 102mg, Total Carbohydrate 10.1g, Dietary Fiber 0g, Protein 6.8g

Almond Bread Puff

This sensational version of French toast is light and lots of fun to eat. The taste is great, and you can vary the flavors by replacing the almond extract with any other favorite extract.

Makes 2 servings

¼ cup liquid egg substitute
2 tablespoons skim milk
1 tablespoon sugar
2 teaspoons vanilla extract
½ teaspoon almond extract
2 slices whole wheat bread (1-ounce slices)
2 egg whites (Do not use egg substitute.)

Preheat oven to 350°. Spray a 4 x 8-inch loaf pan with nonstick cooking spray. In a small bowl, combine egg substitute, milk, *half* the sugar, *half* of the vanilla extract, and *half* of the almond extract. Mix well and pour into prepared pan. Place bread in mixture, turning carefully until all of the liquid has been absorbed. Bake 15 minutes. Remove from oven. In a medium bowl, beat egg whites until stiff, using high speed of an electric mixer. Beat in remaining sugar and extracts. Spread over bread. Return to oven and continue to bake for 10 more minutes, or until nicely browned.

Per Serving: Calories 144, Total Fat 2.2g, Cholesterol 0mg, Sodium 259mg, Total Carbohydrate 21g, Dietary Fiber 2g, Protein 10g

Dutch Apple Pancake

This unique cross between an omelet and a pancake is delicious topped with either maple syrup, confectioners' sugar, or a mix of sugar and cinnamon. It's also good topped with the Vanilla-Rum Topping that's served with the Fruittata on page 43.

Makes 2 servings

2 teaspoons margarine
2 small, sweet apples, peeled and cut into ½-inch cubes
½ cup liquid egg substitute
⅓ cup nonfat dry milk
¼ cup water
3 tablespoons all-purpose flour
2 tablespoons sugar
½ teaspoon ground cinnamon
¼ teaspoon ground nutmeg
¼ teaspoon baking powder
1 teaspoon vanilla extract
¼ teaspoon almond extract

Melt margarine in a 10-inch heavy, ovenproof skillet over medium-high heat. Add apples. Cook, stirring frequently, until apples are tender, about 5 minutes. Remove from heat. Preheat oven to 500°. Combine remaining ingredients in a blender. Blend until smooth. Pour over apples. Bake, uncovered, 10 minutes, or until eggs are set and lightly browned.

Per Serving: Calories 323, Total Fat 6.7g, Cholesterol 5mg, Sodium 307mg, Total Carbohydrate 50g, Dietary Fiber 2.9g, Protein 16.1g

Broccoli and Cheese Pancakes

A light meal of tuna salad, a tossed salad, and these cheesy pancakes is often a welcome change of pace from a heavy meat and potato dinner.

Makes 4 servings (4 pancakes each serving)

1 10-ounce package frozen chopped broccoli, thawed and drained
½ cup liquid egg substitute
⅔ cup low-fat (1%) cottage cheese
¼ cup thinly sliced green onion (green part only)
3 tablespoons all-purpose flour
1 tablespoon grated Parmesan cheese
¼ teaspoon garlic powder
Salt and pepper to taste
Dash ground nutmeg

Place broccoli in a large bowl. In a blender, combine egg substitute and cottage cheese. Blend until smooth. Stir in remaining ingredients and add to broccoli, mixing well. Spray a large nonstick griddle or skillet with nonstick cooking spray. Preheat over medium heat. Drop cheese mixture onto griddle, using 2 tablespoons for each pancake. Cook, turning once, until pancakes are lightly browned on both sides.

Per Serving: Calories 105, Total Fat 2.2g, Cholesterol 3mg, Sodium 256mg, Total Carbohydrate 9.8g, Dietary Fiber 2.5g, Protein 11.8g

Asparagus Cheese Tart

This elegant no-crust, quiche-like pie serves 8 as a side dish or 6 as a light entrée. It's so easy to make with no pie crust to roll.

Makes 8 servings

1 10-ounce package frozen asparagus spears
1⅓ cups low-fat (1%) cottage cheese
⅔ cup nonfat dry milk
½ cup water
¼ cup plus 2 tablespoons all-purpose flour
2 teaspoons baking powder
2 tablespoons plus 2 teaspoons reduced-calorie margarine
¾ cup liquid egg substitute
2 teaspoons minced onion flakes
1 packet low-sodium instant chicken- or vegetable-flavored broth mix
3 tablespoons grated Parmesan cheese (1 ounce)

Cook asparagus according to package directions. Drain. Preheat oven to 350°. Spray a 9-inch pie pan with nonstick cooking spray. Cut each asparagus spear into 3 pieces. Arrange pieces in prepared pan. In a blender, combine remaining ingredients, using only half of the Parmesan cheese. Blend until smooth. Pour over asparagus. Sprinkle with remaining Parmesan cheese. Bake 30 minutes, or until set and lightly browned. Cool 5 minutes before serving.

Per Serving: Calories 241, Total Fat 4.3g, Cholesterol 6mg, Sodium 443mg, Total Carbohydrate 26.5g, Dietary Fiber 6.9g, Protein 24.2g

Easy Cheesy

Yes, it's easy and it's cheesy. This quick casserole is suitable for any meal, from breakfast to dinner. You can add lots of different touches if you wish, such as sliced green onions, sliced olives, imitation bacon bits, chopped jalapeño peppers...

Makes 6 servings

1⅓ cups low-fat (1%) cottage cheese
4 ounces shredded reduced-fat Cheddar cheese (1 cup)
1 cup liquid egg substitute
1½ teaspoons vegetable oil
1 tablespoon all-purpose flour
1 tablespoon minced onion flakes
1 packet low-sodium instant chicken-flavored broth mix
⅛ teaspoon garlic powder

Preheat oven to 350°. Spray an 8-inch square baking pan with nonstick cooking spray. In a blender, combine all ingredients. Blend until smooth. Pour into prepared pan. Bake, uncovered, 30 minutes, or until puffy and lightly browned. Cut into squares and serve hot.

Per Serving: Calories 86, Total Fat 2.9g, Cholesterol 6mg, Sodium 321mg, Total Carbohydrate 3.8g, Dietary Fiber 0.1g, Protein 11g

Broccoli Cheese Puff

Simple, yet elegant, this dish can be prepared up to a day ahead and baked when you are ready. It serves 6 as a side dish or 4 as a delicious, light entrée.

Makes 6 servings

4 slices whole wheat bread (1-ounce slices)
4 ounces shredded reduced-fat Cheddar cheese (1 cup)
1 10-ounce package frozen chopped broccoli, thawed and drained
1 cup liquid egg substitute
2 cups skim milk
2 teaspoons minced onion flakes
½ teaspoon dry mustard
¼ teaspoon salt
⅛ teaspoon pepper
⅛ teaspoon garlic powder

Spray a 4 x 8-inch loaf pan with nonstick cooking spray. Place 2 slices of the bread in the prepared pan. Sprinkle with *half* of the cheese. Spread broccoli over the cheese and top with remaining cheese, followed by remaining bread slices. In a blender, combine egg substitute and remaining ingredients. Blend until smooth. Pour evenly over bread.

Refrigerate at least 1 hour, up to 24 hours. Remove from refrigerator 30 minutes before baking. Preheat oven to 350°. Bake, uncovered, 40 minutes, or until golden brown.

Per Serving: Calories 162, Total Fat 3.8g, Cholesterol 5mg, Sodium 441mg, Total Carbohydrate 16.3g, Dietary Fiber 2.8g, Protein 15.6g

Potato-Cheese Casserole

You can either bake or boil the potatoes for this rich, cheesy casserole. If you are making baked potatoes for dinner one night, why not pop a few extra ones into the oven so you can make this great casserole the next night?

Makes 6 servings

12 ounces cooked potatoes, peeled and thinly sliced (2 small baking potatoes)
3 ounces shredded reduced-fat Cheddar cheese (¾ cup)
½ cup liquid egg substitute
⅔ cup low-fat (1%) cottage cheese
1 teaspoon dried parsley flakes
⅛ teaspoon garlic powder
Salt and pepper to taste
½ cup thinly sliced green onions (green part only)

Preheat oven to 350°. Spray a 1½ -quart baking dish with nonstick cooking spray. Arrange *half* of the potatoes in prepared pan. Top with *half* of the Cheddar cheese, then the remaining potatoes, followed by the remaining Cheddar. In a blender, combine remaining ingredients, except green onions. Blend until smooth. Stir in green onions. Pour over potatoes. Bake, uncovered, 30 minutes, or until hot and lightly browned.

Per Serving: Calories 115, Total Fat 2.1g, Cholesterol 4mg, Sodium 230mg, Total Carbohydrate 13.9g, Dietary Fiber 1.1g, Protein 10.4g

Baked Cauliflower and Cheese

The combination of the ricotta and Parmesan cheeses gives this dish a very rich taste. It makes a lovely buffet dish.

Makes 4 servings

4 cups cauliflower, cut into flowerets (or two 10-ounce packages frozen cauliflower)
½ cup part-skim ricotta cheese
½ cup liquid egg substitute
1 tablespoon grated Parmesan cheese
2 teaspoons minced onion flakes
Salt and pepper to taste

Place cauliflower in a steamer rack over boiling water in a medium saucepan. Cook, covered, 5 minutes. (If using frozen cauliflower, cook according to package directions, choosing the shorter amount of cooking time given.) Preheat oven to 350°. Spray a 1-quart baking dish with nonstick cooking spray. Place cauliflower in prepared pan. Combine remaining ingredients in a small bowl. Beat with a fork or wire whisk until blended. Spoon over cauliflower. Bake, uncovered, 25 minutes, or until lightly browned.

Per Serving: Calories 108, Total Fat 4.1g, Cholesterol 11mg, Sodium 153mg, Total Carbohydrate 7.8g, Dietary Fiber 2.6g, Protein 10g

Spaghetti Squash Kugel

Spaghetti squash takes the place of noodles in this rich, cheesy dish. It can be served warm or cold, and it is a good side dish to serve with the "Pretend" Salmon Salad on page 63.

Makes 8 servings

1 cup liquid egg substitute
1⅓ cups low-fat (1%) cottage cheese
¼ cup sugar
2 teaspoons vanilla extract
½ teaspoon ground cinnamon
3 cups cooked, drained spaghetti squash*

Preheat oven to 350°. Spray an 8-inch square baking pan with nonstick cooking spray. In a large bowl, combine egg substitute, cottage cheese, sugar, vanilla, and cinnamon. Beat with a fork or wire whisk until blended. Add spaghetti squash to egg mixture. Mix well. Spoon into prepared pan. Sprinkle lightly with additional cinnamon. Bake 40 minutes, or until set and lightly browned.

**To cook spaghetti squash, cut squash in half lengthwise. Remove seeds. Bake, cut-side down in a baking pan containing 1 inch of water, at 350°, for 45 minutes, or until tender. Drain halves cut-side down. Pull strands free with a fork.*

Per Serving: Calories 87, Total Fat 1.4g, Cholesterol 2mg, Sodium 215mg, Total Carbohydrate 10.2g, Dietary Fiber 0.5g, Protein 8.5g

Italian Eggplant and Cheese Casserole

Serve this easy favorite with rice or noodles and a green vegetable, and dinner is complete. As an entrée for 6 or a filling side dish for 8, this one will be requested again and again.

Makes 6 servings

1 large eggplant (1¼ pounds), peeled and cut crosswise into ½ -inch slices
2 cups reduced-fat, meatless spaghetti sauce, or marinara sauce
2 cups part-skim ricotta cheese
2 ounces part-skim Mozzarella cheese (½ cup)
1 tablespoon grated Parmesan cheese

Preheat broiler. Arrange eggplant slices in a single layer on a nonstick baking sheet. Broil until lightly browned on both sides, turning slices once. Reduce oven temperature to 375°. Spray a 9 x 13-inch baking pan with nonstick cooking spray. Spread a thin layer of the sauce in the bottom of the prepared pan. Arrange half of the eggplant slices over the sauce. Drop ricotta cheese by spoonfuls onto eggplant. Top with ⅔ cup of sauce. Top with remaining eggplant slices, pressing them down gently. Top with remaining sauce, then sprinkle with Mozzarella and Parmesan cheeses. Bake, uncovered, 35 minutes. Let stand 3 to 5 minutes before serving.

Per Serving: Calories 223, Total Fat 10.2g Cholesterol 31mg, Sodium 511mg, Total Carbohydrate 18.3g, Dietary Fiber 4.1g, Protein 14.4g

Quiche for One

You can enjoy the glorious flavor of quiche without all the muss and fuss. Go ahead—treat yourself.

Makes 1 serving

¼ cup liquid egg substitute
½ cup skim milk
⅛ teaspoon salt
⅛ teaspoon pepper
Dash ground nutmeg
½ cup chopped mushrooms, fresh or canned
1 ounce shredded reduced-sodium Swiss cheese (¼ cup)
2 tablespoons thinly slice green onion (green part only)
1 teaspoon imitation bacon bits

Preheat oven to 350°. Spray a small individual casserole with nonstick cooking spray. In a small bowl, combine egg substitute, milk, salt, pepper, and nutmeg. Beat with a fork or wire whisk until blended. Stir in remaining ingredients. Pour into prepared pan. Bake 30 minutes, or until set. Let stand 5 minutes before serving.

Per Serving: Calories 231, Total Fat 11.3g, Cholesterol 31mg, Sodium 546mg, Total Carbohydrate 10.3g, Dietary Fiber 1g, Protein 22g

Italian Cheese-Stuffed Pita

For cheese lovers, this is an easy sandwich that can be varied by choosing different cheese combinations. For instance, Swiss or Provolone add their own distinctive flavors.

Makes 2 servings

¼ cup part-skim ricotta cheese
2 ounces shredded reduced-fat Cheddar cheese
1 teaspoon grated Parmesan cheese
½ teaspoon dried basil
¼ teaspoon onion powder
Dash garlic powder
Pepper to taste
2 1-ounce whole wheat pita breads
2 slices tomato

Preheat oven to 350°. In a small bowl, combine cheeses with basil, onion powder, garlic powder, and pepper. Mix well. Split open one end of each pita, forming a pocket. Place tomato slices inside pita, then divide cheese mixture and spoon into the pita. Wrap sandwiches in foil and bake 20 minutes.

Per Serving: Calories 185, Total Fat 5.5g, Cholesterol 17mg, Sodium 385mg, Total Carbohydrate 19.5g, Dietary Fiber 2.6g, Protein 13.9g

Orange Upside-Down French Toast

A wonderful orange flavor makes this version of an all-time favorite quite unique. And baking the toast rather than frying makes it puffier and fluffier. For a special company touch, you can dust the toast lightly with confectioners' sugar just before serving.

Makes 4 servings

2 teaspoons margarine
2 tablespoons sugar
½ teaspoon ground cinnamon
1 cup liquid egg substitute
½ teaspoon orange extract
½ teaspoon vanilla extract
½ teaspoon maple extract
¼ cup frozen orange juice concentrate, thawed
¼ cup water
4 slices whole wheat bread (1-ounce slices)

Preheat oven to 400°. Place margarine in an 8-inch square baking pan and place in oven until margarine is melted. Remove pan from oven and spread margarine evenly over bottom of pan. Combine sugar and cinnamon. Sprinkle evenly over margarine. In a shallow bowl, combine egg substitute, extracts, orange juice concentrate, and water. Dip each slice of bread in egg mixture, soaking well. Arrange bread in pan. Spoon any remaining egg mixture on bread. Bake 25 minutes, until eggs are set. Let stand 1 minute, then turn cinnamon-side up to serve.

Per Serving: Calories 197, Total Fat 5.2g, Cholesterol 1mg, Sodium 283mg, Total Carbohydrate 26.8g, Dietary Fiber 2.3g, Protein 10.6g

Cream Cheese and Jelly French Toast

A real favorite among my kids, this is a popular sandwich transformed into a breakfast treat. A real favorite among my kids, this is a popular sandwich transformed into a breakfast treat. Grandchildren love it too!

Makes 2 servings

4 slices thin-sliced whole wheat bread (½ -ounce slices)
4 teaspoons fat-free cream cheese
4 teaspoons fruit-only spread, any flavor
¼ cup liquid egg substitute
¼ cup skim milk
½ teaspoon vanilla extract

Make 2 sandwiches by dividing the cream cheese and fruit spread, spreading it on 2 slices of the bread, and topping with remaining bread. In a shallow bowl, combine egg substitute, milk, and vanilla extract. Beat with a fork until blended. Dip the sandwiches in the egg mixture, turning carefully, until all of the mixture is absorbed. Spray a large nonstick skillet with nonstick cooking spray. Preheat over medium heat. Place sandwiches in skillet. Cook, turning sandwiches several times, until browned on both sides.

Per Serving: Calories 145, Total Fat 2.4g, Cholesterol 1mg, Sodium 273mg, Total Carbohydrate 22.1g, Dietary Fiber 2g, Protein 8.9g

Cottage Cheese Cinnamon Toast

For breakfast or a light, hot lunch, this easy, toasted sandwich can't be beat. For a delicious variation, it can also be made with raisin bread.

Makes 2 servings

⅔ cup low-fat (1%) cottage cheese
1 teaspoon sugar
1 teaspoon vanilla extract
½ teaspoon ground cinnamon
2 slices whole wheat bread (1-ounce slices), lightly toasted

Preheat broiler. Have an ungreased shallow baking pan or baking sheet ready. In a small bowl, combine cottage cheese, sugar, vanilla, and cinnamon. Mix well. Spread on toast. Sprinkle lightly with additional cinnamon. Place toast in pan. Broil 2 to 3 minutes, or until cheese is hot and bubbly. Serve hot.

Per Serving: Calories 138, Total Fat 2g, Cholesterol 3mg, Sodium 455mg, Total Carbohydrate 18g, Dietary Fiber 2.3g, Protein 12g

Pineapple-Orange Danish Toast

This variation of the preceding recipe is also sweet and delicious, and you can make it in no time!

Makes 2 servings

⅔ cup low-fat (1%) cottage cheese
¼ cup canned crushed pineapple (packed in juice), drained
2 tablespoons fruit-only orange marmalade
¼ teaspoon ground cinnamon
2 slices whole wheat bread (1-ounce slices), lightly toasted

Preheat broiler. Have an ungreased shallow baking pan or baking sheet ready. In a small bowl, combine cottage cheese, pineapple, marmalade, and cinnamon. Spread on toast. Place toast in pan. Broil 2 to 3 minutes, or until cheese is hot and bubbly. Serve hot.

Per Serving: Calories 184, Total Fat 2g, Cholesterol 3mg, Sodium 455mg, Total Carbohydrate 29.5g, Dietary Fiber 2.5g, Protein 12.1g

Notes:

Fish and Seafood

Many varieties of fish and seafood are low in fat and fit nicely into a balanced diet. Often, if dishes are high in fat, it is not the seafood that is the culprit, but the way in which it is prepared. So, for my sauces I am careful to choose ingredients such as lemon juice, broth, and vegetables, along with a delectable array of spices. Now you can have all of the flavor without the fat.

Seafood contains no fiber. Therefore, I recommend adding a whole grain, such as brown rice, barley, Quinoa, whole wheat pasta or whole wheat couscous to every meal. In addition, if you serve a salad and a steamed vegetable, you have a beautifully balanced and filling, meal.

My selection of seafood dishes will definitely please your taste buds and delight your family and friends.

Sole and Peppers

In this colorful dish, a delicious blend of herbs are combined with the green peppers and tomato sauce to create a dish fit for a king.

Makes 4 servings

2 teaspoons canola oil
2 medium, green bell peppers, cut into ¼-inch strips
½ cup chopped onion
1 packet low-sodium instant beef- or chicken-flavored broth mix
2 8-ounce cans salt-free (or regular) tomato sauce
½ teaspoon dried oregano
¼ teaspoon dried thyme
⅛ teaspoon garlic powder
1 bay leaf
1¼ pounds sole or flounder fillets

Heat oil in a large nonstick skillet over medium heat. Add green peppers, onion, and broth mix. Cook, stirring frequently, until vegetables are tender. Add small amounts of water if necessary (about a tablespoon at a time) to prevent sticking. Add tomato sauce and spices. Reduce heat slightly and simmer, uncovered, 10 minutes. Remove and discard bay leaf. Preheat oven to 375°. Spray a 7 x 11-inch baking pan with nonstick cooking spray. Arrange fish in pan. Pour sauce evenly over fish. Bake, uncovered, 20 minutes, or until fish flakes easily when tested with a fork.

Per Serving: Calories 216, Total Fat 4.1g, Cholesterol 70mg, Sodium 157mg, Total Carbohydrate 15.9g, Dietary Fiber 3.6g, Protein 29.1g

Flounder Parmigiana

The fish is rolled in seasoned breadcrumbs and topped with a delicately herbed sauce, then sprinkled lightly with Parmesan cheese. It's a very impressive dinner.

Makes 4 servings

¾ cup dry breadcrumbs
2 teaspoons dried oregano
⅛ teaspoon garlic powder
1¼ pounds flounder fillets
1 8-ounce can salt-free (or regular) tomato sauce
2 tablespoons minced onion flakes
¼ teaspoon dried basil
¼ teaspoon dried oregano
⅛ teaspoon garlic powder
3 tablespoons grated Parmesan cheese

Preheat oven to 350°. Spray a 7 x 11-inch baking pan with nonstick cooking spray. In a shallow bowl, combine breadcrumbs, oregano, and garlic powder. Dip fish fillets first into a bowl of water and then in crumbs. Place fish in prepared pan. Sprinkle any remaining crumbs over fish. Spray fish evenly with nonstick spray.

Bake, uncovered, 10 minutes. Combine tomato sauce and spices in a small bowl and pour evenly over fish. Sprinkle with Parmesan cheese. Bake 20 minutes longer, or until fish flakes easily when tested with a fork.

Per Serving: Calories 257, Total Fat 4.3g, Cholesterol 74mg, Sodium 395mg, Total Carbohydrate 22.5g, Dietary Fiber 1.9g, Protein 32.1g

Breaded Fillet of Sole

Fast, with no fuss, this delicious fish needs only a squeeze of fresh lemon to enhance its delicate flavor.

Makes 4 servings

¼ cup plus 2 tablespoons Italian seasoned breadcrumbs
⅓ cup nonfat dry milk
2 tablespoons minced onion flakes
⅛ teaspoon garlic powder
1¼ pounds sole or flounder fillets

Preheat oven to 400°. Spray a 7 x 11-inch baking pan with nonstick cooking spray. In a shallow bowl, combine breadcrumbs, dry milk, onion flakes, and garlic powder. Mix well. Dip each fish fillet first in a bowl of water and then in crumb mixture. Place fillets in prepared pan. Sprinkle any remaining crumb mixture evenly over fish. Spray fish evenly with cooking spray. Bake, uncovered, 10 minutes, or until fish flakes easily when tested with a fork.

Per Serving: Calories 209, Total Fat 2.1g, Cholesterol 72mg, Sodium 468mg, Total Carbohydrate 15.3g, Dietary Fiber 0.7g, Protein 32.1g

Caribbean Fish

The unique blend of flavors is reminiscent of the exotic tastes of the Caribbean. It's delicate and complex at the same time.

Makes 4 servings

1¼ pounds flounder, sole, or orange roughy fillets
1 6-ounce can tomato paste
½ cup water
1½ tablespoons lime juice
1½ teaspoons coconut extract
½ teaspoon dried oregano
½ teaspoon onion powder
¼ teaspoon garlic powder
¼ teaspoon salt
¼ teaspoon pepper
1 bay leaf, crumbled

Preheat oven to 375°. Spray a 7 x 11-inch baking pan with nonstick cooking spray. Place fish fillets in prepared pan. In a small bowl, combine remaining ingredients, mixing well. Spoon evenly over fish. Bake, uncovered, 20 minutes, or until fish flakes easily when tested with a fork.

Per Serving: Calories 167, Total Fat 1.9g, Cholesterol 70mg, Sodium 599mg, Total Carbohydrate 9.2g, Dietary Fiber 1.8g, Protein 28.3g

French Fish

The savory sauce is so easy to make, and it really dresses up this fish. When buying French dressing, choose one that has a deep, dark color—those usually have a richer flavor.

Makes 4 servings

1¼ pounds flounder, sole, or orange roughy fillets
¼ cup bottled fat-free French dressing
2 tablespoons grated Parmesan cheese
2 tablespoons minced onion flakes
1 tablespoon lemon juice
1 tablespoon water

Arrange fish in a single layer in a shallow baking pan. Combine remaining ingredients in a small bowl, mixing well. Spread evenly over fish. Marinate in the refrigerator 4 to 5 hours, or overnight, turning fish several times. Preheat oven to 375°. Bake fish, uncovered, 20 minutes, or until fish flakes easily when tested with a fork. For a crisper fish, place it under the broiler for a few minutes before serving.

Per Serving: Calories 168, Total Fat 2.6g, Cholesterol 72mg, Sodium 324mg, Total Carbohydrate 6g, Dietary Fiber 0.7g, Protein 28.2g

Snapper Creole

You can also use haddock or grouper for this classic Southern dish. The fish is baked first, then heated in a rich, savory sauce. It's perfect over brown rice or noodles.

Makes 4 servings

1¼ pounds snapper fillets
2 teaspoons canola oil
½ cup chopped onion
½ cup celery, thinly sliced
½ medium, green bell pepper, thinly sliced
2 cloves garlic, finely chopped
2 8-ounce cans salt-free (or regular) tomato sauce
½ cup water
1 tablespoon vinegar
1 teaspoon Worcestershire sauce
1 teaspoon sugar
2 bay leaves
1 teaspoon dried oregano
½ teaspoon dried thyme
½ teaspoon chili powder
Bottled hot pepper sauce

Bake fish in a 400° oven for 10 minutes, or until fish flakes easily when tested with a fork. Heat oil in a large saucepan over medium heat. Add onion, celery, green pepper, and garlic. Cook, stirring frequently, until vegetables are tender, about 8 minutes. Add small amounts of water if necessary (about a tablespoon at a time) to prevent sticking. Add remaining ingredients, except hot pepper sauce, to saucepan. When mixture boils, reduce heat to medium-low, cover, and simmer 15 minutes. Add fish. Continue to cook, covered, 10 more minutes. Add hot pepper sauce to taste. Remove and discard bay leaves.

Per Serving: Calories 220, Total Fat 4.3g, Cholesterol 53mg, Sodium 167mg, Total Carbohydrate 14.7g, Dietary Fiber 3.2g, Protein 31.1g

Italian Baked Fish

You can mix the marinade up quickly and put the fish in the refrigerator in the morning; then just pop it in the oven when ready. It's also great on a grill and makes a quick and easy summertime entrée.

Makes 4 servings

1¼ pounds flounder, sole, or orange roughy fillets
¼ cup bottled fat-free Italian dressing
2 tablespoons lemon juice
1 tablespoon Worcestershire sauce
⅛ teaspoon garlic powder

Arrange fish in a single layer in a shallow baking pan. Combine remaining ingredients in a small bowl, mixing well. Spoon over fish. Marinate in the refrigerator 4 to 5 hours, or overnight, turning fish occasionally.

Preheat oven to 375°. Bake fish, uncovered, 20 minutes, or until fish flakes easily when tested with a fork. For a crisper fish, place it under the broiler for a few minutes before serving.

Per Serving: Calories 136, Total Fat 1.7g, Cholesterol 70mg, Sodium 352mg, Total Carbohydrate 3.6g, Dietary Fiber 0g, Protein 26.7g

Springtime Broiled Fish

This easy, herbed fish is also great on a grill and makes a delicious dish for summertime entertaining.

Makes 4 servings

1¼ pounds flounder, sole, or orange roughy fillets
2 tablespoons reduced-calorie margarine
1 tablespoon lemon juice
1 teaspoon dill weed
½ teaspoon onion powder
½ teaspoon grated fresh lemon peel
¼ teaspoon dried oregano
⅛ teaspoon salt
⅛ teaspoon pepper
Dash paprika

Place fish in a shallow broiler pan. Place margarine in a small saucepan and heat over low heat until almost melted. Remove from heat and stir in remaining ingredients. Spread half of the mixture evenly over fish. Place fish, margarine-side up, under a preheated broiler. Cook 3 to 5 minutes, then turn fish, spread with remaining margarine mixture, and broil 3 to 5 minutes more, or until fish flakes easily when tested with a fork.

Per Serving: Calories 144, Total Fat 4g, Cholesterol 70mg, Sodium 234mg, Total Carbohydrate 0.6g, Dietary Fiber 0g, Protein 26.7g

Spicy Fish Cakes

A wonderful stand-in for crab cakes, these delectable patties can be made from any non-oily, mild fish, such as flounder, sole, or orange roughy. You can make them "on purpose," or whenever you have leftover fish.

Makes 4 servings (2 fish cakes each serving)

12 ounces cooked fish, flaked
2 slices whole wheat bread (1-ounce slices), crumbled
2 egg whites
1 tablespoon plus 1 teaspoon reduced-calorie mayonnaise
1 teaspoon Worcestershire sauce
1 teaspoon baking powder
1 teaspoon seafood seasoning (such as Old Bay)
Salt and pepper to taste

In a large bowl, combine fish and breadcrumbs. Combine remaining ingredients in a small bowl and mix well. Add to fish and mix with a fork until well blended. Divide mixture evenly and shape into 8 patties, ½- to ¾-inch thick. Spray a large nonstick skillet or griddle with nonstick cooking spray and preheat over medium heat. Place fish cakes in skillet and cook, turning several times, until nicely browned on both sides.

Per Serving: Calories 151, Total Fat 2.8g, Cholesterol 59mg, Sodium 534mg, Total Carbohydrate 8g, Dietary Fiber 1g, Protein 23.5g

"Pretend" Salmon Salad

Less expensive than salmon, haddock fillets make a wonderful cold salad that will please even the most discriminating gourmet. Make this dish up to a day ahead and chill it thoroughly to blend the wonderful flavors.

Makes 4 servings

1¼ pounds haddock fillets
2 tablespoons lemon juice
½ cup plain nonfat Greek yogurt
¼ cup bottled chili sauce
2 tablespoons reduced-calorie mayonnaise
½ cup finely chopped celery
2 tablespoons finely chopped onion
1 teaspoon sugar
¼ teaspoon celery salt
⅛ teaspoon pepper

Preheat oven to 375°. Place fish in a shallow pan than has been sprayed with nonstick cooking spray. Bake 20 minutes, or until fish flakes easily when tested with a fork. Cool for 15 minutes, then flake fish into a large bowl. Combine remaining ingredients in a small bowl and mix well. Spoon over fish and blend well with a fork. Chill several hours or overnight to blend flavors.

Per Serving: Calories 178, Total Fat 2.6g, Cholesterol 83mg, Sodium 397mg, Total Carbohydrate 9.6g, Dietary Fiber 1.4g, Protein 29.2g

Lemony Stuffed Fish

I used to make this luscious dish with butter and serve it at all of my dinner parties. Now I use reduced-calorie margarine instead, along with some butter flavor, and, even though I've trimmed the fat, the result is still a wonderful party dish. (Look for butter flavor with the extracts in most large grocery stores.)

Makes 4 servings

¼ cup reduced-calorie margarine
½ cup finely chopped onion
½ cup finely chopped celery
½ cup plain nonfat yogurt
2 tablespoons lemon juice
1 tablespoon grated fresh lemon peel
1 teaspoon imitation butter flavor
1 teaspoon paprika
1 teaspoon dill weed
¼ teaspoon salt
4 slices whole wheat bread (1-ounce slices), cubed
1¼ pounds flounder fillets

Preheat oven to 375°. Spray a 1-quart baking dish with nonstick cooking spray. Melt margarine in a small nonstick skillet over medium heat. Add onion and celery and cook, stirring frequently, until tender, about 5 minutes. Transfer to a small bowl. Stir in yogurt, lemon juice, lemon peel, butter flavor, paprika, dill weed, and salt. Add bread cubes, mixing well. Place half of the fillets in prepared baking dish. Spoon stuffing evenly over fish. Top with remaining fillets. Press fish down firmly onto stuffing. Sprinkle with additional paprika. Bake, uncovered, 30 minutes, or until fish flakes easily when tested with a fork.

Per Serving: Calories 269, Total Fat 7.6g, Cholesterol 70mg, Sodium 569mg, Total Carbohydrate 18.9g, Dietary Fiber 3g, Protein 31.6g

Potato-Fish Patties

Affectionately known as "coddies" when I was a kid, these patties were usually topped with mustard and served between saltine crackers. They make a wonderful change-of-pace lunch.

Makes 4 servings (2 patties each serving)

1 pound cod fillets
1 pound cooked potatoes, mashed (2 medium baking potatoes)
¼ cup evaporated skim milk
2 tablespoons grated onion
1 tablespoon plus 1 teaspoon Worcestershire sauce
2 teaspoons canola oil
¼ teaspoon garlic powder
Salt and pepper to taste

Preheat oven to 350°. Bake fish for 30 minutes in a shallow pan that has been sprayed with a nonstick cooking spray, until fish flakes easily when tested with a fork. Set aside to cool. In a large bowl, combine potatoes, milk, and onion. Mix well. Stir in remaining ingredients. Flake fish and add to bowl. Mix well. (Add a little water, a few teaspoons at a time, if mixture is too dry to hold together.) Chill thoroughly.

Shape mixture into 8 patties about ½ - to ¾-inch thick. Spray a large nonstick skillet or griddle with nonstick cooking spray and preheat over medium heat. Place fish cakes in skillet and cook, turning several times, until nicely browned on both sides.

Per Serving: Calories 229, Total Fat 3.2g, Cholesterol 50mg, Sodium 141mg, Total Carbohydrate 26.7g, Dietary Fiber 2.2g, Protein 23.5g

Lemon-Broiled Scallops

Incredibly easy and just as delicious, this dish can also be made on the grill. Served with seasoned rice and steamed broccoli, it makes an elegant meal.

Makes 4 servings

1 pound scallops, uncooked
2 tablespoons reduced-calorie margarine, melted
3 tablespoons lemon juice
1 teaspoon grated fresh lemon peel
1 teaspoon Worcestershire sauce
½ teaspoon dried tarragon
½ teaspoon dried basil
¼ teaspoon salt

Preheat broiler. Place scallops in a shallow baking pan that has been sprayed with a nonstick cooking spray. Combine remaining ingredients in a small bowl. Baste scallops with half of this mixture. Broil three to five minutes, or until edges of scallops begin to crisp. Turn scallops, baste with remaining sauce, and broil 3 to 5 minutes more, or until scallops are done.

Per Serving: Calories 121, Total Fat 3.1g, Cholesterol 38mg, Sodium 389mg, Total Carbohydrate 4.2g, Dietary Fiber 0.2g, Protein 19g

Teriyaki Scallops

Stir-fry some veggies in a little bit of soy sauce, cook some brown rice, broil your scallops, and you have a delectable feast. This versatile marinade also works well with shrimp.

Makes 4 servings

¼ cup reduced-sodium soy sauce
2 tablespoons dry sherry
2 teaspoons sugar
1 teaspoon ground ginger
¼ teaspoon garlic powder
1 pound scallops, uncooked

In a shallow bowl, combine all ingredients except scallops. Mix well. Add scallops. Marinate in the refrigerator for several hours. Drain, reserving marinade. Preheat broiler. Place scallops in a shallow broiler pan. Baste with marinade. Broil 3 to 5 minutes, or until edges of scallops begin to crisp. Turn scallops, baste again with marinade, and broil 3 to 5 minutes more, or until scallops are done.

Per Serving: Calories 114, Total Fat 0.9g, Cholesterol 38mg, Sodium 715mg, Total Carbohydrate 6.7g, Dietary Fiber 0.2g, Protein 19.8g

Crab and Cheddar Casserole

This has been one of my favorite special occasion dishes for years, with the splash of sherry adding a richness and elegance that will win you rave reviews. It can also be made with flaked fish in place of the crab.

Makes 4 servings

3 tablespoons all-purpose flour
⅔ cup nonfat dry milk
¼ teaspoon dry mustard
⅛ teaspoon salt
⅛ teaspoon pepper
1 cup water
3 ounces shredded reduced-fat Cheddar cheese (¾ cup)
2 tablespoons dry sherry
12 ounces crabmeat (1½ cups)

Preheat oven to 350°. Spray a 1-quart casserole with nonstick cooking spray. In a small saucepan, combine flour, dry milk, mustard, salt, and pepper. Mix well. Gradually add water, stirring briskly to avoid lumps. Heat over medium heat, stirring constantly, until mixture thickens. Remove from heat. Stir cheese and sherry into milk mixture, mixing until cheese is completely melted. Stir in crabmeat. Place in prepared casserole. Bake, uncovered, 20 minutes.

Per Serving: Calories 213, Total Fat 3.4g, Cholesterol 94mg, Sodium 551mg, Total Carbohydrate 15.5g, Dietary Fiber 0.2g, Protein 30.3g

French Herbed Shrimp

Serve this deliciously herbed shrimp over rice or any other grain for an elegant and delicious dinner.

Makes 4 servings

2 teaspoons canola oil
½ cup chopped onion
3 cloves garlic, finely minced
3 tablespoons all-purpose flour
2 cups water
1 8-ounce can salt-free (or regular) tomato sauce
2 teaspoons Worcestershire sauce
1 teaspoon lemon juice
2 bay leaves
1 teaspoon sugar
¼ teaspoon salt
¼ teaspoon dried thyme
⅛ teaspoon pepper
Bottled hot pepper sauce to taste
12 ounces cooked, peeled shrimp

Heat oil in a medium saucepan over medium heat. Add onion and garlic. Cook, stirring frequently, 3 to 5 minutes, until tender. Add small amounts of water if necessary, (about a tablespoon at a time) to prevent sticking. Place flour in a small bowl. Gradually add ½ cup of the water, stirring briskly to avoid lumps. Add flour mixture and remaining ingredients except shrimp to saucepan. Mix well. When mixture boils, reduce heat to medium-low and simmer, covered, 25 minutes, stirring occasionally. Remove and discard bay leaves. Add shrimp. Simmer 5 minutes more.

Per Serving: Calories 165, Total Fat 3.9g, Cholesterol 128mg, Sodium 326mg, Total Carbohydrate 13.8g, Dietary Fiber 1.5g, Protein 18.9g

Shrimp Scampi

This classic dish is always a favorite. I've removed most of the oil and substituted white wine instead, adding even more flavor to an already delicious dish.

Makes 4 servings

⅓ cup dry white wine
3 tablespoons lemon juice
2 tablespoons canola oil
2 tablespoons Worcestershire sauce
1 tablespoon water
2 tablespoons grated Parmesan cheese
1 tablespoon dried parsley flakes
1 teaspoon dried oregano
¼ teaspoon garlic powder
¼ teaspoon salt
¼ teaspoon pepper
1¼ pounds cleaned raw shrimp

Combine all ingredients except shrimp in a shallow bowl. Add shrimp. Marinate in the refrigerator for several hours. Remove shrimp from marinade and place in a shallow baking pan. Broil 6 inches from heat for 8 to 10 minutes, turning occasionally, until shrimp are done. While shrimp is broiling, bring marinade to a boil in a small saucepan. Simmer 2 minutes. Place shrimp in a serving bowl and add marinade.

Per Serving: Calories 231, Total Fat 10.2g, Cholesterol 215mg, Sodium 501mg, Total Carbohydrate 4.9g, Dietary Fiber 0.3g, Protein 30.2g

Tuna Noodle Casserole

This homestyle casserole has been a family favorite of mine for years. Although the ingredients have changed (low-fat dairy products in place of the original sour cream), this is still the best tuna casserole I have ever tasted.

Makes 6 servings

6 ounces medium yolk-free noodles, uncooked
1 cup low-fat (1%) cottage cheese
¾ cup plain nonfat Greek yogurt
1 tablespoon all-purpose flour
2 teaspoons Worcestershire sauce
¼ teaspoon salt
⅛ teaspoon pepper
⅛ teaspoon garlic powder
½ cup frozen peas
¼ cup finely minced onion
1 8-ounce can mushroom pieces, drained
2 6½-ounce cans tuna (packed in water), drained and flaked (8 ounces)
3 tablespoons grated Parmesan cheese

Preheat oven to 350°. Spray an 8-inch square baking pan with nonstick cooking spray. Cook noodles according to package directions. Drain. In a large bowl, combine cottage cheese, yogurt, flour, Worcestershire sauce, salt, pepper, and garlic powder. Mix well. Stir in peas, onion, mushrooms, tuna, and noodles. Spoon into prepared baking pan. Sprinkle Parmesan cheese evenly over casserole. Bake, uncovered, 30 minutes, or until hot.

Per Serving: Calories 280, Total Fat 4.2g, Cholesterol 36mg, Sodium 815mg, Total Carbohydrate 29.9g, Dietary Fiber 2.1g, Protein 31.2g

Italian Tuna Casserole

This delicious casserole is so tasty, you won't believe how easy it is to prepare. Even though it's served hot, the leftovers are also delicious cold.

Makes 6 servings

2 6½-ounce cans tuna (packed in water), drained and flaked (8 ounces)
1 1-pound can salt-free (or regular) tomatoes, chopped and drained
1 4-ounce can mushroom pieces, drained
¼ cup chopped onion
¼ cup chopped green bell pepper
1 cup liquid egg substitute
1 cup nonfat dry milk
1¼ cups water
1 tablespoon dry sherry
1½ teaspoons dried oregano
½ teaspoon dried basil
¼ teaspoon salt
¼ teaspoon pepper
2 teaspoons grated Parmesan cheese

Preheat oven to 350°. Spray an 8-inch square baking pan with nonstick cooking spray. Layer tuna, tomatoes, mushrooms, onion, and green pepper in prepared pan. In a small bowl, combine remaining ingredients except Parmesan cheese. Beat with a fork or wire whisk until blended. Pour over tuna and vegetables. Sprinkle with Parmesan cheese. Bake, uncovered, 40 to 45 minutes, until set.

Per Serving: Calories 222, Total Fat 2.6g, Cholesterol 25mg, Sodium 503mg, Total Carbohydrate 16.3g, Dietary Fiber 1.8g, Protein 34g

Tuna Seashell Salad

This easy salad makes an ideal light summer dinner. Add slices of fresh tomatoes and perhaps some corn on the cob, and your dinner is complete.

Makes 4 servings

- 2 6½-ounce cans tuna (packed in water), drained and flaked (8 ounces)
- 2 cups cooked whole wheat macaroni shells.
- 1 cup thinly sliced celery
- ¼ cup finely chopped onion
- 2 tablespoons reduced-calorie mayonnaise
- 2 tablespoons lemon juice
- 1 tablespoon vinegar
- 1 tablespoon dried parsley flakes
- ½ teaspoon celery seed
- ½ teaspoon dill weed
- ¼ teaspoon salt
- ⅛ teaspoon pepper

In a large bowl, combine flaked tuna with macaroni. Add celery and onion and toss to combine. In a small bowl, combine remaining ingredients. Mix well. Pour over tuna mixture. Mix well. Chill several hours to blend flavors.

Per Serving: Calories 259, Total Fat 2.9g, Cholesterol 32mg, Sodium 394mg, Total Carbohydrate 24.2g, Dietary Fiber 1.7g, Protein 34.1g

Superb Salmon Loaf

The leftovers of this delicately flavored loaf make wonderful sandwiches. Try it between 2 slices of whole grain bread with a little ketchup and a slice of pickle for a "banquet on bread."

Makes 4 servings

1 14¾ -ounce can salmon, drained and flaked (12 ounces)
½ cup liquid egg substitute
2 slices whole wheat bread (1-ounce slices), crumbled
⅔ cup nonfat dry milk
½ cup finely chopped green bell pepper
¼ cup finely chopped onion
1 teaspoon lemon juice
1 teaspoon dried basil
½ teaspoon grated fresh lemon peel
½ teaspoon dried parsley flakes
¼ teaspoon salt
¼ teaspoon pepper
¼ teaspoon dry mustard
¼ teaspoon celery seed

Preheat oven to 350°. Spray a 4 x 8-inch loaf pan with nonstick cooking spray. In a large bowl, combine all ingredients, mixing well. Spoon mixture into prepared pan. Press in pan gently with the back of a spoon. Bake, uncovered, 1 hour, or until top of loaf is golden. Let stand 5 minutes, then remove loaf to a serving plate.

Per Serving: Calories 261, Total Fat 5.9g, Cholesterol 73mg, Sodium 724mg, Total Carbohydrate 19.8g, Dietary Fiber 2.3g, Protein 32.5g

Bengal Seafood Salad

This unusual salad has an exotic flavor and a wonderful blend of textures. It's lovely served on a bed of lettuce, accompanied by sliced, fresh pineapple and tomatoes.

Makes 6 servings

12 ounces crabmeat (1½ cups)
4 ounces cooked, peeled shrimp, cut into 1-inch pieces
1 cup thinly sliced celery
¼ cup finely chopped onion
3 ounces sliced water chestnuts
1 cup canned crushed pineapple (packed in juice), undrained
1¼ cup raisins
2 tablespoons sunflower seeds (raw or dry roasted)
¾ cup plain nonfat Greek yogurt
3 tablespoons reduced-calorie mayonnaise
3 tablespoons lemon juice
1 teaspoon coconut extract
2 teaspoons curry powder, or more to taste

In a large bowl, combine crabmeat, shrimp, celery, onion, water chestnuts, pineapple, raisins, and sunflower seeds. Mix well. In a small bowl, combine remaining ingredients. Add to crab mixture and mix well. Chill several hours to blend flavors.

Per Serving: Calories 282, Total Fat 3.8g, Cholesterol 72mg, Sodium 292mg, Total Carbohydrate 44.1g, Dietary Fiber 3g, Protein 18g

Seafood Quiche

Most quiches are made with cream and whole eggs, making them very high in fat and cholesterol. Switching to skim milk and egg substitute lets you keep the fat content low without sacrificing flavor.

Makes 8 servings

To prepare crust:

½ cup all-purpose flour
¼ cup whole wheat flour
¼ teaspoon baking powder
⅛ teaspoon salt
2 tablespoons plus 2 teaspoons margarine
3 tablespoons plus 2 teaspoons ice water

To prepare filling:

8 ounces cooked fish, shrimp, or crabmeat, cut into small chunks
1 4-ounce can mushroom pieces, drained
½ cup thinly sliced green onion
4 ounces shredded reduced-fat Swiss cheese (1 cup)
1 cup liquid egg substitute
1¼ cups water
⅔ cup nonfat dry milk
1 tablespoon dry sherry
1 tablespoon grated Parmesan cheese

Preheat oven to 450°. Have a 9-inch pie pan ready. To prepare crust: In a medium bowl, combine both types of flour, baking powder, and salt, mixing well. Add margarine. Mix with a fork or pastry blender until mixture resembles coarse crumbs. Add water. Mix with a fork until dry ingredients are moistened. Work dough into a ball, using your hands. (Add a little more flour if dough is sticky, or a little more water if dough is too dry.) Roll dough between 2 sheets of wax paper into an 11-inch circle. Remove top sheet of wax paper and invert crust into prepared pan. Fit crust into pan, leaving an overhang. Carefully remove remaining wax paper. Bend edges of crust under and flute dough with your fingers or a fork. Prick the bottom and sides of crust with a fork about 20 times. Bake 8 minutes. Reduce oven temperature to 350°.

To prepare filling: Sprinkle seafood, mushrooms, green onion, and Swiss cheese evenly in crust. In a blender, combine remaining ingredients. Blend until smooth. Pour over seafood. Bake 45 minutes, or until set and lightly browned. Let stand 5 minutes before cutting.

Per Serving: Calories 204, Total Fat 6.4g, Cholesterol 27mg, Sodium 305mg, Total Carbohydrate 15.8g, Dietary Fiber 1.2g, Protein 20.1g

Bouillabaisse

This cross between a soup and a stew is so filling and hearty. All you need is a salad and a loaf of crusty French bread. You'll serve it time and time again.

Makes 6 servings

1 tablespoon olive oil
½ cup chopped carrots
½ cup chopped onion
3 cloves garlic, finely chopped
2 medium leeks, thinly sliced (white part only)
1 1-pound can salt-free (or regular) tomatoes, chopped and drained
4 cups water
1 tablespoon dried parsley flakes
1 bay leaf
½ teaspoon salt
¼ teaspoon saffron, crumbled
¼ teaspoon dried thyme
Pepper to taste
1¾ pounds seafood, uncooked, cut into 1-inch pieces (Use any combination of flounder, sole, haddock, scallops, shrimp, lobster, or crabmeat.)

Heat oil in a large saucepan over medium heat. Add carrots, onion, garlic, and leeks. Cook, stirring frequently, 10 minutes. Add small amounts of water if necessary (about a tablespoon at a time) to keep vegetables from sticking. Add remaining ingredients except seafood. Bring to a boil, then reduce heat to medium-low, cover, and simmer 30 minutes. Add seafood. Continue to cook, uncovered, 15 minutes, or until seafood is thoroughly cooked. Remove and discard bay leaf before serving. Divide seafood evenly into 6 bowls. Spoon soup over seafood.

Per Serving: Calories 169, Total Fat 4g, Cholesterol 65mg, Sodium 323mg, Total Carbohydrate 7.4g, Dietary Fiber 1.6g, Protein 26g

Poultry

The versatility of chicken and turkey have made them universal favorites, with almost every culture having its own traditional favorites.

When buying chicken, the white meat is your best bet, because it is lower in fat than the dark meat. One very important tip in cooking chicken is to remove the skin before cooking. Because the skin itself has a very high fat content, leaving it on can add quite a bit of fat per serving.

Turkey cutlets are one of my quick-cooking favorites, and ground turkey is versatile for use in meat loaves and casseroles. However, when buying ground turkey it is important to read the label carefully, as some brands may contain a high percentage of skin. I recommend 93/7 as ground turkey. My easy-to-prepare poultry recipes will show you that the variations are endless.

I choose my cooking methods carefully (baking and broiling rather than frying) and use lots of herbs and spices, rather than high-fat sauces, to enliven my dishes.

Chicken and Peppers

You can use either red or green bell peppers for this dish depending on the taste you prefer (red peppers are much sweeter than the green). Or, if you like both types of peppers, you can use half red and half green.

Makes 4 servings

1 pound boneless, skinless chicken breasts, cut into 1-inch slices
3 tablespoons reduced-sodium soy sauce
¼ cup dry sherry
2 teaspoons ground ginger
2 teaspoons canola oil
1 cup chopped onion
3 cloves garlic, crushed
4 medium red or green bell peppers, sliced ¼ -inch thick
½ cup water

In a medium bowl, combine chicken with soy sauce, sherry, and ginger. Marinate in the refrigerator several hours, turning chicken several times. Heat oil in a large nonstick skillet over medium heat. Add onion and garlic. Cook, stirring frequently, 3 minutes. Add peppers and continue to cook and stir 3 more minutes. Add chicken and marinade. Cook, stirring frequently, until chicken loses its pink color. Reduce heat to medium-low, add water, cover, and cook 15 minutes, or until chicken is done.

Per Serving: Calories 182, Total Fat 4g, Cholesterol 65mg, Sodium 569mg, Total Carbohydrate 8.9g, Dietary Fiber 1.5g, Protein 27.8g

Chicken Scampi

You've seen it with shrimp. Now try this unique version made with chicken.

Makes 4 servings

¼ cup dry white wine
3 tablespoons lemon juice
2 tablespoons Worcestershire sauce
2 tablespoons grated Parmesan cheese
1 tablespoon canola oil
1 tablespoon dried parsley flakes
1 teaspoon dried oregano
¼ teaspoon garlic powder
¼ teaspoon salt
¼ teaspoon pepper
1 pound boneless, skinless chicken breasts, cut into 1-inch strips

Combine all ingredients, except chicken, in a shallow bowl. Mix well. Add chicken. Turn chicken over several times to coat each piece with marinade. Marinate in the refrigerator for several hours, turning chicken several times.

Preheat broiler. Place chicken in a shallow pan and broil 4 to 5 inches from heat, turning chicken several times. Cook until chicken is no longer pink inside, about 6 to 8 minutes. Baste with any remaining marinade while cooking.

Per Serving: Calories 176, Total Fat 5.7g, Cholesterol 67mg, Sodium 349mg, Total Carbohydrate 3.5g, Dietary Fiber 0.3g, Protein 27.6g

Asian Chicken and Mushrooms

This chicken is delicious served over Asian noodles. Look for the whole grain, dark-colored soba or somen noodles in health food stores and most large grocery stores.

Makes 4 servings

1 pound boneless, skinless chicken breasts
1 tablespoon minced onion flakes
3 tablespoons reduced-sodium soy sauce
2 teaspoons honey
¼ teaspoon garlic powder
½ cup chopped green bell pepper
2½ cups sliced mushrooms
½ cup low-sodium chicken broth (or ½ cup of water and ½ packet low-sodium instant chicken-flavored broth mix)

Preheat oven to 350°. Spray a 7 x 11-inch baking dish with nonstick cooking spray. Place chicken in prepared pan. Sprinkle with onion flakes. In a small bowl, combine soy sauce, honey, and garlic powder and pour evenly over chicken. Cover and bake 30 minutes.

Spread green pepper and mushrooms evenly over chicken. Drizzle broth over chicken and continue to bake, covered, 20 minutes more.

Per Serving: Calories 162, Total Fat 1.7g, Cholesterol 65mg, Sodium 487mg, Total Carbohydrate 8.3g, Dietary Fiber 1g, Protein 28.4g

Chicken in Wine Sauce

This has long been one of my favorite party dishes. It tastes best when made a day ahead and reheated, making it an easy dish for entertaining. It's delicious over couscous.

Makes 4 servings

1 cup rosé wine
3 tablespoons reduced-sodium soy sauce
2 tablespoons water
3 cloves garlic, crushed
1 tablespoon firmly packed brown sugar
1 teaspoon ground ginger
½ teaspoon dried oregano
1 pound boneless, skinless chicken breasts

Combine all ingredients, *except* chicken, in a shallow casserole, mixing well. Add chicken. Marinate in the refrigerator several hours.* Preheat oven to 375°. Bake, covered, 1 hour.

**If chicken is to be served the following day, marinating is not necessary. Just bake and refrigerate. Reheat before serving.*

Per Serving: Calories 146, Total Fat 1.4g, Cholesterol 65mg, Sodium 476mg, Total Carbohydrate 6.2g, Dietary Fiber 0.3g, Protein 27g

Pineapple Mandarin Chicken

The sweetness of orange and pineapple makes a delicious contrast to the tartness of the vinegar in this unusual dish. It really makes an attractive presentation when served on a bed of brown and wild rice.

Makes 4 servings

1 pound boneless, skinless chicken breasts
½ cup canned crushed pineapple (packed in juice), undrained
2 small oranges, peeled and sectioned, white membrane discarded
¼ cup orange juice
1 tablespoon cornstarch
2 tablespoons very finely minced onion
3 tablespoons reduced-sodium soy sauce
1 tablespoon vinegar
½ teaspoon dry mustard
¼ teaspoon garlic powder

Preheat oven to 350°. Spray a shallow baking dish with nonstick cooking spray. Place chicken in prepared dish. Spread crushed pineapple and orange sections evenly over chicken. In a small bowl, combine remaining ingredients, stirring until cornstarch is dissolved. Pour over chicken. Bake, covered, 1 hour.

Per Serving: Calories 195, Total Fat 1.6g, Cholesterol 65mg, Sodium 473mg, Total Carbohydrate 17.4g, Dietary Fiber 2.2g, Protein 27.6g

Golden Crowned Chicken

Apples and carrots make this an outstanding flavor treat, as well as a colorful and attractive way to prepare chicken.

Makes 4 servings

1 pound boneless, skinless chicken breasts
2 small Golden Delicious apples, peeled, cut into 1-inch chunks
1 1-pound can carrots, drained and cut into ½-inch chunks (or 2 cups fresh carrots, steamed)
1 packet low-sodium instant chicken-flavored broth mix
1 tablespoon plus 1 teaspoon honey
¼ cup plus 2 tablespoons dry breadcrumbs
1 tablespoon plus 1 teaspoon reduced-calorie margarine

Preheat oven to 350°. Spray a 1-quart shallow casserole with nonstick cooking spray. Place chicken in prepared pan. In a small bowl, combine apples and carrots. Stir in broth mix and honey. Spoon carrot mixture evenly over chicken. Sprinkle with breadcrumbs. Dot with margarine. Cover tightly and bake 30 minutes. Uncover and continue to bake 30 minutes more.

Per Serving: Calories 269, Total Fat 3.7g, Cholesterol 65mg, Sodium 213mg, Total Carbohydrate 30.5g, Dietary Fiber 3.5g, Protein 28.2g

Orange Barbecue Chicken

Orange marmalade adds a delicious, sweet flavor to this crowd-pleasing version of an all-time favorite. It's delicious and attractive served over fine, yolk-free noodles.

Makes 6 servings

1½ pounds boneless, skinless chicken breasts
1 8-ounce can salt-free (or regular) tomato sauce
3 tablespoons fruit-only orange marmalade
1 tablespoon minced onion flakes
1 teaspoon vinegar
1 teaspoon Worcestershire sauce
¼ teaspoon garlic powder
Bottled hot sauce to taste
Salt and pepper to taste

Preheat oven to 350°. Spray a 7 x 11-inch baking pan with nonstick cooking spray. Place chicken in prepared pan. Combine remaining ingredients and spread *half* of the sauce over chicken. Bake, uncovered, 1 hour, basting with sauce several times. Heat remaining sauce and serve with chicken.

Per Serving: Calories 152, Total Fat 1.4g, Cholesterol 65mg
Sodium 89mg, Total Carbohydrate 7.8g, Dietary Fiber 0.7g, Protein 26.9g

Chicken in White Wine

White wine and herbs give this easy dish a truly gourmet taste. The leftovers make a great sandwich, either hot or cold.

Makes 4 servings

1 pound boneless, skinless chicken breasts
½ cup dry white wine
2 tablespoons grated onion
½ teaspoon celery salt
½ teaspoon pepper
¼ teaspoon dried thyme
¼ teaspoon dried marjoram
¼ teaspoon dried rosemary, crumbled

Place chicken in a shallow baking pan. Combine remaining ingredients in a small bowl and pour over chicken. Marinate in the refrigerator several hours, turning chicken several times. Preheat oven to 350°. Bake chicken, uncovered, 1 hour, basting several times.

Per Serving: Calories 125, Total Fat 1.4g, Cholesterol 65mg, Sodium 74mg, Total Carbohydrate 1.7g, Dietary Fiber 0.2g, Protein 26.3g

Spice-Glazed Chicken

This recipe has been a family favorite for years. When you try it, you'll see why.

Makes 4 servings

1 pound boneless, skinless chicken breasts
⅓ cup ketchup
⅓ cup water
2 tablespoons plus 2 teaspoons sugar
2 tablespoons vinegar
1 tablespoon canola oil
1 teaspoon Worcestershire sauce
¾ teaspoon dry mustard
1 bay leaf
1 cup thinly sliced onion, separated into rings after measuring

Preheat oven to 350°. Spray a 1-quart baking pan with nonstick cooking spray. Place chicken in prepared pan. In a small saucepan, combine remaining ingredients. Bring to a boil over medium heat, then reduce heat to medium-low and simmer 2 minutes, stirring frequently. Baste chicken with a little of the sauce, leaving the onions in the saucepan. Bake chicken, uncovered, 1 hour, basting frequently with the sauce. During the last 20 minutes of baking, arrange onion rings over chicken. Remove and discard bay leaf. Serve any remaining sauce with the cooked chicken.

Per Serving: Calories 230, Total Fat 5.2g, Cholesterol 65mg, Sodium 326mg, Total Carbohydrate 18.3g, Dietary Fiber 1.1g, Protein 27.2g

Chicken Cacciatore

There are many versions of this popular Italian dish, but I'm particularly partial to this one. Serve it over noodles, add a green vegetable, and you have a dinner to be proud of.

Makes 4 servings

2 teaspoons olive oil
1 cup sliced onion
2 cloves garlic, finely chopped
1 1-pound can salt-free (or regular) tomatoes, chopped and undrained
1 8-ounce can salt-free (or regular) tomato sauce
1 teaspoon dried oregano
½ teaspoon celery seed
¼ teaspoon salt
¼ teaspoon pepper
1 bay leaf
1 pound boneless, skinless chicken breasts, cut into quarters
¼ cup dry white wine

Heat oil in a large saucepan over medium heat. Add onion and garlic. Cook, stirring frequently, until onion is tender, about 10 minutes. Add small amounts of water as necessary (about a tablespoon at a time) to prevent sticking. Add tomatoes, tomato sauce, and spices, stirring to blend. Add chicken. Cover, reduce heat to medium-low, and simmer 1 hour, stirring occasionally. Add wine. Cook, uncovered, 15 minutes. Remove and discard bay leaf before serving.

Per Serving: Calories 203, Total Fat 3.9g, Cholesterol 65mg, Sodium 242mg, Total Carbohydrate 13.1g, Dietary Fiber 2.9g, Protein 28.7g

Peachy Spiced Chicken

Very moist and topped with peaches and spices, this is really a special dish. It's delicious with rice or any cooked grain.

Makes 4 servings

1 pound boneless, skinless chicken breasts
3 fresh peaches, peeled and sliced, or 1½ cups canned peach slices (packed in juice), drained
½ cup orange juice
1 tablespoon vinegar
1 tablespoon firmly packed brown sugar
½ teaspoon dried basil
¼ teaspoon ground nutmeg
¼ teaspoon garlic powder

Several hours before baking, place chicken in an 8-inch-square baking pan that has been sprayed with a nonstick cooking spray. Combine peaches with remaining ingredients, mixing well. Pour over chicken. Marinate in the refrigerator for several hours. Preheat oven to 350°. Cover chicken tightly and bake 1 hour.

Per Serving: Calories 204, Total Fat 1.6g, Cholesterol 65mg, Sodium 80mg, Total Carbohydrate 20.6g, Dietary Fiber 1.4g, Protein 26.8g

Honey Crunch Chicken

I found that "painting" the chicken with reduced-calorie mayonnaise seals in the moistness and the cereal on the outside adds a wonderful crunch. You'll choose this one time and again.

Makes 4 servings

1 pound boneless, skinless chicken breasts
2 tablespoons plus 2 teaspoons reduced-calorie mayonnaise
1½ ounces Grape Nuts cereal, crushed (⅓ cup)
1 tablespoon plus 1 teaspoon honey

Preheat oven to 375°. Spray a 1-quart baking pan with nonstick cooking spray. Rinse chicken and pat dry. Place in prepared pan. Using a pastry brush, spread mayonnaise over both sides of the chicken. Sprinkle the cereal evenly over top side of chicken. Drizzle evenly with honey. Let chicken stand at room temperature for 10 minutes. Bake, uncovered, 45 minutes.

Per Serving: Calories 204, Total Fat 3.8g, Cholesterol 68mg, Sodium 224mg, Total Carbohydrate 15g, Dietary Fiber 0.9g, Protein 27.3g

Lazy Day Chicken

This dish got its name due to its incredible ease of preparation. When you're in a hurry or just don't feel like cooking, this dish is ideal.

Makes 4 servings

1 pound boneless, skinless chicken breasts
1 8-ounce can salt-free (or regular) tomato sauce
2 tablespoons minced onion flakes
1 packet low-sodium instant beef-flavored broth mix
¼ teaspoon garlic powder
½ cup water

Preheat oven to 350°. Spray a shallow casserole with nonstick cooking spray. Place chicken in prepared pan. In a small bowl, combine remaining ingredients, mixing well. Spoon over chicken. Cover and bake 30 minutes. Uncover and continue to bake 20 minutes more.

Per Serving: Calories 144, Total Fat 1.4g, Cholesterol 65mg, Sodium 84mg, Total Carbohydrate 5.4g, Dietary Fiber 1.1g, Protein 27.3g

Apricot-Glazed Chicken

My kids' all-time favorite chicken dish, this one is so easy you won't mind making it over and over.

Makes 4 servings

1 pound boneless, skinless chicken breasts
⅓ cup bottled fat-free French dressing
3 tablespoons fruit-only apricot spread
2 tablespoons water
1 tablespoon plus 1 teaspoon canola oil
1 tablespoon minced onion flakes
1 packet low-sodium instant beef-flavored broth mix

Preheat oven to 350°. Spray a shallow casserole with nonstick cooking spray. Place chicken in prepared pan. In a small bowl, combine remaining ingredients, mixing well. Spread sauce evenly over chicken. Bake, uncovered, 1 hour.

Per Serving: Calories 223, Total Fat 5.8g, Cholesterol 65mg, Sodium 275mg, Total Carbohydrate 16.3g, Dietary Fiber 0.8g, Protein 26.3g

Chicken Dijon

Dijon mustard and herbs make this dish spicy and delicious. It's a perfect dinner, for family or guests, served with a baked potato and a pile of steamed fresh broccoli and cauliflower.

Makes 4 servings

1 pound boneless, skinless chicken breasts
2 tablespoons Dijon mustard
1 tablespoon plus 1 teaspoon olive oil
1 teaspoon dried parsley flakes
½ teaspoon dried rosemary, crumbled
½ teaspoon paprika
¼ teaspoon dried thyme
¼ teaspoon salt
¼ teaspoon pepper
⅛ teaspoon garlic powder

Preheat oven to 350°. Spray a shallow casserole with nonstick cooking spray. Place chicken in prepared pan. Combine remaining ingredients in a small bowl. Mix well and spread over chicken. Cover tightly and bake 30 minutes. Uncover, baste chicken, and bake 20 minutes more.

Per Serving: Calories 161, Total Fat 5.8g, Cholesterol 65mg, Sodium 401mg, Total Carbohydrate 0.7g, Dietary Fiber 0.2g, Protein 26.2g

Savory Roast Chicken

This is easy to prepare, and it's ideal even for a small family because the leftovers make such great sandwiches.

Makes 9 servings

1 4½ -pound roasting chicken
1 small celery stalk
½ small onion, peeled
1 lemon wedge (about ¼ of a small lemon)
¼ cup bottled fat-free Italian dressing
1 tablespoon dill weed
¼ teaspoon pepper

Preheat oven to 375°. Place chicken, breast-side up, on a rack in a shallow roasting pan. Place celery, onion, and lemon wedge inside cavity. Combine dressing, dill, and pepper. Brush chicken (including inside cavity) with the sauce. If a meat thermometer is used, insert it in the center of the thigh muscle, making sure it does not touch bone.

Roast, uncovered, 1½ to 2 hours, or until the internal temperature reaches 185° on a meat thermometer. (The drumstick should feel soft and it should move up and down easily in the socket. Also, the juices should run clear when the meat is pierced with a fork.) Remove chicken from oven, cover loosely with foil to keep warm, and let stand 10 minutes before carving. Remove and discard skin before serving.

Per Serving: Calories 239, Total Fat 16.7g, Cholesterol 85mg, Sodium 168mg, Total Carbohydrate 1.2g, Dietary Fiber 0g, Protein 21.1g

Chicken and Broccoli Bake

A perfect use for leftover chicken, this luscious casserole needs only a tossed salad and a slice of whole grain bread to make a delectable meal.

Makes 6 servings

1 10-ounce package frozen chopped broccoli, thawed and drained
1 teaspoon vegetable oil
1 cup finely chopped onion
8 ounces cooked, cubed chicken, skin removed (2 cups)
1 cup liquid egg substitute
1 cup nonfat dry milk
1¼ cups water
¼ cup all-purpose flour
2 teaspoons Worcestershire sauce
1 teaspoon baking powder
¼ teaspoon garlic powder
¼ teaspoon salt
⅛ teaspoon pepper
4 ounces shredded reduced-fat Cheddar cheese (1 cup)

Preheat oven to 350°. Spray an 8-inch square baking pan with nonstick cooking spray. Place broccoli in prepared pan. Heat oil in a small saucepan over medium heat. Add onion. Cook, stirring frequently, until tender, about 5 minutes. Spoon over broccoli. Spread chicken over broccoli and onion.

In a blender, combine remaining ingredients except cheese. Blend until smooth. Pour over chicken. Sprinkle evenly with cheese. Bake, uncovered, 40 minutes, until top is brown and mixture is set. Let stand five minutes before serving.

Per Serving: Calories 248, Total Fat 5.2g, Cholesterol 40mg, Sodium 510mg, Total Carbohydrate 20.2g, Dietary Fiber 2g, Protein 30.6g

Deviled Cornish Hens

A great company dish, these hens can be marinated all day and then baked when needed. Serve them with my Favorite Rice Casserole on page 140 and some steamed fresh asparagus for a dinner they won't forget.

Makes 4 servings

2 ½-pound Cornish hens, skin removed*
½ cup dry red wine
3 tablespoons reduced-sodium soy sauce
2 tablespoons water
2 tablespoons dry sherry
1 tablespoon Dijon mustard
2 teaspoons canola oil
½ teaspoon bottled hot pepper sauce
3 tablespoons dry breadcrumbs

Split hens in half down the back. Place in a shallow baking pan that has been sprayed with nonstick cooking spray. In a small bowl, combine remaining ingredients *except* breadcrumbs. Mix well and pour over hens. Marinate in the refrigerator for 4 to 5 hours, turning hens several times. Preheat oven to 350°. Sprinkle half of the breadcrumbs evenly over hens. Bake, uncovered, 30 minutes. Turn hens. Sprinkle with remaining crumbs. Bake 30 minutes more.

**To remove the skin, first cut the skin down the middle of each breast using kitchen shears. Pull the skin to each side and over each leg. Snip the skin around each wing and pull the skin over each wing. Turn hen over and use a sharp knife to remove the remaining skin on the backs. It helps to grasp the skin firmly with a paper towel when pulling it off.*

Per Serving: Calories 182, Total Fat 6.6g, Cholesterol 108mg, Sodium 678mg, Total Carbohydrate 6g, Dietary Fiber 0.2g, Protein 25.1g

Cranberry-Stuffed Chicken Breasts

Chicken breasts stuffed with a delectable cranberry stuffing make a wonderful holiday meal. But you don't have to wait for a holiday to try them. Just be sure to freeze some cranberries in the fall when they are abundant, and you can enjoy this elegant dish anytime of the year.

Makes 4 servings

- 1 pound boneless, skinless chicken breasts
- 1 cup cranberries
- 3 tablespoons sugar
- 1 teaspoon grated fresh orange peel
- ¼ teaspoon salt
- ¼ teaspoon ground cinnamon
- 4 slices whole wheat bread (1-ounce slices), cut into small cubes and toasted in a 300° oven until dry
- 2 tablespoons raisins
- 2 tablespoons water
- Paprika
- Dried parsley flakes

Preheat oven to 350°. Spray a 10-inch pie pan with nonstick cooking spray. Place each chicken breast between 2 pieces of wax paper and flatten with a mallet until chicken is ¼-inch thick.

Combine cranberries, sugar, orange peel, salt, and cinnamon in a blender or food processor. Process until cranberries are chopped. Spoon mixture into a bowl and add bread cubes, raisins, and water, mixing well. Add a little more water if necessary to moisten stuffing.

Divide stuffing mixture evenly onto the center of each chicken breast. Pull the corners together and fold up the edges to enclose the stuffing. Turn the chicken over and place, smooth-side up, in prepared pan. Sprinkle liberally with paprika and parsley flakes. Cover pan tightly with aluminum foil and bake 40 minutes.

Per Serving: Calories 262, Total Fat 2.7g, Cholesterol 65mg, Sodium 371mg, Total Carbohydrate 30.3g, Dietary Fiber 3.6g, Protein 29.2g

Polynesian Chicken Salad

This delicious salad, with its exotic flair, is really a hit when served in a scooped-out pineapple shell.

Makes 4 servings

1 1-pound can pineapple tidbits (packed in juice), drained (Reserve ½ cup of the juice.)
¼ cup water
2 teaspoons cornstarch
¼ teaspoon dry mustard
2 tablespoons vinegar
2 tablespoons ketchup
2 teaspoons Worcestershire sauce
2 teaspoons reduced-sodium soy sauce
¼ teaspoon paprika
¼ teaspoon garlic powder
12 ounces cooked, cubed chicken, skin removed (3 cups)
½ cup chopped green bell pepper

Set pineapple aside. In a medium saucepan, combine pineapple juice, water, cornstarch, and mustard. Cook over medium heat, stirring constantly, until thick and bubbly. Cool 10 minutes. Stir in vinegar, ketchup, Worcestershire sauce, soy sauce, paprika, and garlic powder. Add chicken, green pepper, and pineapple. Mix well. Chill thoroughly.

Per Serving: Calories 233, Total Fat 3.2g, Cholesterol 72mg, Sodium 263mg, Total Carbohydrate 23.5g, Dietary Fiber 1.3g, Protein 27.4g

Turkey Divan

Chicken can also be used in this slimmed-down version of a popular favorite. It's a delicious dish to serve with cooked couscous or barley.

Makes 6 servings

2 10-ounce packages frozen broccoli
12 ounces cooked, sliced, skinless turkey breast
¼ cup plus 2 tablespoons all-purpose flour
2 cups water
2 packets low-sodium instant chicken-flavored broth mix
½ cup plain nonfat Greek yogurt
½ teaspoon Worcestershire sauce
1 tablespoon plus 1 teaspoon prepared yellow mustard
2 tablespoons minced onion flakes
3 tablespoons grated Parmesan cheese
Pepper to taste

Preheat oven to 400°. Spray an 8-inch square baking pan with nonstick cooking spray. Cook broccoli according to package directions. Drain. Place in prepared pan. Place turkey slices on top of broccoli. Place flour in a small bowl. Gradually add water, stirring to prevent lumps. Add remaining ingredients. Mix well with a fork or wire whisk. Pour mixture over turkey. Bake, uncovered, 30 minutes, or until hot and bubbly.

Per Serving: Calories 176, Total Fat 3.1g, Cholesterol 41mg, Sodium 179mg, Total Carbohydrate 14.4g, Dietary Fiber 3.2g, Protein 23.2g

Rosemary Turkey Cutlets

Rosemary adds a wonderful, delicate flavor to the turkey in this dish that's fit for the fanciest dinner party.

Makes 4 servings

1 pound turkey breast cutlets
1 cup sliced mushrooms
¾ cup plain nonfat Greek yogurt
1 tablespoon all-purpose flour
½ cup dry white wine
2 teaspoons Dijon mustard
1 teaspoon dried rosemary, crumbled
¼ teaspoon garlic powder
Pepper to taste

Preheat oven to 350°. Spray an 8-inch square baking pan with nonstick cooking spray. Place turkey in pan. Top with mushrooms. In a small bowl, combine remaining ingredients, mixing well. Spread evenly over turkey and mushrooms. Bake, uncovered, 45 minutes.

Per Serving: Calories 166, Total Fat 2g, Cholesterol 69mg, Sodium 167mg, Total Carbohydrate 7.1g, Dietary Fiber 0.4g, Protein 29.9g

Oven-Fried Turkey Cutlets

One of my family's favorites, these breaded cutlets can be served as is or topped with spaghetti sauce. They also make great sandwiches, hot or cold.

Makes 4 servings

1 pound turkey breast cutlets
2 tablespoons lemon juice
¾ cup dry breadcrumbs
2 tablespoons grated Parmesan cheese
2 teaspoons dried oregano
½ teaspoon poultry seasoning
¼ teaspoon salt
¼ teaspoon pepper
¼ teaspoon garlic powder

Preheat oven to 350°. Spray a shallow baking pan with nonstick cooking spray. Place turkey cutlets in a medium bowl. Cover with water. Add lemon juice. In a shallow bowl, combine remaining ingredients. Mix well. One at a time, take cutlets from water and dip into crumbs, turning to coat both sides of cutlets. Place in prepared pan. Spray each cutlet lightly and evenly with cooking spray. Bake, uncovered, 30 minutes, or until lightly browned.

Per Serving: Calories 223, Total Fat 3.9g, Cholesterol 70mg, Sodium 451mg, Total Carbohydrate 16.3g, Dietary Fiber 0.8g, Protein 30.6g

French Turkey Cutlets

Ready in no time, these cutlets are perfect alongside a baked potato that is topped with nonfat sour cream and chives. Add some steamed broccoli, and you have a tempting and very healthful dinner.

Makes 4 servings

1 pound turkey breast cutlets
1 teaspoon dry mustard
½ teaspoon salt
½ teaspoon pepper
¼ teaspoon garlic powder
2 teaspoons canola oil
2 tablespoons lemon juice
2 teaspoons Worcestershire sauce
1 tablespoon dried chives

Sprinkle each side of cutlets with mustard, salt, pepper, and garlic powder. Heat oil in a large nonstick skillet over medium heat. Add turkey and cook, turning frequently, until turkey is done and is no longer pink. Sprinkle with lemon juice, Worcestershire sauce, and chives. Cook, turning frequently, 3 minutes more.

Per Serving: Calories 152, Total Fat 4.4g, Cholesterol 68mg, Sodium 387mg, Total Carbohydrate 1.7g, Dietary Fiber 0.2g, Protein 26.9g

Turkey in Dilled Cream Sauce

It sounds unusual, but the combination of sour cream (nonfat, of course) and dill seed makes an exciting, rich-tasting dish.

Makes 4 servings

1 pound turkey breast cutlets
1 cup nonfat sour cream
1 teaspoon dill seed
¼ teaspoon salt
⅛ teaspoon pepper
2 packets low-sodium instant beef-flavored broth mix
1 tablespoon plus 1 teaspoon minced onion flakes

Preheat oven to 350°. Spray a shallow baking pan with nonstick cooking spray. Place turkey in prepared pan. In a small bowl, combine remaining ingredients, mixing well. Spread evenly over turkey. Bake, uncovered, 1 hour.

Per Serving: Calories 183, Total Fat 1.9g, Cholesterol 74mg, Sodium 270mg, Total Carbohydrate 12.7g, Dietary Fiber 0.2g, Protein 28.9g

Country Turkey Loaf

This easy loaf is loaded with vegetables, making it colorful as well as tasty and nutritious. The flavor of the soy sauce blends well with the tomato sauce, giving the taste a nice little boost.

Makes 4 servings

1 pound lean ground turkey
½ cup chopped carrot, in ¼ -inch pieces
½ cup finely chopped onion
½ cup chopped mushrooms
¼ cup finely chopped green pepper
½ cup salt-free (or regular) tomato sauce
2 tablespoons reduced-sodium soy sauce
¼ teaspoon garlic powder
Salt and pepper to taste

Preheat oven to 350°. Have a shallow baking pan ready. In a large bowl, combine turkey with remaining ingredients. Mix well. Shape into a loaf. Place loaf in prepared pan. Bake, uncovered, 1 hour.

Per Serving: Calories 196, Total Fat 9.4g, Cholesterol 89mg, Sodium 385mg, Total Carbohydrate 6.5g, Dietary Fiber 1.8g, Protein 21.4g

Barbecue Turkey Loaf

Brown sugar and vinegar added to the tomato sauce give this moist loaf a wonderful barbecue flavor. It's delicious with my Oven-Baked French "Fries" on page 177 and a pile of steamed mixed vegetables.

Makes 6 servings

1½ pounds lean ground turkey
1 8-ounce can salt-free (or regular) tomato sauce
1 cup finely chopped onion
Salt to taste
¼ teaspoon pepper
¼ teaspoon garlic powder
2 teaspoons Worcestershire sauce
2 tablespoons firmly packed brown sugar
2 tablespoons prepared yellow mustard
1 tablespoon vinegar

Preheat oven to 350°. In a large bowl, combine turkey, ¾ cup of the tomato sauce, onion, salt, pepper, garlic powder, and Worcestershire sauce. Mix well. Shape mixture into a loaf and place on a rack in a shallow baking pan. Bake, uncovered, 20 minutes. Combine remaining tomato sauce, brown sugar, mustard, and vinegar. Spoon over loaf. Bake, uncovered, 40 minutes longer.

Per Serving: Calories 204, Total Fat 9.4g, Cholesterol 90mg, Sodium 190mg, Total Carbohydrate 9.2g, Dietary Fiber 1.1g, Protein 20.9g

Italian Turkey Burgers

Served on a whole grain bun or on a bed of rice or noodles, these burgers will definitely be a hit.

Makes 4 servings

Burgers:
1 pound lean ground turkey
2 tablespoons grated onion
1 teaspoon dried oregano
½ teaspoon dried basil
¼ teaspoon garlic powder

Sauce:
1 8-ounce can salt-free (or regular) tomato sauce
1 4-ounce can mushroom pieces, drained
¼ teaspoon each dried oregano and basil
⅛ teaspoon garlic powder

In a large bowl, combine turkey with remaining burger ingredients. Mix well. Shape into 4 patties. Spray a large nonstick griddle or skillet with nonstick cooking spray. Heat over medium heat. Place burgers on griddle. Cook until burgers are done and nicely browned on both sides. Turn burgers several times while cooking.

While burgers are cooking, combine sauce ingredients in a small saucepan. Heat over medium heat until hot and bubbly. Keep warm over low heat until burgers are ready. Divide sauce evenly and spoon over burgers when serving.

Per Serving: Calories 191, Total Fat 9.5g, Cholesterol 89mg, Sodium 236mg, Total Carbohydrate 5.2g, Dietary Fiber 2g, Protein 21.3g

Roast Turkey Breast with Peach Sauce

The scrumptious peach sauce turns an ordinary turkey breast into an extraordinary dish. Serve it for dinner and slice the rest for sandwiches.

Makes 16 servings

1 5-pound bone-in turkey breast
¾ teaspoon salt
½ teaspoon poultry seasoning
¼ teaspoon pepper
¼ teaspoon dried thyme

Sauce:
1 tablespoon cornstarch
¾ cup water
1 packet low-sodium instant chicken-flavored broth mix
¼ cup fruit-only peach spread
1 tablespoon dry sherry

Preheat oven to 325°. Sprinkle top and bottom of turkey breast with salt, poultry seasoning, pepper, and thyme. Place turkey, skin-side up, on a rack in a shallow roasting pan. Roast 1½ to 2 hours, or until meat is no longer pink. Remove and discard the skin before slicing. Slice and weigh 3 pounds of turkey; reserve any remaining turkey for another use.

Just before serving, prepare sauce: Dissolve cornstarch in water in a small saucepan. Add broth mix and peach spread and mix well. Bring sauce to a boil over medium heat, stirring constantly. Boil, stirring, 2 minutes. Remove from heat and stir in sherry. Spoon sauce over sliced turkey.

Per Serving: Calories 178, Total Fat 5g, Cholesterol 75mg, Sodium 437mg, Total Carbohydrate 4.2g, Dietary Fiber 0g, Protein 29g

Mock-Sausage and Peppers

By refrigerating the turkey with the herbs and allowing the flavors to "marry," these delicious patties taste just like the Italian specialty. Serve with pasta or on a crusty roll, topped with pasta sauce.

Makes 4 servings (2 patties each serving)

1 teaspoon canola oil
½ cup finely minced green bell pepper
½ cup finely minced onion
1 pound lean ground turkey
½ teaspoon fennel seeds, crushed*
¼ teaspoon ground sage
¼ teaspoon dried thyme
¼ teaspoon dried marjoram
¼ teaspoon salt
¼ teaspoon pepper
⅛ teaspoon ground savory

Heat oil in a small nonstick skillet over medium heat. Add green pepper and onion. Cook, stirring frequently, until tender, about 8 minutes. Add small amounts of water as necessary (about a tablespoon at a time) to prevent sticking. In a large bowl, combine turkey with peppers and onions. Add remaining ingredients and mix well. Refrigerate mixture for 1 to 5 hours to blend flavors.

Shape mixture into 8 thin patties. Spray a large nonstick griddle or skillet with nonstick cooking spray. Preheat over medium heat. Place patties on griddle, cooking until patties are done and lightly browned on both sides. Turn patties several times while cooking.

**To crush seeds, place between 2 pieces of wax paper and crush with a rolling pin or mallet.*

Per Serving: Calories 188, Total Fat 10.5g, Cholesterol 89mg, Sodium 255mg, Total Carbohydrate 3.2g, Dietary Fiber 0.8g, Protein 20.2g

Marinated Turkey Roll

A rolled turkey roast is perfect for a family dinner, and, if you have a small family, you have the added bonus of lots of leftovers for sandwiches. Just ask the butcher to bone the turkey breast and remove the skin. The rest is easy.

Makes 12 servings

1 3-pound skinless, boneless turkey breast
¾ teaspoon dried thyme
½ teaspoon ground ginger
¼ teaspoon garlic powder
¼ cup dry sherry
¼ cup reduced-sodium soy sauce
¼ cup orange juice
2 teaspoons honey

Using a sharp knife, make a lengthwise slit in one side of the turkey breast, as if creating a pocket. Do not cut all the way through. Open at the pocket and lay flat.

Place turkey between 2 sheets of wax paper and flatten with a mallet to about 1½-inches thick. Sprinkle *half* of the thyme, ginger, and garlic powder evenly over the turkey. Starting at one end, roll turkey like a jelly roll. Tie with a cord in 3 or 4 places.

Place turkey in a plastic bag and add remaining spices, along with sherry, soy sauce, orange juice, and honey. Close bag tightly and place in a shallow pan. Marinate in the refrigerator several hours, turning bag over several times.

To cook, place turkey and marinade in the bottom of a roasting pan. Preheat oven to 350°. Cook, covered, 2 hours, or until meat is no longer pink. Slice crosswise to serve.

Per Serving: Calories 176, Total Fat 5g, Cholesterol 75mg, Sodium 529mg, Total Carbohydrate 3.5g, Dietary Fiber 0g, Protein 29.3g

Barbecued Turkey Franks

Serve this tangy dish with rice or noodles for a tasty, quick, and very inexpensive dinner. Kids will love it.

Makes 4 servings

9 ounces low-fat turkey frankfurters (up to 2 grams of fat per ounce), cut into 2-inch pieces
1 teaspoon canola oil
½ cup chopped onion
½ cup chopped green bell pepper
2 tablespoons chopped celery
1 8-ounce can salt-free (or regular) tomato sauce
2 tablespoons firmly packed brown sugar
1 tablespoon prepared yellow mustard
1 tablespoon vinegar
2 teaspoons Worcestershire sauce
⅛ teaspoon garlic powder
Bottled hot pepper sauce to taste

Broil frankfurters on a rack under the broiler, until brown on all sides. Heat oil in a large nonstick skillet over medium heat. Add onion, green pepper, and celery. Cook, stirring frequently, until tender, about 8 minutes. Add small amounts of water as necessary (about a tablespoon at a time) to prevent sticking. Add remaining ingredients except frankfurters and mix well. Reduce heat to medium-low. Stir in frankfurters. Cover and cook until hot and bubbly, about 10 minutes.

Per Serving: Calories 125, Total Fat 1.1g, Cholesterol 13mg, Sodium 618mg, Total Carbohydrate 19.5g, Dietary Fiber 1.7g, Protein 9.2g

Notes:

Beans and Tofu

The beans in this section are actually legumes, which are the seeds from certain pod-bearing plants. Among the most popular types of legumes are kidney beans, pinto beans, chickpeas (or garbanzo beans), Great Northern beans, black beans, split peas, and lentils.

Legumes are extremely versatile. They can be used to replace all or part of the meat in stews, they add fiber and texture to soups, and they even appear in some of my desserts! Beans are low in fat, high in fiber, and contain iron, B vitamins, and minerals.

Tofu is a product that is made from soybeans in much the same way that cheese is made from milk. Available in the produce section, tofu is high in protein, low in saturated fat, and contains no cholesterol. Its very mild flavor is a definite advantage, allowing the tofu to blend easily with other ingredients and take on the flavor of whatever it is combined with.

In this section, I offer delicious, creative recipes that will add variety to your meals along with a refreshing change of pace.

Basic Cooking Directions for Legumes

Before cooking, beans need to be soaked in order to restore the water lost in drying. (Split peas and lentils, however, do not require soaking.) Soak the beans first, using either of the two following methods. Then, using 2 to 3 cups of water for each cup of beans, bring water to a boil and add beans. (There should be enough water to cover the beans by 1 inch.) Reduce heat to low, cover partially, and simmer for the amount of time specified, or until beans are tender. Cooking times may vary with the size, quality, and freshness of the legumes.

Quick soaking method: Place beans in a pot and add enough water to cover beans by 3 inches. Bring to a boil over medium heat. Boil 2 minutes. Remove from heat, cover, and let stand 2 hours. Drain and cook as directed.

Overnight soaking method: Place beans in a bowl and add enough water to cover beans by 3 inches. Soak overnight, drain, and cook as directed.

Cooking times for legumes: The following cooking times are for soaked beans, except for split peas and lentils, which do not require soaking:

Black beans	1 to 2 hours
Black-eyed peas	30 to 45 minutes
Garbanzo beans (chickpeas)	2 to 3 hours
Great Northern beans	1 to 1½ hours
Kidney beans	1½ to 2 hours
Lentils	30 to 45 minutes
Lima beans	1 to 1½ hours
Navy beans	1½ to 2 hours
Pinto beans	1½ to 2 hours
Soybeans	2 to 3 hours
Split peas	30 to 45 minutes

Note

Generally, 1 cup of dry legumes will yield 2 to 3 cups cooked legumes. One cup of cooked legumes will weigh approximately 6 ounces. The yield and amount of cooking time may vary with the size and quality of the legumes and the mineral content of the water used.

Prairie Bean Tortillas

Similar to fajitas, but made with corn tortillas rather than flour tortillas, this is a quick, easy meal to prepare.

Makes 4 servings

4 6-inch flour tortillas
1 teaspoon canola oil
1 cup chopped onion
2 cloves garlic, minced
1 1-pound can pinto beans, rinsed and drained (This will yield approximately 9 ounces of beans.)
1 8-ounce can salt-free (or regular) tomato sauce
1 4-ounce can chopped green chilies (hot or mild), drained
1 teaspoon ground cumin
1 teaspoon chili powder
1 teaspoon dried oregano
1 cup shredded lettuce
½ cup chopped tomato
2 ounces shredded reduced-fat Cheddar cheese (½ cup)

Preheat oven to 350°. Stack tortillas and wrap them tightly in foil. Heat in oven for 10 minutes. While tortillas are heating, heat oil in a large nonstick skillet over medium heat. Add onion and garlic. Cook, stirring frequently, until onion is tender, about 5 minutes. Add beans, tomato sauce, chilies, and spices. Cook 5 minutes, stirring occasionally and mashing beans slightly with a fork. Place each tortilla on a serving plate. Divide bean mixture evenly onto tortillas. Top with lettuce, tomato, and cheese. Roll up tortillas and serve right away.

Per Serving: Calories 250, Total Fat 5.4g, Cholesterol 3mg, Sodium 566mg, Total Carbohydrate 38.2g, Dietary Fiber 7g, Protein 11.7g

Bean-Stuffed Eggplant

You'll be proud to serve this elegant meal. It looks so fancy, yet it's so easy to prepare.

Makes 4 servings

2 small eggplants, about 1½ pounds total
2 teaspoons olive oil
1 cup chopped onion
2 cloves garlic, minced
1 1-pound can kidney beans, rinsed and drained (This will yield approximately 10 ounces of beans)
2 cups cooked brown rice
1 teaspoon dried basil
1 teaspoon dried oregano
¼ teaspoon dried thyme
3 ounces shredded reduced-fat Cheddar cheese (¾ cup)
½ cup evaporated skim milk
1 tablespoon grated Parmesan cheese

Preheat oven to 350°. Spray a shallow baking pan with nonstick cooking spray. Cut eggplants in half lengthwise. Scoop out the pulp, using a small knife or melon ball scoop, leaving ¼-inch shells. Chop pulp. Heat oil in a large nonstick skillet over medium heat. Add eggplant pulp, onion, and garlic. Cook, stirring frequently, 3 to 5 minutes, until onion is tender. Remove from heat and stir in remaining ingredients except Parmesan cheese. Stir until mixture is thoroughly combined. Fill eggplant shells with bean mixture. Sprinkle evenly with Parmesan cheese. Bake, uncovered, 30 minutes.

Per Serving: Calories 378, Total Fat 6.2g, Cholesterol 7mg, Sodium 458mg, Total Carbohydrate 62.2g, Dietary Fiber 13.9g, Protein 18.6

Pineapple-Black Bean Salad

As cool as the Caribbean breezes, this refreshing bean salad can be served on a bed of lettuce or piled into a pita for a delicious sandwich.

Makes 4 servings

1 1-pound can black beans, rinsed and drained (This will yield approximately 10 ounces of beans.)
1 8-ounce can pineapple tidbits (packed in juice), drained (Reserve ¼ cup of the juice.)
½ cup finely chopped red bell pepper
½ cup thinly sliced green onion (green and white parts)
2 teaspoons vinegar
½ teaspoon ground cumin
¼ teaspoon salt
Pepper to taste
1 jalapeno pepper, finely chopped, seeds and inner membranes discarded (optional)

Combine all ingredients in a medium bowl, including the reserved pineapple juice. Mix well. Chill thoroughly. Mix before serving.

Per Serving: Calories 115, Total Fat 0.3g, Cholesterol 0mg, Sodium 422mg, Total Carbohydrate 23.1g, Dietary Fiber 6.2g, Protein 4.9g

Bean and Cheese Quesadillas

If you like, you can place some chopped tomato, green onion, or green chilies on top of the cheese before you fold the tortillas. Served with salsa, this makes a great appetizer or lunch dish.

Makes 4 servings

4 6-inch flour tortillas
½ cup canned fat-free refried beans
2 ounces shredded reduced-fat Cheddar or Monterey Jack cheese (½ cup)
Salsa (optional)

Preheat a large nonstick griddle over medium heat. Spray with nonstick cooking spray. Place tortillas on a flat surface. Place 2 tablespoons of beans on each tortilla and spread it evenly, covering just half of each tortilla. Divide cheese evenly and place on top of the beans. Add chopped green onion, etc., if desired. Fold tortillas in half and press down gently. Heat tortillas, flipping them back and forth, until cheese is melted and tortillas are hot and crispy on both sides. Serve right away, topped with salsa if you like.

Per Serving: Calories 160, Total Fat 3.7g, Cholesterol 5mg, Sodium 339mg, Total Carbohydrate 23.5g, Dietary Fiber 2.8g, Protein 8.1g

Cheesy Beans and Rice

Add a tossed salad and some steamed broccoli, and you have a filling, hearty family supper. It's a good idea to keep packets of cooked rice in the freezer. That way they're always ready to use in easy casseroles like this.

Makes 4 servings

2 teaspoons canola oil
½ cup chopped onion
½ cup chopped carrots
½ cup chopped celery
1 tablespoon dried basil
½ teaspoon dried oregano
¼ teaspoon garlic powder
1 1-pound can kidney beans, rinsed and drained (This will yield approximately 10 ounces of beans.)
2 cups chopped fresh tomato
Salt and pepper to taste
2 ounces shredded reduced-fat Cheddar cheese (½ cup)
2 cups cooked brown rice

Heat oil in a large nonstick skillet over medium heat. Add onion, carrots, and celery. Sprinkle with basil, oregano, and garlic powder. Cook, stirring frequently, until vegetables are tender, about 10 minutes. Add small amounts of water while cooking (about a tablespoon at a time) to prevent sticking. Stir in beans, tomato, salt, and pepper. Heat through. Stir in cheese and rice. Heat, stirring, until mixture is hot.

Per Serving: Calories 251, Total Fat 4.6g, Cholesterol 3mg, Sodium 365mg, Total Carbohydrate 41.4g, Dietary Fiber 6.9g, Protein 11g

Herbed Chickpea Patties

Serve these deliciously herbed patties plain or topped with a little ketchup. And use the leftovers, hot or cold, to make wonderful sandwiches.

Makes 4 servings (3 patties each serving)

1 1-pound can chickpeas, rinsed and drained (This will yield approximately 10 ounces of chickpeas.)
⅓ cup nonfat dry milk
½ cup liquid egg substitute
3 tablespoons dry breadcrumbs
2 teaspoons canola oil
1 teaspoon reduced-sodium soy sauce
½ teaspoon dry mustard
½ teaspoon dried oregano
½ teaspoon dried basil
¼ teaspoon garlic powder
Salt and pepper to taste

In a blender, combine all ingredients. Blend until smooth. Spray a large nonstick griddle or skillet with nonstick cooking spray. Preheat over medium heat. Drop chickpea mixture onto griddle, making 12 patties and using about 2 tablespoons for each patty. Cook until edges of patties appear dry and bottoms are lightly browned. Turn, flatten patties with a spatula, and cook until lightly browned on both sides.

Per Serving: Calories 190, Total Fat 4.6g, Cholesterol 2mg, Sodium 410mg, Total Carbohydrate 25.7g, Dietary Fiber 3.5g, Protein 11.7g

Herbed Bean Soufflé

Folding egg whites into the beans makes them light and fluffy in this unusual soufflé. You'll need to serve it right away, before it "sinks."

Makes 4 servings

1 1-pound can cannellini (white kidney beans), rinsed and drained (This will yield approximately 10 ounces of beans.)
½ cup liquid egg substitute
1 tablespoon minced onion flakes
2 teaspoons dried parsley flakes
½ teaspoon dried marjoram
¼ teaspoon dried thyme
⅛ teaspoon dill weed
Salt and pepper to taste
3 egg whites (Egg substitute will not work here.)

Preheat oven to 350°. Spray a 1½-quart soufflé dish or deep baking dish with nonstick cooking spray. In a blender, combine beans, egg substitute, onion flakes, parsley, marjoram, thyme, dill, salt, and pepper. Blend until smooth. Spoon mixture into a large bowl. In another bowl, beat egg whites on high speed of an electric mixer until stiff. Fold into bean mixture, gently but thoroughly. Spoon mixture into prepared baking dish. Bake 40 to 45 minutes, until set and lightly browned. Serve right away.

Per Serving: Calories 97, Total Fat 1.1g, Cholesterol 0mg, Sodium 262mg, Total Carbohydrate 11.4g, Dietary Fiber 3.5g, Protein 10.4g

Cajun Bean Pot

Add as little or as much hot sauce as you like to this easy dish for a crowd. It's perfect over rice or with a chunk of crusty bread for a football Sunday.

Makes 8 servings

2 teaspoons olive oil
1 cup chopped onion
1 cup chopped green bell pepper
½ cup chopped celery
3 cloves garlic, finely chopped
3 1-pound cans kidney beans, rinsed and drained, or you can use a mixture of 3 different kinds of beans (This will yield approximately 30 ounces of beans.)
1 1-pound can stewed tomatoes, undrained
1 6-ounce can tomato paste
1¼ cups water
1 teaspoon Worcestershire sauce
½ teaspoon dried oregano
¼ teaspoon dried thyme
⅛ to ¼ teaspoon bottled hot sauce
2 bay leaves

Heat oil in a large saucepan over medium heat. Add onion, green pepper, celery, and garlic. Cook, stirring frequently, until tender, about 10 minutes. Add small amounts of water as necessary (about a tablespoon at a time) to prevent sticking. Add remaining ingredients, mixing well. When mixture boils, reduce heat to medium-low, cover, and simmer 30 minutes. Remove and discard bay leaves before serving.

Per Serving: Calories 152, Total Fat 1.5g, Cholesterol 0mg, Sodium 608mg, Total Carbohydrate 27.1g, Dietary Fiber 5.9g, Protein 7.4g

Bean Stroganoff

Any variety of bean will work in this creamy dish that tastes delicious spooned over noodles.

Makes 4 servings

1 teaspoon canola oil
1 medium onion, sliced
3 cups sliced mushrooms
3 cloves garlic, minced
3 tablespoons all-purpose flour
1 teaspoon dill weed
1 teaspoon dry mustard
¼ teaspoon salt
⅛ teaspoon pepper
Dash ground nutmeg
1 packet low-sodium instant beef-flavored broth mix
2 tablespoons dry sherry
1 19-ounce can kidney beans, rinsed and drained (This will yield approximately 12 ounces of beans.)
½ cup plain nonfat yogurt

Heat oil in a large nonstick skillet over medium heat. Add onion, mushrooms, and garlic. Cook, stirring frequently and separating onion into rings, until tender, about 5 minutes. Combine flour, spices, and broth mix and sprinkle over mushroom mixture. Add water, a few tablespoons at a time, stirring constantly and mixing well after each addition. Stir in sherry and beans. When mixture is hot and bubbly, stir in yogurt. Heat through but do not boil.

Per Serving: Calories 184, Total Fat 1.8g, Cholesterol 0mg, Sodium 169mg, Total Carbohydrate 30.4g, Dietary Fiber 9.3g, Protein 11.7g

Mushroom Bean Loaf Supreme

And supreme it is! This meatless loaf has the texture of a fine paté. Serve it hot for dinner and serve the leftovers, hot or cold, in a sandwich or on crackers as an appetizer.

Makes 6 servings

1 1-pound can pinto beans, rinsed and drained (This will yield approximately 9 ounces of beans.)
¾ cup liquid egg substitute
2 slices whole wheat bread (1-ounce slices), crumbled
2 teaspoons canola oil
2 packets low-sodium instant chicken-flavored broth mix
1 tablespoon grated onion
¼ teaspoon garlic powder
Salt and pepper to taste
1 8-ounce can mushroom pieces, drained

Preheat oven to 350°. Spray a 4 x 8-inch loaf pan with nonstick cooking spray. In a blender, combine all ingredients *except* mushrooms. Blend until smooth. Stir in mushrooms. Spoon mixture into prepared pan. Bake 50 to 55 minutes, until set and lightly browned. Let loaf stand for 5 minutes, then invert onto a serving plate.

Per Serving: Calories 115, Total Fat 3.3g, Cholesterol 0mg, Sodium 393mg, Total Carbohydrate 13.5g, Dietary Fiber 3.6g, Protein 7.5g

Easy Bean Salad

So zesty and good, this is a perfect salad for backyard picnics. It also makes a great addition to a tossed salad.

Makes 8 servings

2 10-ounces packages frozen cut green beans
1 1-pound can kidney beans, rinsed and drained (This will yield approximately 10 ounces of beans.)
1 1-pound can chickpeas, rinsed and drained (This will yield approximately 10 ounces of chickpeas.)
1 tablespoon plus 1 teaspoon sweet pickle relish*
½ cup finely chopped onion
¼ cup finely chopped green bell pepper
1 tablespoon dried parsley flakes
½ cup bottled fat-free Italian dressing

Cook green beans according to package directions. Drain. In a large bowl, combine all ingredients. Toss until blended. Chill several hours to combine flavors, mixing several times while chilling. **Sweet pickle relish is also available sweetened with Splenda.*

Per Serving: Calories 118, Total Fat 0.6g, Cholesterol 0mg, Sodium 448mg, Total Carbohydrate 22.9g, Dietary Fiber 5.1g, Protein 5g

Bean and Tuna Salad

Pile this delectable, herbed medley into a pita, add some lettuce and a slice of tomato, and you have a delicious, filling sandwich they'll love. It's also good piled onto a bed of lettuce and served with a chunk of crusty bread.

Makes 6 servings

1 1-pound can kidney beans, rinsed and drained (This will yield approximately 10 ounces of beans.)
1 1-pound can chickpeas, rinsed and drained (This will yield approximately 10 ounces of chickpeas.)
1 6½-ounce can tuna (packed in water), drained and flaked (4 ounces)
¼ cup red wine vinegar
2 tablespoons canola oil
½ teaspoon dried marjoram
½ teaspoon dried basil
½ teaspoon dried oregano
¼ teaspoon garlic powder
Salt and pepper to taste

In a large bowl, combine all ingredients. Toss until well blended. Chill several hours, or overnight, to blend flavors. Mix before serving.

Per Serving: Calories 161, Total Fat 5.3g, Cholesterol 6mg, Sodium 369mg, Total Carbohydrate 18.6g, Dietary Fiber 4g, Protein 9.6g

Pepper-Bean Casserole

This easy casserole has an unusual and delicious flavor. It's slightly sweet, and the bacon bits add just the right amount of flavor without the fat of real bacon.

Makes 4 servings

2 10-ounce packages frozen lima beans
2 teaspoons canola oil
2 medium green bell peppers, cut into 1 ¼-inch strips
1 1-pound can salt-free (or regular) tomatoes, chopped, undrained
1 tablespoon imitation bacon bits
1 tablespoon molasses
2 teaspoons minced onion flakes
1 tablespoon firmly packed brown sugar
1 teaspoon dry mustard
¼ teaspoon dried oregano
¼ teaspoon garlic powder

Preheat oven to 350°. Spray a 1½-quart casserole with nonstick cooking spray. Cook beans according to package directions. Drain. Place in prepared casserole. Heat oil in a medium nonstick skillet over medium heat. Add green peppers. Cook, stirring frequently, until tender, about 8 minutes. Add small amounts of water if necessary (about a tablespoon at a time) to prevent sticking. Add peppers to casserole. In a small bowl, combine remaining ingredients, mixing well. Pour over beans and peppers. Toss to combine. Cover and bake 30 minutes, or until hot and bubbly.

Per Serving: Calories 295, Total Fat 3.6g, Cholesterol 0mg, Sodium 124mg, Total Carbohydrate 52.4g, Dietary Fiber 11.1g, Protein 13.4g

Cranberry Beans

Served over rice, this dish creates a deliriously different taste sensation.

Makes 4 servings

1 cup cranberries
½ cup canned crushed pineapple (packed in juice), drained slightly
½ cup orange juice
¼ cup plus 2 tablespoons red currant jelly
1 tablespoon Dijon mustard
2 teaspoons cornstarch
1 tablespoon water
1 1-pound can kidney beans, rinsed and drained (This will yield approximately 10 ounces of beans.)

In a small saucepan, combine cranberries, pineapple, orange juice, jelly, and mustard. Mix well. Bring to a boil over medium heat. Reduce heat slightly and simmer 10 minutes. Spoon mixture into a blender and blend until smooth. Return to saucepan. Combine cornstarch and water in a small bowl or custard cup. Mix until cornstarch is dissolved. Stir into cranberry mixture. Add beans to saucepan and mix well. Bring to a boil over medium heat. Cook, stirring constantly, 3 to 4 minutes, until sauce has thickened.

Per Serving: Calories 350, Total Fat 0.5g, Cholesterol 0mg, Sodium 341mg, Total Carbohydrate 82.2g, Dietary Fiber 4.2g, Protein 4.3g

Barbecue Black-Eyed Peas

This quick dish can be put together fast and is delicious spooned over brown rice or noodles.

Makes 6 servings

2 1-pound cans black-eyed peas, rinsed and drained (This will yield approximately 20 ounces of beans.)
2 8-ounces cans salt-free (or regular) tomato sauce
⅓ cup molasses
1 tablespoon plus 1 teaspoon minced onion flakes
1 teaspoon dry mustard
½ teaspoon paprika
½ teaspoon Worcestershire sauce
⅛ teaspoon garlic powder
Salt and pepper to taste

Preheat oven to 350°. Spray a 1½ -quart baking dish with nonstick cooking spray. Combine all ingredients, mixing well. Place in prepared baking dish. Bake, covered, 1 hour.

Per Serving: Calories 175, Total Fat 1.3g, Cholesterol 0mg, Sodium 356mg, Total Carbohydrate 32.5g, Dietary Fiber 4.6g, Protein 8g

Baked Lentils and Tomatoes

Lentils are relatively quick-cooking legumes and, unlike most other beans, they don't have to be soaked before cooking. This delicious casserole makes a great accompaniment to pasta or noodles.

Makes 4 servings

1 cup lentils, uncooked (7½ ounces)
4 cups boiling water
2 teaspoons canola oil
½ cup chopped onion
½ cup chopped celery
½ cup chopped green bell pepper
1 1-pound can salt-free (or regular) tomatoes, chopped and undrained
1 teaspoon dried oregano
1 teaspoon dried basil
¼ teaspoon garlic powder
Salt and pepper to taste
2 tablespoons Italian-seasoned breadcrumbs
2 teaspoons grated Parmesan cheese

Add lentils to boiling water in a medium saucepan over medium heat. Cover, reduce heat to medium-low, and simmer 40 to 45 minutes, until tender. Drain. Heat oil in a medium nonstick skillet over medium heat. Add onion, celery, and green pepper. Cook, stirring frequently, until vegetables are tender, about 5 minutes. Preheat oven to 350°. Spray a 1½-quart casserole with nonstick cooking spray. In a large bowl, combine lentils, onion mixture, tomatoes, and spices. Mix well. Spoon into prepared casserole. Combine breadcrumbs and Parmesan cheese and sprinkle evenly over the top. Cover and bake 30 minutes, then uncover and continue to bake 15 minutes more.

Per Serving: Calories 267, Total Fat 3.3g, Cholesterol 1mg, Sodium 155mg, Total Carbohydrate 41.8g, Dietary Fiber 18.9g, Protein 17.4g

Tangy Baked Kidney Beans

Apples and honey add a sweetness to this unusual and very delicious bean dish.

Makes 4 servings

2 teaspoons canola oil
½ cup chopped onion
1 packet low-sodium instant chicken-flavored broth mix
1 small apple, unpeeled, coarsely shredded
¼ cup tomato paste
2 tablespoons vinegar
2 teaspoons honey
½ teaspoon dry mustard
½ teaspoon dried oregano
1 19-ounce can red or white kidney beans, rinsed and drained (This will yield approximately 12 ounces of beans.)

Preheat oven to 350°. Spray a 1-quart casserole with nonstick cooking spray. Heat oil in a medium nonstick skillet over medium heat. Add onion and broth mix. Cook, stirring frequently, until onion is tender, about 5 minutes. Stir in apple and continue to cook, stirring, 2 minutes more. Add remaining ingredients, mixing well. Transfer mixture to prepared casserole. Cover and bake 40 minutes, or until hot and bubbly.

Per Serving: Calories 155, Total Fat 2.9g, Cholesterol 0mg, Sodium 550mg, Total Carbohydrate 27.1g, Dietary Fiber 5.3g, Protein 5.5g

Italian Tofu "Meatballs"

Although these don't taste anything like real meatballs, they're fun to serve and yes, they're even delicious over pasta.

Makes 4 servings

1 pound medium or firm tofu, sliced and drained well between layers of towels
2 slices whole wheat bread (1-ounce slices), crumbled
2 tablespoons minced onion flakes
2 egg whites
1 tablespoons dried parsley flakes
¼ teaspoon dried oregano
⅛ teaspoon garlic powder
⅛ teaspoon salt
⅛ teaspoon pepper
2 cups reduced-fat, meatless spaghetti sauce
1 tablespoon grated Parmesan cheese

Preheat oven to 375°. Spray a shallow baking pan with nonstick cooking spray. In a large bowl, combine all ingredients except spaghetti sauce and Parmesan cheese. Mix well, mashing the ingredients with a fork, until well blended. Shape mixture into small balls, squeezing tightly. Place tofu balls in prepared pan in a single layer. Spoon half of the sauce evenly over tofu. Sprinkle with Parmesan cheese. Bake, uncovered, 20 minutes. Heat remaining sauce and serve it with the "meatballs."

Per Serving: Calories 275, Total Fat 10.2g Cholesterol 1mg, Sodium 285mg, Total Carbohydrate 31.9g, Dietary Fiber 5.1g, Protein 14g

Kidney Beans Provencal

Simple and straightforward, this dish can be thrown together in no time. It can be served as an entrée or side dish and either alone or over noodles or rice.

Makes 4 servings

2 teaspoons olive oil
2 cloves garlic, minced
½ cup chopped onion
1 cup chopped mushrooms
1 1-pound can salt-free (or regular) tomatoes, chopped, drained (Reserve liquid.)
1 tablespoon cornstarch
1 teaspoon dried basil
1 teaspoon dried oregano
1 19-ounce can white kidney beans, rinsed and drained (This will yield approximately 12 ounces of beans.)
1 tablespoon imitation bacon bits
1 tablespoon Italian-seasoned breadcrumbs
1 teaspoon grated Parmesan cheese

Preheat oven to 350°. Spray a 1-quart casserole with nonstick cooking spray. Heat oil in a large nonstick skillet over medium heat. Add garlic, onion, and mushrooms. Cook, stirring frequently, until vegetables are tender, 8 to 10 minutes. Add tomatoes. Place reserved tomato liquid in a small bowl and add cornstarch, stirring until dissolved. Add to skillet along with basil and oregano. Cook, stirring, until mixture comes to a boil. Remove skillet from heat and stir in beans and bacon bits. Spoon mixture into prepared casserole. Combine breadcrumbs and Parmesan cheese and sprinkle evenly over the top. Bake, uncovered, 30 minutes.

Per Serving: Calories 153, Total Fat 3.2g, Cholesterol 0mg, Sodium 403mg, Total Carbohydrate 24.2g, Dietary Fiber 5.4g, Protein 7.4g

Asian Tofu Fish Cakes

An unusually tasty combo, both the tofu and the fish have mellow flavors that make them wonderfully adaptable to Asian dishes.

Makes 6 servings

Fish Cakes
12 ounces cooked sole or flounder, flaked
1 pound medium or firm tofu, sliced and drained well between layers of towels
2 slices whole wheat bread (1-ounce slices), crumbled
2 egg whites
3 tablespoons reduced-sodium soy sauce
2 tablespoons minced onion flakes
1 tablespoon dry sherry
2 teaspoons honey
¼ teaspoon garlic powder
¼ teaspoon ground ginger
¼ cup plus 2 tablespoons dry breadcrumbs

Sauce
¼ cup fruit-only peach spread
1 teaspoon reduced-sodium soy sauce
1 teaspoon vinegar
1 teaspoon water
½ teaspoon dry mustard

Preheat oven to 400°. Spray a baking sheet with nonstick cooking spray. Combine all fish cake ingredients except dry breadcrumbs in a large bowl. Mix well, mashing the ingredients with a fork until well blended. Shape into 6 patties, pressing firmly. Dip each patty in breadcrumbs and place on prepared baking sheet. Bake 20 minutes, or until lightly browned. While patties are baking, combine all sauce ingredients in a small bowl or custard cup and mix well. Add a little more water if a thinner sauce is desired. Serve sauce over patties.

Per Serving: Calories 208, Total Fat 3.7g, Cholesterol 38mg, Sodium 509mg, Total Carbohydrate 20.9g, Dietary Fiber 1.3g, Protein 22.5g

Tofu Cheddar Squares

One of my quickest, easiest favorites, this dish is a perfect introduction to tofu for people who have never tried it before. It makes a filling dinner or an elegant brunch dish.

Makes 6 servings

1 tablespoon margarine, melted
3 tablespoons dry breadcrumbs
12 ounces medium or firm tofu, drained slightly
1 cup liquid egg substitute
4 ounces shredded reduced-fat Cheddar cheese (1 cup)
2 tablespoons minced onion flakes
1 tablespoon all-purpose flour
2 teaspoons honey
1 teaspoon dried parsley flakes
½ teaspoon dry mustard
Salt and pepper to taste

Preheat oven to 350°. Spray an 8-inch square baking pan with nonstick cooking spray. Spread margarine in bottom of prepared pan. Sprinkle evenly with 2 tablespoons of the breadcrumbs. Bake 5 minutes. In a blender, combine tofu with remaining ingredients except remaining breadcrumbs. Blend until smooth. Pour mixture over the baked crumbs. Sprinkle with remaining crumbs. Bake 25 to 30 minutes, until set and lightly browned. Let stand 5 minutes before serving.

Per Serving: Calories 150, Total Fat 6.4g, Cholesterol 4mg, Sodium 239mg, Total Carbohydrate 8.9g, Dietary Fiber 0.4g, Protein 14.2g

Cauliflower-Tofu Bake

This tasty side dish really shows how versatile tofu can be. It adds protein while it dresses up the cauliflower. Add a salad and a baked potato, and you have a perfect light dinner or lunch.

Makes 4 servings

1 10-ounce package frozen cauliflower
6 ounces medium or firm tofu, sliced and drained well between layers of towels
2 ounces shredded reduced-fat Cheddar cheese (½ cup)
¼ cup bottled fat-free Italian dressing

Cook cauliflower according to package directions. Drain. Preheat oven to 375°. Spray a 1-quart baking dish with nonstick cooking spray. Place cauliflower in prepared baking dish. In a small bowl, combine remaining ingredients, mixing well. Spoon over cauliflower. Bake, uncovered, 20 minutes.

Per Serving: Calories 79, Total Fat 2.3g, Cholesterol 3mg, Sodium 314mg, Total Carbohydrate 6.6g, Dietary Fiber 1.6g, Protein 7.8g

Tofu Parmigiana

One of my favorite ways to enjoy tofu, these crispy breaded slices can be served with pasta or rice, or used to make a wonderful submarine sandwich.

Makes 4 servings

¼ cup plus 2 tablespoons Italian-seasoned breadcrumbs
2 teaspoons dried oregano
Pepper to taste
1 pound firm tofu, sliced ¼ -inch thick
1 8-ounce can salt-free (or regular) tomato sauce
½ teaspoon dried basil
⅛ teaspoon garlic powder
4 ounces shredded part-skim Mozzarella cheese
1 tablespoon grated Parmesan cheese

In a small, shallow bowl, combine breadcrumbs, 1 teaspoon of the oregano, and pepper, mixing well. Place tofu slices in a bowl of water. One at a time, remove slices from water and dip in crumb mixture. Pat with a fork to press crumbs to tofu. Spray a large nonstick skillet with nonstick cooking spray. Heat over medium heat. Cook tofu slices in skillet until browned and crisp on both sides, spraying both sides of tofu evenly with nonstick cooking spray. Preheat oven to 400°. Spray a shallow baking pan with nonstick cooking spray.

Combine tomato sauce, basil, garlic powder, and remaining oregano in a small bowl. Mix well. Spread a thin layer of sauce in prepared pan. Top with tofu slices, arranging them in a single layer. Spoon remaining sauce over tofu. Top with both cheeses. Bake, uncovered, 20 minutes.

Per Serving: Calories 208, Total Fat 8.5g, Cholesterol 17mg, Sodium 509mg, Total Carbohydrate 14.9g, Dietary Fiber 1.9g, Protein 17.9g

Silken Banana Fritters

Sure to become a breakfast favorite, these moist, tender little pancakes are perfect drizzled with a little maple syrup and topped with sliced bananas and strawberries.

Makes 6 servings (5 pancakes each serving)

1 10-ounce package silken (or soft) tofu
⅓ cup nonfat dry milk
½ cup liquid egg substitute
¼ cup plus 2 tablespoons all-purpose flour
2 tablespoons sugar
1 teaspoon baking powder
1 teaspoon vanilla extract
¼ teaspoon banana extract
1 medium ripe banana, sliced

Place all ingredients in a blender and blend until smooth. Spray a large nonstick skillet or griddle with nonstick cooking spray. Preheat over medium heat. Drop mixture onto skillet, using 1 tablespoonful for each pancake. Turn pancakes when edges appear dry and bottoms are lightly browned. Cook until lightly browned on both sides.

Per Serving: Calories 131, Total Fat 2.3g, Cholesterol 1mg, Sodium 156mg, Total Carbohydrate 20g, Dietary Fiber 0.7g, Protein 8.2g

Notes:

Beef, Pork, and Lamb

Although there's no need to give up meat when planning a healthy diet, most health professionals do recommend that you limit the amount of meat you consume. It's also important to choose the cuts of meat carefully, choosing the leanest cuts. Extra lean ground beef, flank steak, and pork tenderloin are among the leanest choices. In addition, it is important to trim away all visible fat before cooking.

Meat contains no fiber, so it is always important to serve meat with ample portions of whole grains and vegetables. To reduce your overall fat intake, I also recommend using smaller portions of meat and larger portions of grains and vegetables.

Even though a few of my meat dishes contain more than the recommended 30% of calories from fat, remember that it should be figured by the day, not the individual food, so if you eat a little more fat in one meal or one dish, you can compensate by eating less fat in the other meals or dishes. Ideally, you should evaluate your daily or weekly diet rather than single foods.

In the following recipes, I've lowered the fat content and increased the flavor by emphasizing the use of herbs and spices. I know these dishes will delight the entire family.

Steak Diane

A lot of fine restaurants serve this elegant dish, often prepared right at the table. Now you can prepare my version at home with a lot less fat and fuss.

Makes 4 servings

1 pound boneless beef top sirloin steaks, sliced ½-inch thick, all visible fat removed
Salt and pepper to taste
1 teaspoon dry mustard
1 tablespoon plus 1½ teaspoons lemon juice
1 tablespoon plus 1½ teaspoons tub-style (not diet) margarine
1 tablespoon dry sherry
2 teaspoons dried chives
1 teaspoon Worcestershire sauce

Using a meat mallet, pound the steaks to ¼-inch thick. Sprinkle each side with salt, pepper, and a little of the dry mustard. Rub the seasonings into the meat. Preheat broiler. Place meat on a rack in a broiler pan. Broil until meat is lightly browned on each side, turning meat once.

Place meat on a serving dish. While meat is browning, heat remaining ingredients to boiling in a small skillet over medium-low heat. Pour sauce over meat and serve.

Per Serving: Calories 189, Total Fat 9.5g, Cholesterol 68mg, Sodium 154mg, Total Carbohydrate 1.4g, Dietary Fiber 0.1g, Protein 24.3g

Teriyaki Flank Steak

This is my very favorite dish for cookouts. I usually serve it with a tossed salad, the Favorite Rice Casserole on page 140 and a pile of steamed fresh green beans.

Makes 6 servings

1 1½-pound flank steak
¼ cup reduced-sodium soy sauce
¼ cup dry sherry
¼ teaspoon garlic powder
¼ teaspoon ground ginger

Score meat diagonally on both sides, making several cuts about ¼-inch deep. Place meat in a shallow bowl or baking dish. Combine remaining ingredients and pour over meat. Marinate in the refrigerator 4 to 5 hours, turning meat several times.

Preheat broiler. Place meat on a broiler rack and broil until done to taste. Turn meat several times while cooking and baste with marinade. To slice, tilt knife blade slightly and slice meat, across the grain, into paper-thin slices.

Per Serving: Calories 206, Total Fat 12g, Cholesterol 60mg, Sodium 498mg, Total Carbohydrate 1.8g, Dietary Fiber 0.1g, Protein 22.8g

Chinese Pepper Steak

A favorite in Chinese restaurants, this delicious dish is usually served over rice. The meat is best when sliced very thin, which is easier to do if it is partially frozen.

Makes 6 servings

2 teaspoons canola oil
1¼ pounds boneless beef top round steak, sliced across the grain into very thin strips
½ cup chopped onion
3 cloves garlic, finely chopped
1 packet low-sodium instant beef-flavored broth mix
1¼ cups water
1 1-pound can salt-free (or regular) tomatoes, chopped and drained
2 large, green bell peppers, sliced vertically into ½-inch strips
1 tablespoon plus 1 teaspoon cornstarch dissolved in ¼ cup water
2 tablespoons reduced-sodium soy sauce
⅛ teaspoon pepper

Heat oil in a large nonstick skillet over medium-high heat. Add beef. Cook until browned, then remove beef from skillet and place in a covered bowl to keep warm. Add onion and garlic to skillet. Cook, stirring frequently, about 3 minutes, until onion starts to brown. Return meat to skillet. Add broth mix, water, tomatoes, and green pepper. Reduce heat to medium, cover skillet, and simmer 5 minutes, stirring occasionally.

Combine cornstarch mixture, soy sauce, and pepper. Add to skillet. Reduce heat to medium-low and cook, stirring, until mixture has thickened slightly and is hot and bubbly, about 3 minutes.

Per Serving: Calories 226, Total Fat 10.6g, Cholesterol 58mg, Sodium 288mg, Total Carbohydrate 10.1g, Dietary Fiber 1.9g, Protein 22.3g

Chili Meat Loaf

Chili powder and garlic add a wonderful zip to this easy dish. Serve it with a baked potato topped with plain nonfat Greek yogurt or fat free sour cream and salsa, add a tossed salad, and dinner is complete. The leftovers make great sandwiches.

Makes 6 servings

1 pound lean ground beef (10% fat)
3 slices whole wheat bread (1-ounce slices), crumbled
1 cup salsa (hot or mild)
1 egg white
2 tablespoons grated onion
1 tablespoon prepared yellow mustard
1 teaspoon chili powder (or more to taste)
½ teaspoon dry mustard
¼ teaspoon garlic powder

Preheat oven to 350°. In a large bowl, combine beef with remaining ingredients, mixing well. Shape mixture into a loaf. Place the loaf on a rack in a shallow baking pan. Bake, uncovered, 1 hour.

Per Serving: Calories 187, Total Fat 8.3g, Cholesterol 48mg, Sodium 407mg, Total Carbohydrate 9.3g, Dietary Fiber 1.3g, Protein 18.7g

Meat Loaf Florentine

A delightful filling of spinach and cheese awaits you as you dig into this moist meat loaf. Using bread as a "filler" lets you have bigger portions with less fat per serving.

Makes 6 servings

1 8-ounce can salt-free (or regular) tomato sauce
1 teaspoon dried oregano
1 teaspoon dried basil
¼ teaspoon garlic powder
1 pound lean ground beef (10% fat)
3 slices whole wheat bread (1-ounce slices), crumbled
1 egg white
Salt and pepper to taste
1 10-ounce package frozen chopped spinach, thawed and drained (Press most of the water out, but do not squeeze until too dry.)
4 ounces shredded part-skim Mozzarella cheese (1 cup)
1 tablespoon grated Parmesan cheese

Preheat oven to 350°. In a small bowl, combine tomato sauce, oregano, basil, and garlic powder. In a large bowl, combine beef, bread crumbs, egg white, salt, pepper, and half of the tomato sauce mixture. Mix well.

Spread meat on a sheet of wax paper, forming a rectangle about 8 x 10 inches. Spread spinach over half of the meat. Top with Mozzarella cheese, still covering only half of the meat. Fold meat over so that spinach and cheese are inside. Pinch edges of meat to seal. Place the meat on a rack in a shallow baking pan. Top with remaining tomato sauce. Sprinkle with Parmesan cheese. Bake, uncovered, 1 hour.

Per Serving: Calories 248, Total Fat 11.4g, Cholesterol 60mg, Sodium 279mg, Total Carbohydrate 11.3g, Dietary Fiber 3.2g, Protein 24.9g

Meat Sauce and Spaghetti Squash

Spaghetti squash is a fun vegetable that is so often neglected. Its mild flavor and noodle-like texture make it a perfect accompaniment to the meat sauce in this scrumptious casserole.

Makes 4 servings

½ pound lean ground beef (10% fat)
1 cup chopped onion
3 cloves garlic, finely chopped
2 8-ounce cans salt-free (or regular) tomato sauce
2 teaspoons dried oregano
1 teaspoon dried basil
Dash cayenne pepper
4 cups cooked, drained spaghetti squash*
1 tablespoon grated Parmesan cheese

Heat a large nonstick skillet over medium heat. Add beef, onion, and garlic. Cook, stirring frequently, until meat is browned. Break up the meat with a spoon while cooking. Spoon mixture onto a paper towel-lined plate to drain. Return meat to skillet. Add tomato sauce, oregano, basil, and pepper. Cover skillet and cook 10 minutes, stirring occasionally. Preheat oven to 375°. Spray a 2-quart casserole with nonstick cooking spray. Remove skillet from heat and stir in squash, tossing to blend well. Spoon mixture into prepared casserole. Sprinkle with Parmesan cheese. Bake, uncovered, 20 minutes.

*To cook spaghetti squash, cut squash lengthwise, remove seeds, and place cut-side down in a shallow baking pan containing 1 inch of water. Bake at 350° for 45 minutes, or until squash is tender. Remove squash from pan and drain cut-side down. Pull strands free with a fork.

Per Serving: Calories 187, Total Fat 6.3g, Cholesterol 37mg, Sodium 101mg, Total Carbohydrate 17.5g, Dietary Fiber 4g, Protein 15.2g

French Herbed Pork Roast

This elegant dish is made with pork tenderloin, which is one of the leanest cuts of pork. This tender roast can also be made on a grill.

Makes 4 servings

½ cup water
1 packet instant low-sodium chicken- or onion-flavored broth mix
⅛ teaspoon dried rosemary, crumbled
⅛ teaspoon dried oregano
⅛ teaspoon dried thyme
⅛ teaspoon garlic powder
⅛ teaspoon salt
⅛ teaspoon pepper
1 bay leaf
1 1-pound boneless lean pork tenderloin, trimmed of all visible fat

In a small bowl, combine all ingredients except meat. Pour into a large plastic bag. Add meat to bag and close tightly. Set bag in a shallow bowl and refrigerate overnight, turning bag over several times. Preheat oven to 325°. Remove meat from bag and place it on a rack in a shallow roasting pan. Bake, uncovered, 45 minutes to 1 hour, or until meat is done.

Per Serving: Calories 133, Total Fat 3.9g, Cholesterol 72mg, Sodium 132mg, Total Carbohydrate 0.6g, Dietary Fiber 0g, Protein 23.8g

Pork Chops Italiano

This delicious and easy to put together dinner adds a Mediterranean flavor when combined with your favorite noodles.

Makes 4 servings

1 pound boneless center-cut loin pork chops, trimmed of all visible fat
2 cups sliced mushrooms
2 medium, green bell peppers, cut into thin strips
½ cup chopped onion
2 8-ounce cans salt-free (or regular) tomato sauce
½ teaspoon dried oregano
½ teaspoon dried basil
¼ teaspoon garlic powder

Lightly spray a large nonstick skillet with nonstick cooking spray. Heat over medium heat. Add chops and brown on both sides. Transfer chops to a shallow baking dish that has been sprayed with nonstick spray. Preheat oven to 350°. Place mushrooms, green pepper, and onion in skillet. Cook, stirring frequently, 5 minutes. Add remaining ingredients, mixing well. Continue to cook, stirring frequently, 5 more minutes. Spoon mixture evenly over chops. Bake, uncovered, 45 minutes to 1 hour, or until chops are done.

Per Serving: Calories 202, Total Fat 4.7g, Cholesterol 55mg, Sodium 231mg, Total Carbohydrate 13.7g, Dietary Fiber 4.1g, Protein 26.3g

Deviled Pork Chops

Tasty and tangy, these delectable chops can also be made on the grill for a terrific summertime barbecue. Add a baked potato (also great on the grill) and a tossed salad, and enjoy.

Makes 4 servings

1 pound boneless center-cut loin pork chops, trimmed of all visible fat
2 tablespoons Dijon mustard
1 tablespoon Worcestershire sauce
1 teaspoon canola oil
¼ teaspoon garlic powder

Preheat broiler. Place chops in a shallow pan that has been sprayed with nonstick cooking spray. Combine remaining ingredients in a small bowl. Mix well. Spread half of the mixture on one side of the chops. Broil 3 inches from heat for about 5 minutes, or until chops are lightly browned and cooked through. Turn meat and spread with remaining mixture. Broil until meat is done.

Per Serving: Calories 145, Total Fat 5.6g, Cholesterol 55mg, Sodium 424mg, Total Carbohydrate 0.7g, Dietary Fiber 0g, Protein 23g

Italian Grilled Pork Kabobs

Delicious and colorful, these kabobs are perfect over rice. Feel free to add other vegetables to the skewers, such as onions and slices of corn on the cob.

Makes 4 servings

⅓ cup fat-free Italian dressing
½ teaspoon dried oregano
1 pound boneless center cut loin pork chops, trimmed of all visible fat, cut into 1 ½-inch cubes
2 medium zucchini, unpeeled, cut into 1- to 1½-inch cubes
2 medium red or green bell peppers, cut into 1-inch squares

In a medium bowl, combine dressing and oregano. Add pork. Marinate in the refrigerator 4 to 5 hours, stirring occasionally. Preheat broiler. Remove meat from marinade. Alternately thread pork, zucchini, and peppers on 4 skewers. Place on a broiler rack. Broil 3 inches from heat for about 10 minutes, or until pork is done. Turn skewers frequently and baste with any remaining marinade while broiling.

Per Serving: Calories 179, Total Fat 4.7g, Cholesterol 55mg, Sodium 473mg, Total Carbohydrate 9.7g, Dietary Fiber 2.3g, Protein 24.5g

Asian Pork

Tender slices of pork loin, simmered in a delectable soy and pineapple sauce, make a perfect dish to serve with the Fried Rice on page 139.

Makes 4 servings

2 teaspoons canola oil
2 medium, green bell peppers, cut into thin strips
1 pound thinly sliced pork loin, trimmed of all visible fat
2 tablespoons reduced-sodium soy sauce
2 tablespoons sugar
2 tablespoons very finely minced onion
Bottled hot pepper sauce to taste
1 cup canned pineapple chunks (packed in juice), drained (Reserve ¼ cup of the juice.)

Heat oil in a large nonstick skillet over medium heat. Add peppers and cook, stirring frequently, until slightly tender. Add pork. Cook, turning pork frequently, until it is white on both sides. Reduce heat to medium-low and add remaining ingredients to skillet, including the reserved pineapple juice. Cover and simmer until pork is cooked through, about 8 to 10 minutes.

Per Serving: Calories 269, Total Fat 8.8g, Cholesterol 67mg, Sodium 327mg, Total Carbohydrate 21.7g, Dietary Fiber 2g, Protein 25.7g

Grilled Ham Steak

The smoky ham flavor is a perfect match for the sweet preserves in this easy meal. Use any flavor preserves you like, and whether made in the broiler or on the outside grill, it's sure to be a hit.

Makes 6 servings

½ cup canned crushed pineapple (packed in juice), drained
¼ cup fruit-only spread (choose any flavor; my favorites are peach, apricot, or raspberry)
1 tablespoon lemon juice
2 teaspoons dry mustard
1 teaspoon grated fresh orange peel
½ teaspoon cornstarch
1 1-pound slice boneless ham, cut 1½ inches thick, trimmed of all visible fat

In a small saucepan, combine all ingredients except ham. Bring to a boil over medium heat, stirring constantly. Continue to cook, stirring, 2 minutes. Remove from heat. Broil ham to desired doneness on both sides. Spread preserve mixture over top. Return to broiler until hot and bubbly.

Per Serving: Calories 136, Total Fat 3.6g, Cholesterol 35mg, Sodium 959mg, Total Carbohydrate 10.9g, Dietary Fiber 0.4g, Protein 15.2g

Ham Barbecue on a Bun

This is a perfect Sunday football supper. Add a bowl of soup and a salad, and enjoy the game.

Makes 6 sandwiches

1 teaspoon canola oil
1 cup chopped onion
3 cloves garlic, finely chopped
1 8-ounce can salt-free (or regular) tomato sauce
¼ cup vinegar
1 tablespoon plus 1 teaspoon lemon juice
2 tablespoons prepared yellow mustard
2 tablespoons firmly packed brown sugar
1 teaspoon Worcestershire sauce
Bottled hot pepper sauce to taste
1 pound cooked boneless ham, sliced paper-thin, all visible fat removed
6 2-ounce hamburger buns

Heat oil in a large nonstick skillet over medium heat. Add onion and garlic. Cook, stirring frequently, until onion is tender, about 5 minutes. Add remaining ingredients except ham and buns. Reduce heat to medium-low and cook, stirring frequently, 5 minutes. Add ham and heat through. Serve on buns.

Per Serving: Calories 308, Total Fat 6.7g, Cholesterol 35mg, Sodium 1327mg, Total Carbohydrate 40.2g, Dietary Fiber 2.4g, Protein 21.8g

Roast Leg of Lamb

The rosemary adds a touch of distinction to this delicious dish. It's a favorite company dish and goes well with mashed potatoes, steamed broccoli, and a tossed salad. Add a light fruit dessert, and you have a low-fat meal fit for royalty.

Makes 10 servings

1 6-pound leg of lamb
6 large cloves garlic, peeled, cut in half lengthwise
2 teaspoons seasoned salt
1 teaspoon dried rosemary, crumbled
1 teaspoon dried thyme
½ teaspoon onion powder
¼ teaspoon pepper
¼ teaspoon garlic powder

Preheat oven to 450°. Place lamb on a rack in a shallow roasting pan. With a sharp knife, make twelve 1-inch-deep cuts in lamb. Place a garlic half in each cut. Combine seasonings and rub into meat, covering entire surface. Place pan in oven.

Reduce heat to 325°. Roast 2 to 2½ hours, or until done to taste. Remove all visible fat before slicing. Serve 3 ounces of sliced lamb per portion, reserving remaining lamb for another time.

Per Serving: Calories 338, Total Fat 12.3g, Cholesterol 173mg, Sodium 473mg, Total Carbohydrate 1g, Dietary Fiber 0.1g, Protein 56.1g

Pasta

Everyone's favorite, pasta is a versatile food that can change dramatically, taking on a new character with the addition of each delectable sauce. Pasta is high in carbohydrates, which is our bodies' main source of fuel. In fact, athletes are now turning to pasta for meals rather than the heavy, high-protein meals they used to consume.

I've avoided butter and cream sauces in my recipes, proving to my mother that it isn't the pasta that adds pounds but what we put on top of it. In addition, when noodles are called for, I always choose the yolk-free variety, thereby reducing the amount of cholesterol in the dishes. I also recommend trying whole wheat pasta for a dish that's higher in carbohydrates, vitamins, minerals, and fiber than the original version.

With its variety of shapes and colors, this nutritious food can be an important part of a healthful diet.

Greek Eggplant and Macaroni Casserole

Similar to the Greek favorite pastitsio, this enjoyable casserole has layers of cheese, macaroni, and a thick tomato and eggplant sauce.

Makes 6 servings

2 teaspoons olive oil
1 medium eggplant, peeled and cut into ½-inch cubes (about 1 pound)
½ cup chopped onion
1 6-ounce can tomato paste
½ cup dry white wine
¼ cup water
1 teaspoon dried basil
¼ teaspoon ground cinnamon
¼ teaspoon salt
8 ounces elbow macaroni, uncooked
½ cup liquid egg substitute
1⅓ cups low-fat (1%) cottage cheese
2 tablespoons grated Parmesan cheese

Heat oil in a large nonstick skillet over medium heat. Add eggplant and onion. Cook 10 minutes, stirring frequently. Add small amounts of water if necessary (a few tablespoons at a time) to prevent sticking. Reduce heat to low. Stir in tomato paste, wine, water, basil, cinnamon, and salt. Cover and simmer 15 minutes, stirring occasionally. While eggplant is cooking, cook macaroni according to package directions. Drain.

Preheat oven to 350°. Spray a 9-inch square baking pan with nonstick cooking spray. In a small bowl, combine egg substitute and cheeses. Spread 1 cup of the eggplant mixture in bottom of prepared pan. Top with macaroni, then cheese, and then remaining eggplant mixture. Bake, uncovered, 30 minutes.

Per Serving: Calories 270, Total Fat 4.2g, Cholesterol 4mg, Sodium 607mg, Total Carbohydrate 41.8g, Dietary Fiber 4.4g, Protein 16.4g

Cheese and Noodle Casserole

Served with a colorful tossed salad, this casserole makes a perfect dish for a luncheon or light dinner.

Makes 4 servings

6 ounces medium or thin noodles (yolk-free), uncooked
1 cup low-fat (1%) cottage cheese
3 ounces reduced-fat Cheddar cheese (¾ cup)
¾ cup plain nonfat yogurt
2 tablespoons grated Parmesan cheese
1 tablespoon minced onion flakes
¼ teaspoon garlic powder
½ teaspoon Worcestershire sauce
1 8-ounce can mushroom pieces, drained

Cook noodles according to package directions. Drain. Preheat oven to 350°. Spray an 8-inch square baking pan with nonstick cooking spray. Place noodles in prepared pan. In a blender, combine cottage cheese, Cheddar cheese, yogurt, half of the Parmesan cheese, onion flakes, garlic powder, and Worcestershire sauce. Blend until smooth. Stir in mushrooms. Pour over noodles and mix together lightly. Sprinkle remaining Parmesan cheese over noodles. Bake, uncovered, 25 to 30 minutes, until hot and lightly browned.

Per Serving: Calories 292, Total Fat 4.1g, Cholesterol 10mg, Sodium 708mg, Total Carbohydrate 41g, Dietary Fiber 2.3g, Protein 23.3g

Parmesan Noodles

Turn noodles into an easy side dish by simply tossing them with a few ingredients.

Makes 6 servings

6 ounces medium noodles (yolk-free), uncooked (about 1½ cups)
1 tablespoon plus 1 teaspoon tub-style (not diet) margarine
1 tablespoon plus 1 teaspoon grated Parmesan cheese
⅛ teaspoon garlic powder Freshly ground black pepper to taste (lots!)

Cook noodles according to package directions. Drain. Place noodles in a serving bowl and add remaining ingredients. Toss until blended.

Per Serving: Calories 140, Total Fat 3.5g, Cholesterol 1mg, Sodium 60mg, Total Carbohydrate 22.4g, Dietary Fiber 1.1g, Protein 4.7g

Macaroni with Cheddar and Tomatoes

An easy dinner awaits you when you alternate layers of macaroni, Cheddar cheese, and stewed tomatoes. If you like spicy food, add a finely minced jalapeno pepper to one of the tomato layers.

Makes 4 servings

1 cup elbow macaroni, uncooked (4 ounces)
1 1-pound can salt-free (or regular) stewed tomatoes, drained
4 ounces shredded reduced-fat Cheddar cheese (1 cup)
1 tablespoon grated Parmesan cheese
¼ teaspoon oregano
¼ teaspoon dried basil
⅛ teaspoon pepper
1 tablespoon all-purpose flour
1 cup evaporated skim milk
2 tablespoons dry breadcrumbs

Cook macaroni according to package directions. Drain. Preheat oven to 375°. Spray a 1-quart casserole with nonstick cooking spray. Place half of the macaroni in the prepared baking dish. Top with half each of the stewed tomatoes, Cheddar, Parmesan, oregano, basil, and pepper. Repeat, using remaining tomatoes, cheeses, and spices. Place flour in a small bowl. Gradually add milk, stirring briskly to avoid lumps. Pour milk over casserole. Sprinkle with breadcrumbs. Spray lightly and evenly with nonstick cooking spray. Bake, uncovered, 35 minutes, or until set. Let stand 5 minutes before serving.

Per Serving: Calories 254, Total Fat 3.2g, Cholesterol 9mg, Sodium 336mg, Total Carbohydrate 39.1g, Dietary Fiber 2.7g, Protein 17.2

Pasta à Pesto

This delicious side dish has always been one of my family's favorite ways to enjoy pasta. Any leftovers make a delicious cold salad.

Makes 4 servings

4 ounces thin spaghetti, uncooked
1 tablespoon plus 1 teaspoon olive oil
1 packet low-sodium instant chicken- or vegetable-flavored broth mix
¼ cup water
2 tablespoons grated Parmesan cheese
1 tablespoon dried parsley flakes
1 tablespoon dried basil
1 clove garlic, chopped
⅛ teaspoon ground nutmeg

Break pasta strands in half and cook according to package directions. Drain. While pasta is cooking, combine remaining ingredients in a blender. Blend until smooth. Place hot pasta in a serving bowl. Add herb mixture and toss. Serve right away.

Per Serving: Calories 165, Total Fat 5.8g, Cholesterol 2mg, Sodium 62mg, Total Carbohydrate 22.8g, Dietary Fiber 1.3g, Protein 5.2g

Pacific Pasta Sauce with Salmon

In the Pacific Northwest, where salmon is plentiful, this tender fish is added to lots of dishes—even pasta. This one starts with already prepared sauce. Choose your favorite low-fat brand and just add the rest.

Makes 6 servings (¾ cup each serving)

1 28-ounce jar reduced-fat, meatless spaghetti or marinara sauce
1 tablespoon dried parsley flakes
1 teaspoon grated fresh lemon peel
Pepper to taste
1 14 ½-ounce can salmon, drained and flaked, skin and bones discarded (12 ounces)

Combine spaghetti sauce, parsley, lemon peel, and pepper in a medium saucepan. Bring to a boil over medium heat. Reduce heat to medium-low, cover, and simmer 15 minutes. Add salmon. Serve over pasta or noodles.

Per Serving: Calories 156, Total Fat 6.2g, Cholesterol 34mg, Sodium 415mg, Total Carbohydrate 11.8g, Dietary Fiber 2.2g, Protein 13.4g

Mediterranean Pasta Sauce with Artichokes

If you love artichoke hearts, this one is for you. The sauce is thick, chunky, and just loaded with the flavors of the Mediterranean. Serve it over pasta or any cooked grain.

Makes 6 servings (¾ cup each serving)

2 teaspoons canola oil
1 cup chopped onion
1 cup chopped green bell pepper
3 cloves garlic, finely chopped
1 1-pound can artichoke hearts, drained (2 cups)
6 large, black pitted olives, sliced
1 26-ounce jar reduced-fat, meatless spaghetti sauce (3 cups)
1 teaspoon dill weed

Heat oil in a medium saucepan over medium heat. Add onion, green pepper, and garlic. Cook, stirring frequently, 8 to 10 minutes, or until vegetables are tender. Add small amounts of water (about a tablespoon at a time) to prevent sticking. Add remaining ingredients, mixing well. When sauce boils, reduce heat to medium-low, cover, and simmer 10 minutes.

Per Serving: Calories 140, Total Fat 2.1g, Cholesterol 0mg, Sodium 475mg, Total Carbohydrate 24.7g, Dietary Fiber 7.3g, Protein 5.3g

Quick 'n' Chunky Tomato Sauce

Canned stewed tomatoes form the base for this tangy sauce. Throw in a little wine and a few spices, cook the pasta, and dinner is ready.

Makes 6 servings (⅔ cup each serving)

2 14 ½-ounce cans salt-free (or regular) stewed tomatoes
⅓ cup tomato paste
¼ cup dry red wine
1 teaspoon sugar
1 teaspoon dried basil
½ teaspoon dried oregano
2 tablespoons grated Parmesan cheese

In a medium saucepan, combine all ingredients except Parmesan cheese. Bring to a boil over medium heat, stirring frequently. Reduce heat to medium-low, cover, and simmer 15 minutes. Spoon sauce over cooked pasta. Sprinkle each serving with 1 teaspoon of the Parmesan cheese.

Per Serving: Calories 70, Total Fat 0.7g, Cholesterol 2mg, Sodium 188mg, Total Carbohydrate 13.3g, Dietary Fiber 3.1g, Protein 2.5g

Pasta Sauce with Rosemary and Lemon

You feel the wonderful tang on your lips when you enjoy this tasty sauce. Spoon it over your favorite pasta, add a side dish of steamed broccoli and yellow peppers, and your dinner is colorful as well as delicious.

Makes 4 servings (½ cup each serving)

1 1-pound can salt-free (or regular) tomatoes, chopped and undrained
1 8-ounce can salt-free (or regular) tomato sauce
1 tablespoon tomato paste
2 cloves garlic, crushed
½ teaspoon dried rosemary, crumbled
½ teaspoon grated fresh lemon peel
½ teaspoon sugar
¼ teaspoon dried basil
⅛ teaspoon pepper
Salt to taste

Combine all ingredients in a medium saucepan. Bring to a boil over medium heat. Reduce heat to medium-low, cover, and simmer 30 minutes.

Per Serving: Calories 54, Total Fat 0.1g, Cholesterol 0mg, Sodium 61mg, Total Carbohydrate 11.3g, Dietary Fiber 2.3g, Protein 1.9g

Fruit and Noodle Kugel

Noodle puddings have so many variations. Some are sweet, others are not so sweet. Some contain fruit, others do not. This one is sweet and it's filled with fruit. It can be served as a side dish, a brunch entrée, or even a delicious dessert.

Makes 8 servings

6 ounces fine noodles (yolk-free), uncooked (3 cups)
2 small, sweet apples, peeled and coarsely shredded
1 cup canned crushed pineapple (packed in juice), drained
¼ cup plus 2 tablespoons raisins
1⅓ cups low-fat (1%) cottage cheese
1 cup liquid egg substitute
½ cup orange juice
¼ cup sugar
2 teaspoons vanilla extract
½ teaspoon ground cinnamon

Cook noodles according to package directions. Drain. Preheat oven to 350°. Spray an 8-inch square baking pan with nonstick cooking spray. In a large bowl, combine cooked noodles, apples, pineapple, and raisins. Toss to combine. In a blender, combine remaining ingredients. Blend until smooth. Add noodles and mix well. Spoon into prepared pan. Bake 45 minutes, or until set. Serve warm or cold, cut into squares.

Per Serving: Calories 217, Total Fat 1.9g, Cholesterol 2mg, Sodium 213mg, Total Carbohydrate 38.5g, Dietary Fiber 1.2g, Protein 11.9g

Little Pineapple Kugel

Have some leftover noodles that you don't know what to do with? This easy kugel is a smaller version of my Fruit and Noodle Kugel and is perfect for a small family. If you like, you can use a coarsely chopped apple in place of the pineapple.

Makes 2 servings

⅓ cup low-fat (1%) cottage cheese
2 egg whites
¼ cup vanilla nonfat or Greek yogurt
1 tablespoon sugar
1 teaspoon vanilla extract
½ teaspoon almond or rum extract
⅛ teaspoon ground cinnamon
½ cup canned crushed pineapple (packed in juice), undrained
½ cup cooked thin or medium noodles, (yolk-free)

Preheat oven to 325°. Spray a small baking dish with nonstick cooking spray. In a blender, combine cottage cheese, egg whites, yogurt, sugar, extracts, and cinnamon. Blend until smooth. Add pineapple. Blend 2 seconds. Pour mixture into a bowl and stir in noodles. Pour mixture into prepared pan. Sprinkle with additional cinnamon. Bake, uncovered, 40 minutes, or until set. Serve warm or cold.

Per Serving: Calories 162, Total Fat 0.6g, Cholesterol 3mg, Sodium 223mg, Total Carbohydrate 28.5g, Dietary Fiber 0.9g, Protein 10.7g

Notes:

Grains

Grains are an important building block in the foundation of a healthy diet. However, many well-meaning, health-conscious eaters often eat a limited selection of grains. While there is nothing wrong with the popular choices of whole wheat bread, rice, and oatmeal, there are so many other delicious—and nutritious—possibilities.

Grains are rich in complex carbohydrates. They also provide protein, vitamin E, B vitamins, magnesium, iron, copper, and zinc. Whole grains are an excellent source of fiber and therefore may help to lower blood cholesterol and maintain bowel regularity. A cup of cooked grains provides from 3 to 11 grams of fiber, depending on the grain.

Grains are also low in fat and calories, with a cup of cooked grains providing about 200 calories. And grains are so versatile. They're not just for dinner. Cooked grains also make a filling, nutritious breakfast.

So, try them all. Some of the popular ones are barley, cornmeal, couscous, millet, oats, rice, rye, and wheat. Many health food stores also carry little-known grains such as triticale, quinoa, and teff. Be adventurous and enjoy the many delicious possibilities grains have to offer.

BASIC COOKING DIRECTIONS FOR GRAINS

Unless the recipe specifies another method, grains are usually cooked by stirring them into boiling water or broth, covering the pot, reducing the heat, then simmering the grains until they are tender and most of the liquid has been absorbed.

The following chart is a guide; however, cooking times may vary slightly depending on the size and quality of the grains. Grains with similar cooking times may be combined and cooked together.

Cooking Chart for Grains

Grain	Uncooked Amount	Amount of Water	Cooking	Approximate Yield
Barley	1 cup	4 cups	45 minutes	3½ cups
Bulgur	1 cup	2 cups	15 minutes	3 cups
Brown rice	1 cup	2½ cups	45 minutes	3½ cups
Converted rice	1 cup	2¼ cups	20 minutes	3½ cups
Kasha	1 cup	3 cups	15 minutes	3½ cups
Cornmeal	1 cup	3 cups	25 minutes	4 cups
Millet	1 cup	2 cups	20 minutes	3 cups
Wheat berries	1 cup	3½ cups	40 to 60 min.	3 cups

Spinach and Rice Bake

Rosemary lends a delicate flavor to this easy casserole. It makes 8 side-dish servings and can also be used as an entrée for 6.

Makes 8 servings

- 2 10-ounce packages frozen chopped spinach, thawed and drained
- 2 cups cooked brown rice
- 6 ounces shredded reduced-fat Cheddar cheese (1½ cups)
- ½ cup thinly sliced green onion (green and white parts)
- 1 teaspoon dried rosemary, crushed
- ½ teaspoon garlic powder
- ¼ teaspoon salt
- ⅛ teaspoon pepper
- 2 cups evaporated skim milk
- 1 cup liquid egg substitute
- 1 teaspoon Worcestershire sauce

Preheat oven to 350°. Spray an 8-inch square baking pan with nonstick cooking spray. In a large bowl, combine spinach, rice, cheese, green onion, and rosemary. Toss to combine well. Place mixture in prepared pan. In another bowl, combine remaining ingredients. Beat with a fork or wire whisk until blended. Pour over spinach mixture. Bake, uncovered, 35 minutes, or until set.

Per Serving: Calories 189, Total Fat 3.2g, Cholesterol 7mg, Sodium 394mg, Total Carbohydrate 23g, Dietary Fiber 3.3g, Protein 17.1g

Raisin Rice Patties

These delectable patties make a great breakfast or a special light dinner when accompanied by soup and salad. You can even make them smaller and serve them as hors d'oeuvres. They're scrumptious topped with raspberry jam.

Makes 4 servings (three 4-inch patties each serving)

½ cup part-skim ricotta cheese
½ cup liquid egg substitute
1 tablespoon plus 1 teaspoon sugar
1 tablespoon all-purpose flour
2 teaspoons vanilla extract
1 teaspoon baking powder
¼ teaspoon ground cinnamon
1 cup cooked white or brown rice
¼ cup raisins

In a blender, combine all ingredients except rice and raisins. Blend until smooth. Pour mixture into a bowl. Stir in rice and raisins, mixing well. Spray a large nonstick skillet or griddle with nonstick cooking spray. Preheat over medium heat. Drop rice mixture into griddle, using 2 tablespoonfuls for each patty. Turn patties when the bottoms are lightly browned and the tops are slightly dry and bubbly. Cook until golden brown on both sides.

Per Serving: Calories 182, Total Fat 3.8g, Cholesterol 10mg, Sodium 186mg, Total Carbohydrate 27.8g, Dietary Fiber 1.5g, Protein 8.9g

Fried Rice

In fine Chinese style, this delicious dish tastes just like the rice in your favorite restaurant.

Makes 4 servings

2 tablespoons reduced-sodium soy sauce
⅛ teaspoon garlic powder
⅛ teaspoon ground ginger
2 teaspoons canola oil
½ cup liquid egg substitute
4 ounces cooked chicken (1 cup), cut into small pieces*
½ cup thinly sliced green onion
2 cups cooked white or brown rice

In a small bowl or custard cup, combine soy sauce, garlic powder, and ginger. Set aside. Preheat a large nonstick skillet over medium heat. Add 1 teaspoon of the oil. Pour in egg substitute, tilting pan to coat bottom evenly. Cook until egg is set, then remove egg from pan and cut into thin 1-inch strips. Set aside. Add remaining oil to skillet. Add chicken, green onion, and rice. Cook, stirring, until well blended. Stir in soy sauce mixture and egg. Cook, stirring constantly, until rice is hot and sizzly.

*If desired, substitute cooked shrimp for the chicken.

Per Serving: Calories 206, Total Fat 5.1g, Cholesterol 24mg, Sodium 346mg, Total Carbohydrate 24.8g, Dietary Fiber 2.2g, Protein 15.5g

Favorite Rice Casserole

This long-time favorite has dressed my table at many dinner parties and family gatherings. It goes with almost any entrée and always adds just the right touch.

Makes 8 servings

4 teaspoons margarine
1 cup brown rice, uncooked (8 ounces)
1 8-ounce can mushroom pieces, drained
2 packets low-sodium instant beef-flavored broth mix
2 tablespoons minced onion flakes
2¾ cups boiling water

Preheat oven to 350°. Spray a 1-½-quart casserole with nonstick cooking spray. Melt margarine in a medium nonstick skillet over medium heat. Stir in rice. Cook, stirring constantly, until rice is golden, 3 to 5 minutes. Remove from heat and add remaining ingredients, mixing well. Place mixture in prepared casserole. Bake, covered, 1 hour and 5 minutes, stirring once after 45 minutes of cooking.

Per Serving: Calories 121, Total Fat 2.7g, Cholesterol 0mg, Sodium 133mg, Total Carbohydrate 20.9g, Dietary Fiber 1.6g, Protein 3g

Tri-Color Rice

The confetti-like appearance of the different peppers makes this a colorful dish to serve alongside almost any entrée.

Makes 4 servings

2 teaspoons canola oil
½ cup chopped onion
½ cup chopped green bell pepper
½ cup chopped red bell pepper
½ cup chopped yellow bell pepper
2 cups water
1 teaspoon dried oregano
¼ teaspoon dried basil
¼ teaspoon garlic powder
2 packets low-sodium instant chicken- or vegetable-flavored broth mix
Salt and pepper to taste
¾ cup converted rice, uncooked (6 ounces)

Heat oil in a medium saucepan over medium heat. Add onion and peppers. Cook 5 minutes, stirring frequently. Add water, oregano, basil, garlic powder, broth mix, salt and pepper. When water boils, stir in rice. Cover, reduce heat to medium-low, and simmer 20 minutes or until most of the water has been absorbed. Remove from heat and let stand 5 minutes. Fluff rice with a fork before serving.

Per Serving: Calories 207, Total Fat 2.6g, Cholesterol 0mg, Sodium 6mg, Total Carbohydrate 42.1g, Dietary Fiber 2.3g, Protein 3.8g

Israeli Eggplant and Rice

The unusual flavor and subtle sweetness of this side dish make it quite unique. It blends well with almost entrée.

Makes 6 servings

2 teaspoons olive oil
4 cups eggplant, peeled and cut into ½-inch pieces (about ¾ pound)
8 large pitted dates, finely chopped
2 small, sweet apples, unpeeled, chopped into ½-inch pieces
1 cup chopped mushrooms
½ cup chopped onion
2 teaspoons sugar
¼ teaspoon salt
⅛ teaspoon ground allspice
½ teaspoon ground cinnamon
1½ cups cooked brown rice
2 tablespoons chopped walnuts or almonds (½ ounce)

Heat oil in a large nonstick skillet over medium heat. Add eggplant, dates, apples, mushrooms, and onion, mixing well. Sprinkle with sugar, salt, allspice, and half of the cinnamon. Cook, stirring frequently, until vegetables are tender, about 10 to 12 minutes. Add rice and chopped nuts and sprinkle with remaining cinnamon. Cook, stirring, until rice is heated through. Serve hot.

Per Serving: Calories 221, Total Fat 3.7g, Cholesterol 0mg, Sodium 101mg, Total Carbohydrate 43.5g, Dietary Fiber 5.5g, Protein 3.3g

Herbed Barley Casserole

The wonderful, bouncy texture of barley makes it one of my favorite grains. Baking it with herbs and spices makes an easy way to enjoy this often-neglected grain.

Makes 6 servings

2 teaspoons canola oil
½ cup finely chopped celery
1 cup barley, uncooked (6 ¾ ounces)
2½ cups low-sodium chicken or vegetable broth or 2½ cups of water and 2 packets low-sodium instant chicken- or vegetable-flavored broth mix
½ cup thinly sliced green onions (green and white parts)
1 teaspoon dried parsley flakes
¼ teaspoon garlic powder
Pepper to taste

Preheat oven to 350°. Spray a 1 ¾-quart casserole with nonstick cooking spray. Heat oil in a medium nonstick skillet over medium heat. Add celery. Cook, stirring frequently, 4 to 5 minutes, until tender. Add barley to skillet. Cook, stirring frequently, 2 minutes. Place in pre-pared casserole. Stir in 1 cup of the broth, along with remaining ingredients. Bake, covered, 25 minutes, then stir in remaining broth and continue to bake, covered, 40 minutes more, or until the liquid is absorbed and the barley is tender.

Per Serving: Calories 148, Total Fat 2.1g, Cholesterol 2mg, Sodium 57mg, Total Carbohydrate 27.3g, Dietary Fiber 5.6g, Protein 4.9g

Barley-Cheddar Sauté

Any cooked grain will work in this delicious medley, but barley seems to add just the right texture.

Makes 6 servings

2 teaspoons olive oil
½ cup chopped onion
½ cup chopped green bell pepper
2 cloves garlic, minced
1 cup eggplant, peeled and chopped
1 cup zucchini, unpeeled, chopped
2 cups cooked barley
1 1-pound can salt-free (or regular) tomatoes, chopped, drained slightly
1 teaspoon dried oregano
Salt and pepper to taste
4 ounces shredded reduced-fat Cheddar cheese (1 cup)

Heat oil in a large nonstick skillet over medium heat. Add onion, green pepper, and garlic. Cook, stirring frequently, 5 minutes. Add eggplant and zucchini to skillet. Cook, stirring frequently, 5 minutes. Add barley, tomatoes, oregano, salt, and pepper. Cook, stirring frequently, until mixture is hot and bubbly and eggplant and zucchini are tender, about 10 minutes. Sprinkle cheese evenly over vegetables. Remove from heat, cover skillet, and let stand 5 minutes to melt cheese.

Per Serving: Calories 146, Total Fat 3.1g, Cholesterol 4mg, Sodium 127mg, Total Carbohydrate 22.4g, Dietary Fiber 3.8g, Protein 7.2g

Buckwheat-Cheese Bake

Hearty and satisfying, this is almost a meal in itself. All you really need to add is a salad and a steamed vegetable, and you have a filling and delicious meatless meal.

Makes 6 servings

1⅓ cups low-fat (1%) cottage cheese
1 cup liquid egg substitute
1 tablespoon all-purpose flour
2 teaspoons minced onion flakes
1 teaspoon dried parsley flakes
1 teaspoon dried basil
½ teaspoon dried thyme
1 packet low-sodium instant chicken-flavored broth mix
Salt and pepper to taste
2 cups cooked buckwheat groats (kasha). Cook kasha according to package directions, eliminating the margarine completely and using an egg white (added) in place of the whole egg that is usually recommended.

Preheat oven to 375°. Spray an 8-inch square baking pan with nonstick cooking spray. In a blender, combine all ingredients except buckwheat. Blend until smooth. Pour into a large bowl and stir in buckwheat. Mix well. Pour mixture into prepared pan. Bake, uncovered, 30 minutes, or until set and lightly browned.

Per Serving: Calories 135, Total Fat 2.2g, Cholesterol 2mg, Sodium 289mg, Total Carbohydrate 15.1g, Dietary Fiber 1.7g, Protein 13.7g

Baked Bulgur Wheat

Look for bulgur wheat with either the cereals or grains in most large grocery stores. It has a wonderful texture and makes a nice change of pace from rice.

Makes 4 servings

2 teaspoons canola oil
½ cup chopped onion
1 large clove garlic, finely chopped
⅔ cup bulgur wheat (4 ounces), uncooked
½ teaspoon dried marjoram
1⅓ cups boiling water
2 packets low-sodium instant beef-flavored broth mix
1 4-ounce can mushroom pieces, drained

Preheat oven to 350°. Spray a 1-quart baking dish with nonstick cooking spray. Heat oil in a small nonstick skillet over medium heat. Add onion and garlic. Cook, stirring frequently, until onion is lightly browned. Remove from heat and stir in remaining ingredients. Mix well and spoon into prepared baking dish. Bake, covered, 20 to 25 minutes, or until liquid has been absorbed. Fluff with a fork before serving.

Per Serving: Calories 124, Total Fat 2.7g, Cholesterol 0mg, Sodium 126mg, Total Carbohydrate 21.5g, Dietary Fiber 5.4g, Protein 3.6g

Bombay Millet

Millet offers another nice change of pace from rice. Its small size allows it to cook more quickly than brown rice, while still offering the high quality and fiber of a whole grain. Look for millet in health food stores and many large grocery stores.

Makes 4 servings

1½ cups low-sodium chicken broth or 1½ cups of water and 1 packet low-sodium instant chicken-flavored broth mix
½ cup millet, uncooked (3 ounces)
1 teaspoon curry powder
¼ teaspoon ground cumin
¼ teaspoon ground ginger
⅛ teaspoon ground allspice
⅛ teaspoon each salt and pepper

Bring broth to a boil in a small saucepan over medium heat. Stir in remaining ingredients. When water returns to a boil, reduce heat to medium-low, cover, and simmer 25 minutes, or until the broth has been absorbed. Fluff with a fork before serving.

Per Serving: Calories 103, Total Fat 1.4g, Cholesterol 1mg, Sodium 115mg, Total Carbohydrate 19g, Dietary Fiber 2.3g, Protein 4g

15-Minute Muesli

This traditional Swiss breakfast is just the right way to start the day. It needs to soak for at least 15 minutes, so you can put it together and let it sit while you get dressed. There's no cooking involved, and it's ready when you are.

Makes 2 servings

½ cup rolled oats, uncooked (1½ ounces)
1 cup orange juice
⅓ cup nonfat dry milk
1 small apple, unpeeled, coarsely shredded
2 tablespoons raisins
2 teaspoons firmly packed brown sugar
½ teaspoon vanilla extract
¼ teaspoon ground cinnamon
⅛ teaspoon almond extract
Dash ground allspice

Combine all ingredients in a bowl and mix well. Let stand at least 15 minutes. Stir again and serve. Leftovers should be refrigerated and can be served cold.

Per Serving: Calories 297, Total Fat 2g, Cholesterol 4mg, Sodium 112mg, Total Carbohydrate 58.2g, Dietary Fiber 4.4g, Protein 11.8g

Notes:

Vegetables

Low in fat, high in fiber, and loaded with vitamins and minerals, vegetables are virtual powerhouses of nutrition. With health professionals recommending that vegetables play a major role in our daily meals, it is wise to include a wide variety of vegetables in your diet.

For the best flavor and nutritional value, cook vegetables until just tender-crisp and leave the skin on whenever possible. Fresh vegetables are best, with frozen vegetables being my second choice. Canned vegetables often contain high amounts of salt and also tend to be overcooked.

My creative vegetable dishes are good enough for company, yet they are easy to prepare.

BASIC COOKING DIRECTIONS FOR VEGETABLES

Steaming is a cooking method that preserves much of the flavor and texture of the vegetables and keeps vitamin loss to a minimum.

Always wash and trim vegetables before using. Place a steamer basket or rack in the bottom of a saucepan and add water almost up to, but not touching, the rack. Bring the water to a boil and add the vegetables. Cover and cook just until vegetables are tender-crisp. Our chart is a guideline; however, cooking times will vary, depending on the freshness and variety of the vegetables.

A word of caution: When removing the cover from a steaming pot, always open it away from you.

VEGETABLE COOKING TIME SUGGESTED SPICES

Asparagus spears 8 minutes lemon peel, basil, thyme, Asparagus, 2-inch pieces 3 to 5 minutes sesame seed

---

Green beans, whole 15 to 25 minutes basil, oregano, dill weed, thyme,
Green beans, 2-inch pieces 10 to 15 minutes rosemary, tarragon

---

Broccoli spears 10 to 15 minutes dill weed, basil, thyme,
Broccoli, flowerets 5 to 8 minutes lemon peel, oregano, garlic

---

Brussels sprouts 10 to 20 minutes mace, garlic, lemon peel, dill weed

---

Cabbage wedges 10 to 15 minutes savory, fennel, dill seed, caraway seed

---

Carrots, whole 20 minutes basil, orange peel,
Carrots, sliced 10 to 12 minutes cinnamon, ginger, allspice, mint, savory, nutmeg

---

Cauliflower, whole 10 to 15 minutes dill weed, basil, thyme,
Cauliflower, flowerets 5 to 8 minutes tarragon, marjoram, paprika, rosemary

---

Parsnips, sliced 10 to 15 minutes allspice, orange peel, dill weed

---

Turnips, chunks 20 minutes bay leaves, oregano, allspice, rosemary

---

Yellow summer squash, 5 to 8 minutes basil, marjoram, sliced oregano, garlic, sage, Zucchini, sliced thyme

Eggplant Supreme

Everyone who tastes this delicious dish agrees that it is, indeed, supreme. It can be served as a side dish, either hot or cold, or on crackers or toast points as an elegant appetizer.

Makes 8 side-dish servings

1 tablespoon plus 1 teaspoon olive oil
1 small eggplant (about ¾ pound), unpeeled, finely chopped (3 cups)
½ cup finely chopped onion
½ cup finely chopped green bell pepper
1 cup chopped mushrooms
3 cloves garlic, finely minced
1 6-ounce can tomato paste
½ cup water
2 tablespoons red wine vinegar
1½ teaspoons sugar
½ teaspoon dried oregano
½ teaspoon salt
¼ teaspoon pepper
10 small, stuffed green olives, chopped
3 tablespoons sunflower seeds (raw or dry roasted)

Heat oil in a large nonstick skillet over medium heat. Add eggplant, onion, green pepper, mushrooms, and garlic. Mix well. Cover and cook 10 minutes, stirring occasionally. Add small amounts of water if necessary (a few tablespoons at a time) to prevent sticking. Add remaining ingredients, mixing well. Reduce heat to medium-low, cover, and simmer 30 minutes, stirring occasionally. Serve hot, or chill and serve cold.

Per Serving: Calories 111, Total Fat 6.1g, Cholesterol 0mg, Sodium 560mg, Total Carbohydrate 11.8g, Dietary Fiber 2.8g, Protein 2.3g

Ratatouille

Fancy and delicious but easy to prepare, this is a classic dish. It's meant to be served hot, but the leftovers, along with a slice of reduced-fat cheese, make a great sandwich.

Makes 8 servings

2 teaspoons olive oil
1 cup sliced onion
2 large cloves garlic, finely chopped
2 cups eggplant, peeled, cut into ½-inch cubes
2 cups zucchini, unpeeled, sliced ½-inch thick
1 medium green bell pepper, cut into ¼-inch strips
1 1-pound can salt-free (or regular) tomatoes, chopped and drained (reserve juice)
1 teaspoon dried basil
1 teaspoon dried parsley flakes
1 teaspoon salt
⅛ teaspoon pepper

Heat oil in a large saucepan over medium heat. Add onion and garlic. Cook, stirring frequently, 3 minutes. Add remaining ingredients. Cover and simmer 20 minutes, or until vegetables are tender. Add the reserved tomato juice as necessary to prevent drying. (Mixture should be moist, but not soupy.)

Per Serving: Calories 48, Total Fat 1.2g, Cholesterol 0mg, Sodium 305mg, Total Carbohydrate 7.8g, Dietary Fiber 2.3g, Protein 1.5g

Warm Eggplant Salad

I call this a salad because the eggplant is served in an oil and vinegar dressing; however, I really consider it a side dish. It's a nice complement to a chicken or fish dinner.

Makes 6 servings

¼ cup red wine vinegar
1 tablespoon plus 1½ teaspoons vegetable oil
1½ tablespoons water
1 tablespoon plus 1 teaspoon sugar
1 teaspoon dried parsley flakes
1 teaspoon dried basil
½ teaspoon dried mint
1 large eggplant (about 1¼ pound), unpeeled, sliced crosswise into ½ -inch slices
Salt and pepper to taste

Preheat broiler. In a small bowl, combine vinegar, oil, water, sugar, and herbs. Mix well and set aside. Place eggplant slices on a nonstick baking sheet. Sprinkle them lightly with salt and pepper. Broil about 5 minutes on each side, or until browned. Sprinkle the other side with salt and pepper after turning slices over. In the bottom of a deep bowl or soufflé dish, put one third of the warm eggplant slices. Top with about one third of the vinegar mixture. Top with another layer of the eggplant and more of the vinegar mixture. Top with remaining eggplant and remaining vinegar mixture. Serve right away or cover until serving time and serve at room temperature.

Per Serving: Calories 70, Total Fat 3.6g, Cholesterol 0mg, Sodium 3mg, Total Carbohydrate 8.6g, Dietary Fiber 2.5g, Protein 1g

Italian Spinach Bake

This delectable dish combines the flavors of Italy in an easy side dish casserole. You can turn this into a filling meal by spooning the finished spinach over a baked potato. Accompanied by some sliced fresh tomatoes and cucumbers, that's all you need for a healthful, delicious dinner.

Makes 6 servings

2 teaspoons olive oil
½ cup chopped onion
2 10-ounce packages frozen, chopped spinach, thawed and drained well
¾ cup part-skim ricotta cheese
2 tablespoons grated Parmesan cheese
¼ teaspoon ground nutmeg
¼ teaspoon garlic powder
Salt and pepper to taste
1 8-ounce can salt-free (or regular) tomato sauce
1 teaspoon dried basil
½ teaspoon dried oregano

Heat oil in a large nonstick skillet over medium-high heat. Add onion. Cook, stirring frequently, until lightly browned, about 5 minutes. Remove from heat. Preheat oven to 350°. Spray a 9-inch pie pan or shallow casserole with nonstick cooking spray. Add spinach, both cheeses, nutmeg, garlic powder, salt, and pepper to skillet. Mix well. Spoon mixture into prepared pan. Smooth the top with the back of a spoon. Combine tomato sauce, basil, and oregano, and spread evenly over spinach mixture. Bake, uncovered, 25 minutes. Let stand 5 minutes before serving.

Per Serving: Calories 112, Total Fat 4.8g, Cholesterol 12mg, Sodium 153mg, Total Carbohydrate 8.9g, Dietary Fiber 3.8g, Protein 8g

Dilled Carrots in Wine

If ever there was a "comfort food" vegetable, this is it. Mild and sweet, with the subtle flavor of dill, these carrots enhance, yet never compete with, almost any entrée.

Makes 6 servings

2 cups carrots, sliced crosswise into ¼-inch slices
1 cup chopped onion
½ cup chopped celery
½ cup chopped celery leaves
⅓ cup dry white wine
½ teaspoon dill weed
Salt and pepper to taste

Combine all ingredients except salt and pepper in a medium saucepan. Bring to a boil over medium heat, stirring occasionally. Reduce heat slightly, cover, and simmer 15 to 20 minutes, or until carrots are just tender. Sprinkle each serving with salt and pepper to taste.

Per Serving: Calories 34, Total Fat 0.1g, Cholesterol 0mg, Sodium 25mg, Total Carbohydrate 7.5g, Dietary Fiber 2g, Protein 0.8g

Golden Carrot Loaf

The golden loaf is sweet, moist, and delicious. It provides an excellent way to get them to eat their vegetables.

Makes 6 servings

1 cup liquid egg substitute
2 tablespoons dry sherry
1 packet low-sodium instant chicken- or vegetable-flavored broth mix
½ cup plus 1 tablespoon all-purpose flour
1 1-pound bag of carrots, grated or finely shredded (The food processor, using the steel blade, does the best job; cut the carrots into large chunks first.)
1 small onion, grated (or put in the food processor with the carrots)

Preheat oven to 350°. Spray a 4 x 8-inch loaf pan with nonstick cooking spray. Combine egg substitute, sherry, and broth mix in a large bowl. Stir in flour, using a wire whisk. Whisk until smooth. Add carrots and onion. Mix well. Spoon mixture into prepared pan. Bake, uncovered, 50 to 55 minutes, until set. Cool in pan on a wire rack for 5 minutes, then invert onto a serving plate. Cut into slices to serve.

Per Serving: Calories 118, Total Fat 1.6g, Cholesterol 0mg, Sodium 133mg, Total Carbohydrate 18.9g, Dietary Fiber 2.9g, Protein 7.2g

Apricot-Glazed Carrots

This elegant dish combines the flavors of apricot, orange, and nutmeg. It looks so pretty and makes a nice accompaniment to chicken or turkey.

Makes 4 servings

4 cups carrots, sliced crosswise into ¼-inch slices
¼ cup fruit-only apricot spread
½ teaspoon grated fresh orange peel
¼ teaspoon ground nutmeg
2 teaspoons lemon juice

Place a steamer rack in the bottom of a medium saucepan. Add enough water to come almost up to the bottom of the rack. Place saucepan over medium heat. When water boils, add carrots, cover saucepan, and cook 10 minutes, or until carrots are tender. Drain. While carrots are cooking, combine remaining ingredients in a small bowl. Mix well. Add a little water or orange juice (a teaspoon at a time) if sauce is too thick. Place carrots in a serving bowl. Spoon sauce over carrots. Toss and serve.

Per Serving: Calories 101, Total Fat 0.3g, Cholesterol 0mg, Sodium 45mg, Total Carbohydrate 23.4g, Dietary Fiber 3.8g, Protein 1.3g

Carrot and Apple Pudding

This sweet-tasting dish is served warm, as a side dish for dinner or brunch. The leftovers make a delicious cold side dish or snack.

Makes 4 servings

1 cup finely shredded carrots
2 small, sweet apples, unpeeled, shredded
¼ cup raisins
½ cup liquid egg substitute
¼ cup plus 2 tablespoons all-purpose flour
1 tablespoon plus 1 teaspoon firmly packed brown sugar
2 teaspoons lemon juice
1 teaspoon ground cinnamon
3 egg whites (Egg substitute will not work here.)

Preheat oven to 350°. Spray a 1½-quart casserole with nonstick cooking spray. In a medium bowl, combine carrots, apples, raisins, egg substitute, flour, brown sugar, lemon juice, and cinnamon. Mix well. In another bowl, beat egg whites on high speed of an electric mixer until stiff. Fold into carrot mixture. Spoon mixture into prepared casserole. Spray the top lightly and evenly with nonstick cooking spray. Bake, uncovered, 30 to 40 minutes, or until set and lightly browned.

Per Serving: Calories 183, Total Fat 1.4g, Cholesterol 0mg, Sodium 107mg, Total Carbohydrate 34.4g, Dietary Fiber 3.5g, Protein 8.1g

Orange-Glazed Green Beans

So elegant, yet so easy to do, these green beans are at home with the family or with guests. The rich orange glaze, accented with basil, really turns a popular vegetable into a gourmet's delight.

Makes 6 servings

¾ cup orange juice
1 tablespoon cornstarch
1 teaspoon dried basil
½ teaspoon lemon juice
Salt and pepper to taste
1 pound green beans, ends trimmed and strings removed

In a small saucepan, combine all ingredients except green beans. Mix well, stirring until cornstarch is dissolved. Set aside. Place a steamer rack in the bottom of a medium saucepan. Add enough water to come almost up to the bottom of the rack. Place saucepan over medium heat. When water boils, add green beans, cover saucepan, and cook about 15 minutes, or until beans are tender. Drain. When beans are almost done, heat orange juice mixture over medium heat, stirring constantly, until mixture boils. Continue to cook and stir for 1 minute. Place green beans in a shallow serving bowl. Pour glaze evenly over beans.

Per Serving: Calories 48, Total Fat 0.2g, Cholesterol 0mg, Sodium 5mg, Total Carbohydrate 9.9g, Dietary Fiber 2.8g, Protein 1.6g

Green Beans and Tomatoes

This colorful, tasty blend of vegetables and spices couldn't be easier. It goes with almost any entrée and also looks great on a buffet.

Makes 4 servings

1 10-ounce package frozen cut green beans
1 1-pound can salt-free (or regular) tomatoes, chopped, undrained
½ teaspoon dried oregano
⅛ teaspoon garlic powder
Salt and pepper to taste

Cook beans according to package directions. Drain. Return beans to saucepan and add remaining ingredients. Bring to a boil over medium heat, then reduce heat to medium-low and simmer 5 minutes, uncovered.

Per Serving: Calories 54, Total Fat 0.2g, Cholesterol 0mg, Sodium 13mg, Total Carbohydrate 10.6g, Dietary Fiber 3.2g, Protein 2.3g

Baked Cabbage Packets

Cabbage wedges wrapped in individual foil packages are an easy, delicious way to enjoy this often-neglected vegetable. The packets can also be cooked on the grill.

Makes 6 servings

1 medium cabbage (about 1¼ pounds), cut vertically into 6 wedges
Salt and pepper to taste
½ cup plus 1 tablespoon evaporated skim milk
1½ teaspoons grated Parmesan cheese

Preheat oven to 350°. Place each cabbage wedge on a 10-inch square of aluminum foil. Sprinkle each wedge lightly with salt and pepper on each side. Spoon 1½ tablespoons of milk over each wedge. Bring the foil up around the sides of the cabbage and roll the edges together securely to seal the packets. Place packets directly on the middle oven rack. Bake 45 minutes. Sprinkle each wedge with ¼ teaspoon of the Parmesan cheese just before serving.

Per Serving: Calories 48, Total Fat 0.5g, Cholesterol 1mg, Sodium 55mg, Total Carbohydrate 7.8g, Dietary Fiber 2.2g, Protein 3.4g

Cabbage with Mustard Sauce

The horseradish adds a wonderful zip to this dish, turning cabbage into a special-event vegetable. In the original version, I used cream and butter, which I've learned I can replace with evaporated skim milk and reduced-calorie margarine.

Makes 6 servings

1 small head of cabbage, cut vertically into 6 wedges
1 tablespoon reduced-calorie margarine
2 tablespoons grated onion
3 tablespoons all-purpose flour
3 tablespoons water
1 cup evaporated skim milk
Salt and pepper to taste
1 tablespoon prepared yellow mustard
2 teaspoons prepared horseradish

Place a steamer rack in the bottom of a medium saucepan. Add enough water to come almost up to the bottom of the rack. Place saucepan over medium heat. When water boils, add cabbage, cover saucepan, and cook 10 to 15 minutes, or until cabbage is tender. Drain. While cabbage is cooking, melt margarine in a small saucepan over medium heat. Stir in onion. Place flour in a small bowl. Gradually stir in water, mixing briskly to avoid lumps. Then gradually stir in milk, salt, and pepper. Stir into margarine. Cook, stirring constantly, until mixture has thickened and is hot and bubbly. Remove from heat and stir in mustard and horseradish, mixing well. Place cabbage into 6 individual serving bowls. Divide sauce evenly and spoon over cabbage.

Per Serving: Calories 90, Total Fat 1.1g, Cholesterol 2mg, Sodium 119mg, Total Carbohydrate 14.5g, Dietary Fiber 2.9g, Protein 5.3g

Cheese Herbed Onions

If you keep a few jars of these little onions in the pantry, they'll always be available to add to soups and stews and for making easy side dishes like this one.

Makes 6 servings

2 1-pound jars pearl onions, drained
1 cup low-fat (1%) cottage cheese
1 tablespoon grated Parmesan cheese
1 tablespoon all-purpose flour
½ teaspoon dried marjoram
½ teaspoon dried basil
½ teaspoon dried oregano
⅛ teaspoon salt
⅛ teaspoon pepper
1 tablespoon dry breadcrumbs

Preheat oven to 375°. Spray a 1-quart baking dish with nonstick cooking spray. Place onions in prepared baking dish. In a small bowl, combine cottage cheese, Parmesan cheese, flour, herbs, salt, and pepper. Mix well and spoon over onions, spreading evenly. Sprinkle with breadcrumbs. Bake, uncovered, 25 minutes, or until lightly browned.

Per Serving: Calories 71, Total Fat 0.9g, Cholesterol 3mg, Sodium 792mg, Total Carbohydrate 9.1g, Dietary Fiber 2g, Protein 6.6g

Sweet and Sour Braised Onions

Hot or cold, this unique blend of flavors adds a spark to any meal. This is a great dish for a buffet or summer cookout.

Makes 6 servings

2 cups small white pearl onions, peeled*
1 1-pound can salt-free (or regular) tomatoes, chopped and drained
1 cup water
¼ cup raisins
1 tablespoon plus 1½ teaspoons red wine vinegar
1 tablespoon plus 1 teaspoon sugar
1 clove garlic, crushed
1 packet low-sodium instant chicken-flavored broth mix
1 teaspoon dry mustard
¼ teaspoon dried thyme
¼ teaspoon salt
⅛ teaspoon pepper
1 bay leaf

Combine all ingredients in a medium saucepan. Bring to a boil over medium heat, stirring occasionally. Reduce heat to medium-low, cover, and simmer 1 hour or until onions are tender. Remove and discard bay leaf before serving. Serve hot or cold.

*To make peeling onions easier, drop them into a saucepan of boiling water. Boil 1 minute to loosen skin. Drain and peel.

Per Serving: Calories 102, Total Fat 0.3g, Cholesterol 0mg, Sodium 121mg, Total Carbohydrate 22.8g, Dietary Fiber 1.2g, Protein 2g

Baked Onions

My favorite onions for this recipe are the wonderful, sweet Vidalia onions. If they're not available, then any large onion will do. You'll find that baking makes the onions taste sweeter. This makes a nice, extra accompaniment to almost any entrée, especially dishes like oven-fried chicken and fish.

Makes 4 servings

4 medium onions, unpeeled
Freshly ground black pepper

Preheat oven to 350°. Place onions directly on oven rack. Bake 1 hour, or until onions are fork-tender. Cut each onion into 4 wedges and sprinkle with pepper before serving.

Per Serving: Calories 63, Total Fat 0.2g, Cholesterol 0mg, Sodium 5mg, Total Carbohydrate 13.5g, Dietary Fiber 2.8g, Protein 1.8g

Broiled Peppers

Have you seen the long, thin, light green peppers called cubanelle or cubanella in the grocery store and wondered what to do with them? Here's a nice, easy way to prepare them, making a delicious addition to any meal, especially one with an Italian or Mexican theme.

Makes 4 servings

4 medium cubanelle peppers

Preheat broiler. Place whole peppers on a broiler pan or baking sheet. Broil until peppers are charred on both sides, turning once. Serve hot.

Per Serving: Calories 20, Total Fat 0g, Cholesterol 0mg, Sodium 4mg, Total Carbohydrate 4g, Dietary Fiber 1g, Protein 1g

Beets à l'Orange

Serve these delicious beets hot as a side dish, then refrigerate the leftovers and enjoy them cold. Either way, they're sure to please the beet lovers in the family.

Makes 8 servings

2 1-pound cans small whole beets, undrained
1 cup orange juice
2 tablespoons cornstarch
1 tablespoon lemon juice
2 teaspoons vinegar
1 teaspoon grated fresh orange peel
⅛ teaspoon ground nutmeg
Dash salt and pepper

Drain beets, reserving ½ cup liquid. Place liquid in a medium saucepan. Add remaining ingredients except beets. Stir to dissolve cornstarch. Bring mixture to a boil over medium heat, stirring constantly. Continue to cook, stirring, 1 minute. Add beets. Heat through. Serve hot or cold.

Per Serving: Calories 58, Total Fat 0.2g, Cholesterol 0mg, Sodium 323mg, Total Carbohydrate 12.8g, Dietary Fiber 1.5g, Protein 1.1g

Mushrooms, Onions, and Peppers

This delectable medley can be served as a side dish or used as a topping for baked chicken, fish, or omelets. It also makes a great addition to a sandwich. Enjoy the wonderful natural flavors the vegetables have to offer.

Makes 4 servings

2 teaspoons canola oil
1 large green bell pepper, thinly sliced
1 large onion, thinly sliced
2 cups sliced mushrooms
Salt and pepper to taste

Heat oil in a large nonstick skillet over medium-high heat. Add vegetables. Cook, stirring frequently, until vegetables begin to brown, about 5 minutes. Sprinkle with salt and pepper to taste.

Per Serving: Calories 64, Total Fat 2.6g, Cholesterol 0mg, Sodium 3mg, Total Carbohydrate 8.6g, Dietary Fiber 2.1g, Protein 1.7g

Snow Peas Surprise

The surprise is that the often-neglected snow peas make an unusual, and very tasty, side dish.

Makes 4 servings

1 tablespoon reduced-sodium soy sauce
⅛ teaspoon garlic powder
⅛ teaspoon ground ginger
½ teaspoon canola oil
½ teaspoon sesame oil
½ cup chopped onion
3 cups fresh snow peas

In a small bowl or custard cup, combine soy sauce, garlic powder, and ginger. Set aside. Heat both oils in a large nonstick skillet over medium-high heat. Add onion. Cook, stirring frequently, 1 minute. Add snow peas and soy sauce mixture. Cook, stirring, 1 minute more.

Per Serving: Calories 52, Total Fat 1.3g, Cholesterol 0mg, Sodium 137mg, Total Carbohydrate 7.7g, Dietary Fiber 2.3g, Protein 2.5g

Tomatoes Provencal

A delicious and colorful side dish, this one is great for a party. I usually make it in the summer when fresh, vine-ripened tomatoes are plentiful.

Makes 6 servings

1 teaspoon olive oil
1 cup chopped onion
1 cup sliced mushrooms
⅛ teaspoon garlic powder
½ teaspoon seasoned salt
Pepper to taste
1 tablespoon imitation bacon bits
2 pounds fresh, ripe tomatoes, sliced crosswise into ½-inch slices (6 medium tomatoes)
2 tablespoons grated Parmesan cheese

Preheat oven to 350°. Spray a 9-inch round or square baking dish with nonstick cooking spray. Heat oil in a large nonstick skillet over medium heat. Add onion and mushrooms. Cook, stirring frequently, until onion is tender, about 5 minutes. Remove from heat and stir in garlic powder, seasoned salt, pepper, and bacon bits. Place half of the tomato slices in the bottom of the prepared baking dish. Spread onion mixture evenly over tomatoes. Sprinkle with half of the Parmesan cheese, then top with remaining tomatoes. Sprinkle with remaining cheese. Cover tightly and bake 34 to 40 minutes.

Per Serving: Calories 73, Total Fat 2.2g, Cholesterol 2mg, Sodium 203mg, Total Carbohydrate 10g, Dietary Fiber 2.3g, Protein 2.9g

Best Stewed Tomatoes

If you like, you can add bread cubes, plain or toasted, to the stewed tomatoes just before serving. The tomatoes are also delicious served over rice.

Makes 6 servings

2 1-pounds can salt-free (or regular) tomatoes, chopped, undrained
¼ cup very finely minced celery
1 tablespoon minced onion flakes
1 tablespoon sugar
½ teaspoon salt
½ teaspoon dried oregano
¼ teaspoon dried basil
Pepper to taste
1 tablespoon cornstarch dissolved in 1 tablespoon water

Combine all ingredients except dissolved cornstarch in a medium saucepan. Bring to a boil over medium heat, stirring occasionally. Reduce heat to medium-low and simmer, uncovered, 15 minutes. Stir in cornstarch and water mixture. Continue to cook, stirring constantly, 2 to 3 more minutes.

Per Serving: Calories 35, Total Fat 0.1g, Cholesterol 0mg, Sodium 208mg, Total Carbohydrate 7.6g, Dietary Fiber 1.1g, Protein 0.8g

Savory Sprouts

Fresh Brussels sprouts also work in this easy recipe. Steam them first over boiling water until they are just tender-crisp, about 10 to 15 minutes, and proceed with the rest of the recipe. You may find that your family does like this often-neglected vegetable after all.

Makes 4 servings

1 10-ounce package frozen Brussels sprouts
2 teaspoons margarine
1 packet low-sodium instant chicken- or vegetable-flavored broth mix
¼ teaspoon dried basil
⅛ teaspoon ground savory
⅛ teaspoon pepper
Dash nutmeg
Salt to taste

Cook Brussels sprouts according to package directions. Drain. Place sprouts in a serving bowl. Add remaining ingredients. Toss and serve.

Per Serving: Calories 56, Total Fat 2.2g, Cholesterol 0mg, Sodium 30mg, Total Carbohydrate 6.2g, Dietary Fiber 2.7g, Protein 2.7g

Simmered Sauerkraut

Sauerkraut is extremely high in sodium, so I always rinse it several times and eat very small portions. This dish provides a nice accent to a simple entrée of baked chicken or fish.

Makes 6 servings

1 1-pound can sauerkraut, rinsed several times and drained
1 1-pound can salt-free (or regular) tomatoes, chopped, undrained
1 small apple, peeled and coarsely shredded
¼ cup very finely minced onion
1 packet low-sodium instant beef-flavored broth mix
1 tablespoon plus 1 teaspoon firmly packed brown sugar

Combine all ingredients in a medium saucepan. Bring to a boil over medium heat, stirring occasionally. Then reduce heat to medium-low, cover, and simmer 30 minutes.

Per Serving: Calories 56, Total Fat 0.2g, Cholesterol 0mg, Sodium 184mg, Total Carbohydrate 12.3g, Dietary Fiber 2.9g, Protein 1.2g

Cauliflower Puree

This scrumptious way of serving cauliflower tastes amazingly like mashed potatoes. Fresh cauliflower also works well. Just steam it over boiling water until it is tender enough to puree.

Makes 4 servings

2 10-ounce packages frozen cauliflower
1 tablespoon plus 1 teaspoon reduced-calorie margarine
1 tablespoon minced onion flakes
1 packet low-sodium instant beef-flavored broth mix
⅛ teaspoon pepper

Cook cauliflower according to package directions. Continue to cook until cauliflower is very tender. Drain. Preheat oven to 375°. Spray a 1-quart baking dish with nonstick cooking spray. Combine cauliflower and remaining ingredients in a food processor or blender. Process until mixture is pureed. Spoon into prepared baking dish. Bake, uncovered, 10 minutes, or until hot.

Per Serving: Calories 65, Total Fat 1.8g, Cholesterol 0mg, Sodium 64mg, Total Carbohydrate 9.2g, Dietary Fiber 3.5g, Protein 3.1g

Lemon Broccoli

Lemon makes a great accent for broccoli, enhancing its deep flavor and making it a very special vegetable. Fresh broccoli works just as well in this recipe. Steam it over boiling water until tender-crisp, about 10 to 15 minutes.

Makes 4 servings

1 10-ounce package frozen broccoli spears
2 tablespoons reduced-calorie margarine
2 teaspoons lemon juice
2 tablespoons thinly sliced green onions (green part only)
¼ teaspoon grated fresh lemon peel
Salt and pepper to taste

Cook broccoli according to package directions. Drain. While broccoli is cooking, heat margarine until almost melted. (Placing it in a custard cup in the microwave does it nicely.) Stir in lemon juice. Place broccoli in a serving dish. Spoon margarine mixture over broccoli. Sprinkle with green onions, lemon peel, salt, and pepper.

Per Serving: Calories 48, Total Fat 2.4g, Cholesterol 0mg, Sodium 57mg, Total Carbohydrate 4.2g, Dietary Fiber 2.2g, Protein 2.3g

Italian Veggie Bake

An easy way to prepare vegetables is to bake them. If you like them tender-crisp, bake them for less time, and if you like them softer, just bake them longer.

Makes 6 servings

1 cup zucchini, unpeeled, cut into 1-inch cubes
1 cup mushrooms, quartered
1 cup broccoli, cut into flowerets
½ cup yellow squash, unpeeled, cut into 1-inch cubes
½ cup cauliflower, cut into flowerets
½ cup chopped onion
½ medium green bell pepper, sliced
1 1-pound can salt-free (or regular) tomatoes, chopped, undrained
1 teaspoon dried basil
½ teaspoon dried oregano
½ teaspoon garlic powder
⅛ teaspoon pepper
Salt to taste
6 ounces shredded part-skim Mozzarella cheese (1½ cups)
2 tablespoons grated Parmesan cheese

Preheat oven to 375°. Spray a 7 x 11-inch baking pan with nonstick cooking spray. Combine vegetables and spices in a large bowl and mix well. Spoon into prepared pan. Cover tightly and bake 45 minutes, or until vegetables are tender, stirring once halfway through cooking time. Uncover vegetables and sprinkle with cheeses. Continue to bake, uncovered, 10 minutes, or until cheese is melted and begins to brown.

Per Serving: Calories 125, Total Fat 5.3g, Cholesterol 18mg, Sodium 186mg, Total Carbohydrate 9.4g, Dietary Fiber 2.5g, Protein 9.9g

Zucchini Cheese Bake

Cheese and oregano give new dimensions to zucchini in this easy dish. Although I usually serve it as a side dish for 6, it can also serve 4 as a nice light luncheon entrée.

Makes 6 servings

5 cups zucchini, unpeeled, sliced crosswise into thin slices
⅔ cup low-fat (1%) cottage cheese
2 ounces shredded reduced-fat Cheddar cheese (½ cup)
1 tablespoon minced onion flakes
1 teaspoon dried oregano
Salt and pepper to taste

Preheat oven to 375°. Spray a 1-quart baking dish with nonstick cooking spray. Steam zucchini on a rack in a covered saucepan 5 minutes, or until just tender-crisp. Arrange in prepared baking dish. In a blender, combine the remaining ingredients. Blend until smooth. Spoon evenly over zucchini. Bake, uncovered, 20 minutes, or until hot and lightly browned.

Per Serving: Calories 77, Total Fat 3.5g, Cholesterol 10mg, Sodium 107mg, Total Carbohydrate 4.8g, Dietary Fiber 1.4g, Protein 6.7g

Zucchini-Mozzarella Casserole

The wonderful flavors of Italy, accented with a little Dijon mustard, make this delightful dish a favorite they'll ask for over and over again. The mild-mannered zucchini really shines here.

Makes 6 servings

2 teaspoons olive oil
4 cups zucchini, unpeeled, sliced crosswise into thin slices
½ cup finely chopped onion
1 tablespoon dried parsley flakes
½ teaspoon dried oregano
¼ teaspoon dried basil
⅛ teaspoon garlic powder
Salt and pepper to taste
½ cup liquid egg substitute
4 ounces shredded part-skim Mozzarella cheese (1 cup)
1 teaspoon Dijon mustard

Heat oil in a large nonstick skillet over medium heat. Add zucchini and onion. Cook, stirring frequently, until vegetables are tender-crisp, about 5 minutes. Add small amounts of water if necessary (about a tablespoon at a time) to prevent sticking. Remove from heat. Preheat oven to 350°. Spray a l-quart casserole dish with nonstick cooking spray. Sprinkle parsley, oregano, basil, garlic powder, salt, and pepper over zucchini. Mix gently. In a large bowl, combine egg substitute, Mozzarella cheese, and mustard. Mix well. Add zucchini and stir until mixture is combined. Spoon into prepared casserole dish. Bake, uncovered, 35 minutes, until lightly browned.

Per Serving: Calories 98, Total Fat 5.3g, Cholesterol 11mg, Sodium 148mg, Total Carbohydrate 4.4g, Dietary Fiber 1.4g, Protein 8.3g

Savory Zucchini Fritters

This versatile vegetable, with its mild flavor, can be used in so many recipes. It can be used to make delicious fritters that are either savory, as in this recipe, or sweet, as in the next recipe. Why not enjoy them both?

Makes 4 servings (4 fritters each serving)

½ cup liquid egg substitute
⅔ cup low-fat (1%) cottage cheese
¼ cup plus 2 tablespoons all-purpose flour
1 tablespoon minced onion flakes
½ teaspoon baking powder
¼ teaspoon dried marjoram
¼ teaspoon dried thyme
⅛ teaspoon salt
⅛ teaspoon pepper
⅛ teaspoon garlic powder
1 cup (packed) finely shredded zucchini, unpeeled

In a blender, combine all ingredients except zucchini. Blend until smooth. Spoon mixture into a bowl. Drain zucchini in a strainer, pressing out liquid with the back of a spoon. Stir into first mixture. Spray a large nonstick skillet or griddle with nonstick cooking spray. Preheat over medium-high heat. Drop batter into skillet, making 16 fritters, using about 2 tablespoons for each fritter. Turn fritters carefully and cook until nicely browned on both sides. (To make turning fritters easier, spray spatula lightly with nonstick cooking spray.)

Per Serving: Calories 103, Total Fat 1.5g, Cholesterol 2mg, Sodium 329mg, Total Carbohydrate 12.4g, Dietary Fiber 0.8g, Protein 10.2g

Sweet Zucchini Fritters

These tender fritters provide a great way to get the finicky eaters to eat their vegetables. They make a delicious side dish and can even be drizzled with maple syrup and served as a unique brunch dish.

Makes 4 servings (4 fritters each serving)

½ cup liquid egg substitute
⅔ cup low-fat (1%) cottage cheese
¼ cup plus 2 tablespoons all-purpose flour
2 tablespoons sugar
1 teaspoon vanilla extract
½ teaspoon baking powder
½ teaspoon ground cinnamon
¼ teaspoon ground nutmeg
⅛ teaspoon ground allspice
1 cup (packed) finely shredded zucchini, unpeeled
¼ cup raisins

In a blender, combine all ingredients except raisins and zucchini. Blend until smooth. Spoon mixture into a bowl. Drain zucchini in a strainer, pressing out liquid with the back of a spoon. Stir zucchini and raisins into first mixture. Spray a large nonstick skillet or griddle with nonstick cooking spray. Preheat over medium-high heat. Drop batter into skillet, making 16 fritters, using about 2 tablespoons for each fritter. Turn fritters carefully and cook until nicely browned on both sides. (To make turning fritters easier, spray spatula lightly with nonstick cooking spray.)

Per Serving: Calories 159, Total Fat 1.6g, Cholesterol 2mg, Sodium 256mg, Total Carbohydrate 26g, Dietary Fiber 1.3g, Protein 10.4g

Italian Baked Spaghetti Squash

Kids love the spaghetti-like strands of this unique vegetable. This easy casserole can be assembled ahead, refrigerated, and baked when needed. If you have a large squash, you can easily double the recipe.

Makes 4 servings

2 cups cooked spaghetti squash*
1 8-ounce can salt-free (or regular) tomato sauce
½ teaspoon dried oregano
⅛ teaspoon garlic powder
Pepper to taste
1 tablespoon plus 1 teaspoon grated Parmesan cheese

Preheat oven to 375°. Spray a 1-quart baking dish with nonstick cooking spray. Place spaghetti squash in prepared baking dish. Combine tomato sauce, oregano, garlic powder, and pepper. Spoon evenly over squash. Sprinkle with Parmesan cheese. Bake, uncovered, 20 minutes, until hot and bubbly.

*To cook spaghetti squash, cut squash in half lengthwise. Remove seeds. Bake cut-side down in a baking pan containing 1 inch of water at 350° for 45 minutes, or until tender. Remove squash from pan and drain cut-side down. Pull strands free with a fork.

Per Serving: Calories 38, Total Fat 0.6g, Cholesterol 2mg, Sodium 55mg, Total Carbohydrate 6.5g, Dietary Fiber 1.5g, Protein 1.7g

Dilled Yellow Squash

This simple, herbed dish makes a delicious complement to almost any meal. For the best flavor, let the onions get nice and brown before adding the squash.

Makes 6 servings

2 teaspoons olive oil
1 cup chopped onion
3 cloves garlic, finely chopped
4 cups yellow summer squash, unpeeled, slice crosswise into ½-inch slices
1 teaspoon dill weed
½ teaspoon salt
⅛ teaspoon pepper

Heat oil in a large nonstick skillet over medium heat. Add onion and garlic. Cook, stirring frequently, until onion is lightly browned, 8 to 10 minutes. Add squash. Sprinkle evenly with dill, salt, and pepper. Cover and cook until squash is lightly browned and tender-crisp, about 5 to 7 minutes. Turn squash several times while cooking to brown both sides.

Per Serving: Calories 45, Total Fat 1.7g, Cholesterol 0mg, Sodium 199mg, Total Carbohydrate 6.4g, Dietary Fiber 2.1g, Protein 1.2g

Baked Squash Southern Style

An adaptation of an old Southern recipe, this dish has been a family favorite for years.

Makes 6 servings

2 10-ounce packages frozen yellow summer squash
1 tablespoon minced onion flakes
2 tablespoons reduced-calorie margarine
2 egg whites
1½ teaspoons sugar
½ teaspoon salt
⅛ teaspoon pepper
3 tablespoons Italian-seasoned breadcrumbs

Cook squash according to package directions, cooking until it is very tender. Drain. Preheat oven to 350°. Spray a 1-quart baking dish with nonstick cooking spray. Place squash in a large bowl. Mash well, using a fork or a potato masher. Add onion flakes, half of the margarine, egg whites, sugar, salt, pepper, and half of the breadcrumbs. Mix well. Spoon mixture into prepared baking dish. Sprinkle with the remaining crumbs. Dot with remaining margarine. Bake, uncovered, 45 minutes, or until set and lightly browned.

Per Serving: Calories 61, Total Fat 1.7g, Cholesterol 0mg, Sodium 347mg, Total Carbohydrate 8.9g, Dietary Fiber 1.4g, Protein 2.5g

Italian Stuffed Squash

Zucchini or yellow summer squash will work in this elegant dish. It's so easy to prepare, yet it looks—and tastes—like you've worked for hours. For extra servings, it's easy to double the recipe.

Makes 4 servings

2 zucchini or yellow summer squash, about 8 ounces each
2 teaspoons olive oil
½ cup chopped onion
1 tablespoon Italian-seasoned breadcrumbs
2 teaspoons grated Parmesan cheese
½ teaspoon dried oregano
¼ teaspoon dried basil
Dash garlic powder
Dash pepper

Steam whole squash in 1 inch of boiling water for 5 minutes. Drain. Cut squash in half lengthwise. Carefully scoop out pulp, using a spoon or melon ball scoop, leaving a ¼- to ½-inch shell. Save squash shells. Chop pulp. Preheat oven to 350°. Spray a shallow baking pan with nonstick cooking spray. Heat oil in a small nonstick skillet over medium heat. Add onion. Cook, stirring frequently, until lightly browned, about 4 minutes. Remove from heat and stir in squash pulp, breadcrumbs, Parmesan cheese, and spices. Mix well. Pile mixture into squash shells. Place in prepared pan. Bake, uncovered, 30 minutes, or until lightly browned.

Per Serving: Calories 59, Total Fat 2.7g, Cholesterol 1mg, Sodium 73mg, Total Carbohydrate 6.6g, Dietary Fiber 2g, Protein 2.2g

Notes:

Starchy Vegetables

The starchy vegetables include white potatoes, sweet potatoes, corn, peas, parsnips, and all varieties of winter squash. These vegetables are higher in carbohydrates than other vegetables. Starchy vegetables, like other vegetables, are packed with vitamins, minerals, and fiber.

I always recommend leaving the skin on potatoes whenever possible, which provides extra nutrients and fiber. And remember that contrary to what our mothers may have told us, it's not the potato that is fattening but the fatty toppings and deep-frying!

Baked Orange Squash

The complementary flavors of orange and cinnamon really enhance the squash in this delicious casserole. It's good for holidays or any day.

Makes 4 servings

2 cups mashed, cooked butternut or acorn squash*
¼ cup frozen orange juice concentrate, thawed
1 tablespoon plus 1 teaspoon firmly packed brown sugar
½ teaspoon grated fresh orange peel
⅛ teaspoon ground cinnamon
Dash ground ginger

Preheat oven to 375°. Spray a 1-quart baking dish with nonstick cooking spray. Combine all ingredients in a medium bowl. Mix well. Spoon into prepared baking dish. Bake, uncovered, 20 minutes.

*To cook winter squash, cut squash into halves or quarters and remove the seeds. Place squash, cut-side down, in a shallow baking pan. Cover with foil and bake at 350° for 30 minutes. Then turn squash cut-side up and continue to bake until tender, about 30 minutes. Remove peel.

Per Serving: Calories 112, Total Fat 0.1g, Cholesterol 0mg, Sodium 6mg, Total Carbohydrate 26.3g, Dietary Fiber 4.6g, Protein 1.5g

Pineapple-Filled Acorn Squash

Acorn squash cut in half makes a perfect "basket" for fruits or other vegetables. In this dish, I've filled the squash halves with pineapple, making a deliciously sweet side dish. You can turn this into a nice light lunch by topping each half with a scoop of cottage cheese just before serving.

Makes 4 servings

2 acorn squash (about 10 ounces each)
1 8-ounce can crushed pineapple (packed in juice), drained slightly
1 tablespoon plus 1 teaspoon firmly packed brown sugar
1 teaspoon ground cinnamon
½ teaspoon vanilla extract
¼ teaspoon rum extract

Preheat oven to 400°. Cut squash in half lengthwise and remove seeds. Place squash cut-side down in a shallow baking pan. Pour hot water around squash to a depth of ½ inch. Bake, uncovered, 30 to 40 minutes, or until squash is tender. Carefully remove pulp from squash using a spoon, and leave a ½-inch shell. Place pulp in a small bowl and mash with remaining ingredients. Pile mixture back into shells. Return squash to pan. Bake, uncovered, 10 minutes, or until heated through.

Per Serving: Calories 121, Total Fat 0.1g, Cholesterol 0mg, Sodium 6mg, Total Carbohydrate 28.7g, Dietary Fiber 2.9g, Protein 1.3g

Butternut Squash with Apples and Leeks

This recipe can be made with any type of winter squash, such as hubbard, turban, or pumpkin. It seems like an unusual combination of ingredients, but it's a very tasty one.

Makes 6 servings

1 teaspoon canola oil
1 large leek, white part only, chopped (1 cup)
2 cloves garlic, crushed
1 2-pound butternut squash, cut into wedges, peeled, seeded, then sliced into ⅛-inch slices
¼ cup water
2 small Granny Smith apples, unpeeled, cut into wedges, and sliced into ⅛-inch slices
2 tablespoons honey
¼ teaspoon salt
¼ teaspoon ground nutmeg
⅛ teaspoon ground allspice
Freshly ground black pepper

Heat oil in a large nonstick skillet over medium heat. Add leek and garlic. Cook, stirring frequently, 2 minutes. Add squash and water. Mix well. Cover, reduce heat slightly, and cook 6 to 7 minutes, until squash is tender-crisp. Stir once while cooking. Add remaining ingredients *except* pepper. Mix well. Cover and cook 5 minutes, until squash and apples are tender. Spoon into a serving bowl and sprinkle with freshly ground pepper to taste.

Per Serving: Calories 132, Total Fat 1g, Cholesterol 0mg, Sodium 107mg, Total Carbohydrate 29.4g, Dietary Fiber 4.2g, Protein 1.3g

Whipped Spiced Parsnips

An often-forgotten vegetable, parsnips have a wonderful flavor and texture and make a delicious side dish. They look like white carrots and can also be chopped and added to soups and stews.

Makes 4 servings

12 ounces parsnips, peeled and sliced crosswise into ⅛-inch slices
2 teaspoons firmly packed brown sugar
1 teaspoon margarine
¼ teaspoon grated fresh orange peel
Dash ground nutmeg *or* allspice
Dash salt
¼ cup orange juice
¼ cup canned crushed pineapple (packed in juice), drained slightly

Place a steamer rack in the bottom of a medium saucepan. Add enough water to come almost up to the bottom of the rack. Place saucepan over medium heat. When water boils, add parsnips, cover saucepan, and cook 15 to 20 minutes, or until parsnips are very tender. Drain.

Preheat oven to 350°. Spray a 1-quart baking dish with nonstick cooking spray. Place parsnips in a large bowl. Add brown sugar, margarine, orange peel, nutmeg, salt, and *half* of the orange juice. Mash with a fork or potato masher, then beat on medium speed of an electric mixer until smooth. Add remaining orange juice as needed, until the desired consistency is reached. Stir in pineapple. Spoon mixture into prepared baking dish. Bake, uncovered, 15 minutes, or until hot.

Per Serving: Calories 102, Total Fat 1.2g, Cholesterol 0mg, Sodium 60mg, Total Carbohydrate 21.5g, Dietary Fiber 4.3g, Protein 1.2g

Peas New Orleans

As colorful as Mardi Gras, this easy recipe turns ordinary peas into a gourmet side dish. It makes a lovely dish for a buffet.

Makes 4 servings

1 10-ounce package frozen peas
2 teaspoons canola oil
¼ cup chopped onion
¼ cup chopped green bell pepper
1 1-pound can salt-free (or regular) tomatoes, chopped and drained (reserve liquid)
1 teaspoon sugar
Salt and pepper to taste
2 teaspoons cornstarch

Cook peas according to package directions. Drain. Heat oil in a small saucepan over medium heat. Add onion and green pepper. Cook, stirring frequently, until tender. Add small amounts of water as necessary (about a tablespoon at a time) to prevent sticking. Add peas, tomatoes, sugar, salt, and pepper to saucepan.

In a small bowl, stir a few tablespoons of the tomato liquid into the cornstarch, stirring to dissolve the cornstarch. Add cornstarch mixture and remaining tomato liquid to saucepan. Bring to a boil, stirring constantly, then continue to cook, stirring, 1 minute.

Per Serving: Calories 119, Total Fat 2.7g, Cholesterol 0mg, Sodium 91mg, Total Carbohydrate 18.9g, Dietary Fiber 4.9g, Protein 5g

Savory Peas and Mushrooms

Here's a quick, easy way to dress up a package of peas.

Makes 4 servings

1 10-ounce package frozen peas
1 4-ounce can mushroom pieces, drained
2 teaspoons margarine
1 teaspoon onion powder
⅛ teaspoon ground savory
Salt and pepper to taste

Cook peas according to package directions, adding mushrooms during the last half of the cooking time. Drain. Place peas in a serving bowl. Add remaining ingredients. Toss and serve.

Per Serving: Calories 83, Total Fat 2.3g, Cholesterol 0mg, Sodium 199mg, Total Carbohydrate 11.5g, Dietary Fiber 4g, Protein 4.3g

Potato Kugel

A dish my mother always made, this potato pudding is moist and delicious. I like it with lots of pepper, but you can let your own taste buds be your guide. It's a perfect side dish to serve with just about any entrée.

Makes 6 servings

1½ pounds potatoes, unpeeled (3 medium potatoes), grated or finely shredded
½ cup liquid egg substitute
1 small onion, grated
3 tablespoons all-purpose flour
1 tablespoon canola oil
¾ teaspoon salt, or to taste
¼ teaspoon pepper, or to taste
¼ teaspoon baking powder

Preheat oven to 375°. Spray a 1-quart baking pan with nonstick cooking spray. Place the potatoes in a bowl and set aside for 10 minutes, then place them in a strainer and press out as much liquid as you can. Return potatoes to bowl. Add remaining ingredients. Mix well. Spoon mixture into prepared pan. Bake, uncovered, 1 hour and 10 minutes, until set and lightly browned.

Per Serving: Calories 146, Total Fat 3.1g, Cholesterol 0mg, Sodium 359mg, Total Carbohydrate 24.5g, Dietary Fiber 2.1g, Protein 5.3g

Buttermilk Mashed Potatoes

Mashed potatoes become a special dish when buttermilk, mushrooms, and herbs are added.

Makes 4 servings

15 ounces potatoes, unpeeled, quartered
¼ cup buttermilk
1 tablespoon minced onion flakes
¼ teaspoon dried thyme
⅛ teaspoon pepper
⅛ teaspoon garlic powder
Salt to taste
1 8-ounce can mushroom pieces, drained
1 tablespoon wheat germ *or* dry breadcrumbs
1 tablespoon plus 1 teaspoon reduced-calorie margarine

Place potatoes in 2 inches of boiling water, cover, and cook over medium heat 15 to 20 minutes, or until potatoes are tender. Drain potatoes and remove skin.

Preheat oven to 400°. Spray a 1-quart casserole with nonstick cooking spray. Place cooked potatoes in a large bowl and add buttermilk, onion flakes, thyme, pepper, garlic powder, and salt. Mash with a fork or potato masher. Beat on medium speed of an electric mixer until smooth. Add water or a little more buttermilk if potatoes are too dry. Stir in mushrooms. Place mixture in prepared casserole. Sprinkle evenly with wheat germ. Dot with margarine. Bake, uncovered, 15 minutes, until hot and lightly browned.

Per Serving: Calories 140, Total Fat 2.3g, Cholesterol 1mg, Sodium 269mg, Total Carbohydrate 24.5g, Dietary Fiber 3.4g, Protein 5.4g

Oven-Baked French "Fries"

Can you believe it? These taste so much like the real thing, you'll make them over and over again. Just a spray of nonstick spray and you still have all of the taste without the gobs of fat.

Makes 4 servings

4 medium baking potatoes, unpeeled (about 5 ounces each)
Salt and pepper to taste

Preheat oven to 450°. Spray a baking sheet with nonstick cooking spray. Cut potatoes into strips to resemble French fries. Place on prepared sheet in a single layer. Spray potatoes lightly with nonstick spray. Sprinkle with salt and pepper to taste. Bake 10 minutes, then stir potatoes and bake 10 minutes more, or until desired crispness is reached.

Per Serving: Calories 115, Total Fat 0.1g, Cholesterol 0mg, Sodium 9mg, Total Carbohydrate 25.5g, Dietary Fiber 2.3g, Protein 2.9g

Potato Latkes (Pancakes)

Top these tender delicacies with applesauce, and you create a side dish or brunch dish that's really special.

Makes 6 servings (3 pancakes each serving)

1½ pounds potatoes, unpeeled (3 medium potatoes), grated or finely shredded
½ cup liquid egg substitute
1 small onion, grated
2 tablespoons all-purpose flour
¾ teaspoon salt, or to taste
¼ teaspoon pepper, or to taste

Place the potatoes in a bowl and set aside for 10 minutes, then place them in a strainer and press out as much liquid as you can. Return potatoes to bowl. Add remaining ingredients. Mix well.

Spray a large nonstick skillet or griddle with nonstick cooking spray. Preheat over medium heat. Drop potato mixture onto skillet, making 18 pancakes, using about 2 tablespoons for each pancake. Flatten each one slightly with a spatula. Turn fritters carefully and cook until nicely browned on both sides.

Per Serving: Calories 121, Total Fat 0.8g, Cholesterol 0mg, Sodium 339mg, Total Carbohydrate 23.4g, Dietary Fiber 2.1g, Protein 5.2g

Sweet Potatoes and Apples

Alternate slices of sweet potatoes and apples, baked in a spiced orange sauce, make a holiday favorite that you'll want to make throughout the year.

Makes 4 servings

12 ounces cooked sweet potatoes, peeled and sliced into thin slices (Bake the sweet potatoes in a 350° oven for about 1 hour, or microwave for 8 to 10 minutes, until tender, but not mushy.)
2 small, sweet apples, peeled and cored, cut in half, and cut into very thin slices
¼ cup frozen orange juice concentrate, thawed
¼ cup water
2 tablespoons firmly packed brown sugar
¼ teaspoon ground cinnamon
⅛ teaspoon ground nutmeg
⅛ teaspoon ground ginger
1 tablespoon plus 1 teaspoon reduced-calorie margarine

Preheat oven to 350°. Spray a 1-quart baking dish with nonstick cooking spray. Arrange alternate slices of sweet potatoes and apples in prepared baking dish. Combine orange juice, water, brown sugar, and spices. Pour mixture evenly over sweet potatoes and apples. Dot with margarine. Bake, covered, 1 hour. (If a crisper dish is desired, remove cover during last half of cooking time.)

Per Serving: Calories 172, Total Fat 1.7g, Cholesterol 0mg, Sodium 64mg, Total Carbohydrate 37.1g, Dietary Fiber 4g, Protein 2.2g

Island Sweet Potato Pudding

The sweet, moist banana adds flavor and texture to this delicious casserole that's laced with the flavors of nutmeg and rum and baked until golden.

Makes 4 servings

12 ounces cooked sweet potatoes, peeled and cut into chunks (Bake the sweet potatoes in a 350° oven for about 1 hour, or microwave for about 8 to 10 minutes, until very tender.)
1 medium, very ripe banana, mashed
1 tablespoon firmly packed brown sugar
¼ teaspoon ground nutmeg
1 teaspoon rum extract
1 egg white

Preheat oven to 350°. Spray a 1-quart casserole with nonstick cooking spray. In a large bowl, combine sweet potatoes, banana, brown sugar, nutmeg, and rum extract. Beat on low speed of an electric mixer until smooth. Add small amounts of water or orange juice, if necessary, to get a smooth consistency.

In a separate bowl, using clean, dry beaters, beat egg white until stiff. Fold into sweet potato mixture. Spoon mixture into prepared casserole. Bake, uncovered, 45 to 50 minutes, until lightly browned.

Per Serving: Calories 114, Total Fat 0.3g, Cholesterol 0mg, Sodium 44mg, Total Carbohydrate 25.3g, Dietary Fiber 3.5g, Protein 2.7g

Corn Soufflé

This easy soufflé is so creamy and rich-tasting, you won't believe it's so low in fat.

Makes 4 servings

¼ cup liquid egg substitute
1 1-pound can salt-free (or regular) cream-style corn
½ cup skim milk
3 tablespoons all-purpose flour
2 teaspoons sugar
1 teaspoon minced onion flakes
½ teaspoon dry mustard
2 egg whites (Egg substitute will not work here.)

Preheat oven to 350°. Spray a 2-quart soufflé dish or baking dish with nonstick cooking spray. In a medium bowl, combine all ingredients except egg whites. Beat with a fork or wire whisk until blended. In another bowl, beat egg whites with an electric mixer until stiff. Fold into corn mixture. Pour mixture into prepared baking dish. Bake, uncovered, 45 minutes, until puffed and lightly browned. Serve right away.

Per Serving: Calories 158, Total Fat 1.3g, Cholesterol 0mg, Sodium 72mg, Total Carbohydrate 29.5g, Dietary Fiber 1.7g, Protein 7.2g

Mexi-Corn

The sprinkle of fresh cilantro at the end is optional, but I do hope you'll try it that way. Its unusual flavor really enhances the flavors of Mexican food.

Makes 4 servings

2 teaspoons canola oil
¼ cup finely chopped green bell pepper
¼ cup finely chopped red bell pepper
¼ cup finely chopped onion
¼ cup water
1 1-pound can salt-free (or regular) corn, drained
Pepper to taste
1 tablespoon chopped fresh cilantro (optional)

Heat oil in a small saucepan over medium heat. Add peppers and onion. Cook, stirring frequently, until vegetables are tender, about 8 minutes. Add small amounts of water if necessary (about a tablespoon at a time) to prevent sticking. Add water and corn. Heat through and add pepper to taste. Sprinkle with cilantro, if desired.

Per Serving: Calories 113, Total Fat 2.8g, Cholesterol 0mg, Sodium 13mg, Total Carbohydrate 19.6g, Dietary Fiber 2.5g, Protein 2.5g

Notes:

Breads and Muffins

Breads and muffins can be an excellent source of fiber in our diet. Versatile and delicious, they can be served with any meal and also make great snacks. While many bakeries sell breads and muffins, most commercial varieties are high in fat and low in fiber. Often made with white flour, butter, and whole eggs, they are often laden with fat and calories.

Most of the breads and muffins in this section are made with a combination of all-purpose flour and whole wheat flour. This, along with the addition of fruits and vegetables, adds vitamins, minerals, and fiber as well as a delectable texture to the recipes.

To keep the fat down, I use skim milk and low-fat buttermilk in my breads and muffins. To reduce the amount of cholesterol, I use egg whites or liquid egg substitute in place of whole eggs. I also use as little oil as possible and, instead, add moistness by using applesauce, yogurt, or fruits in place of most of the shortening. When I do use oil, I choose one that is mostly monounsaturated, such as canola oil.

All of my breads are quick breads. My muffins are baked in standard muffin pans with 2½-inch cups. I prefer nonstick pans for breads and muffins and spray them lightly with nonstick cooking spray. Remember that oven temperatures may vary slightly, so it is wise to test breads and muffins for doneness by inserting a toothpick in the center. It will come out clean when the breads or muffins are done.

Most breads and muffins taste best when served warm. If this is not possible, let them cool completely before wrapping. Because these homemade delicacies are not made with preservatives, they have a shorter shelf life than many commercially baked goods. Therefore, I advise refrigerating them on the second day and reheating them briefly before serving.

From Beer Bread to Banana Date-Nut Muffins, from sweet to savory, my wonderful variety of breads and muffins are all made "light" for you.

Pumpkin Raisin Bread

This special bread has a mild, spiced flavor and just a hint of orange. It's perfect for holiday gift-giving.

Makes 8 servings

¾ cup whole-wheat flour
¾ cup all-purpose flour
1½ teaspoons baking powder
½ teaspoon baking soda
1 teaspoon pumpkin pie spice
¼ cup plus 2 tablespoons raisins
2 egg whites
1 cup canned pumpkin
⅓ cup sugar
¼ cup plus 2 tablespoons skim milk
2 tablespoons canola oil
1 teaspoon vanilla extract
½ teaspoon orange extract

Preheat oven to 350°. Spray a 4 x 8-inch loaf pan with nonstick cooking spray. In a large bowl, combine both types of flour, baking powder, baking soda, and pumpkin pie spice. Mix well. Stir in raisins. In another bowl, combine remaining ingredients. Beat with a fork or wire whisk until blended. Add to dry mixture, mixing until all ingredients are moistened. Spoon batter into prepared pan. Bake 40 to 50 minutes, until a toothpick inserted in the center of the bread comes out clean. Cool in pan on a wire rack 5 minutes, then turn out onto rack to finish cooling.

Per Serving: Calories 193, Total Fat 3.8g, Cholesterol 0mg, Sodium 191mg, Total Carbohydrate 35.1g, Fiber 2.8g, Protein 4.4g

Irish Soda Bread

This bumpy, crusty bread is traditionally made in a round shape and sliced into thin wedges to serve. Its nice texture and mild caraway flavor make it a perfect accompaniment to any meal.

Makes 16 servings

3 cups all-purpose flour
2 tablespoons sugar
1 tablespoon caraway seeds
1 teaspoon baking soda
1 teaspoon baking powder
1 teaspoon salt
½ cup raisins
1¼ cups plus 2 tablespoons skim milk
1 tablespoon vinegar
2 tablespoons plus 2 teaspoons canola oil

Preheat oven to 375°. Spray an 8-inch cake pan with nonstick cooking spray. In a large bowl, combine flour, sugar, caraway seeds, baking soda, baking powder, and salt. Mix well. Stir in raisins. In a small bowl, combine milk and vinegar. Let stand 3 to 5 minutes. Stir in oil. Add to flour mixture, mixing until all ingredients are moistened. Place dough in prepared pan and, with lightly floured hands, spread dough in pan. Bake 30 minutes, until golden brown. Transfer the bread to a wire rack, cover with a clean dish towel, and let cool.

Per Serving: Calories 136, Total Fat 2.6g, Cholesterol 0mg, Sodium 267mg, Total Carbohydrate 24.9g, Fiber 0.9g, Protein 3.4g

Orange-Raisin Tea Loaf

The chopped orange and raisins give this bread a delicate flavor and moistness you'll love. Be sure to discard the white membrane of the orange, since it is quite bitter.

Makes 10 servings

- ½ cup boiling water
- ½ cup raisins
- 1 small orange
- ¼ cup plus 2 tablespoons sugar
- 2 egg whites
- 1 tablespoon plus 2 teaspoons canola oil
- 1 teaspoon vanilla extract
- 1 cup minus 2 tablespoons all-purpose flour
- 1 cup whole wheat flour
- 1 teaspoon baking powder
- 1 teaspoon baking soda
- 1 teaspoon ground cinnamon
- ½ teaspoon ground nutmeg
- ½ teaspoon ground ginger

Preheat oven to 350°. Spray a 4 x 8-inch loaf pan with nonstick cooking spray. Pour boiling water over raisins in a small bowl. Set aside. Grate the orange, saving the peel. Peel orange, discarding the white membrane. Cut up the orange pulp. Place the orange pulp, raisins, and water in a blender. Blend for a few seconds, until raisins are just chopped. Do not puree.

In a large bowl, combine raisin mixture, orange peel, sugar, egg whites, oil, and vanilla. Mix well. In another bowl, combine remaining ingredients. Mix well. Add to orange mixture, mixing until all ingredients are moistened. Spoon batter into prepared pan. Bake 40 to 45 minutes, until a toothpick inserted in the center of the bread comes out clean. Cool in pan on a wire rack for 5 minutes, then turn out onto rack to finish cooling.

Per Serving: Calories 165, Total Fat 2.6g, Cholesterol 0mg, Sodium 186mg, Total Carbohydrate 32.1g, Fiber 2.2g, Protein 3.5g

Skillet Cheese Corn Bread

You can bake and serve this delicious corn bread right in the skillet. For a Mexican flavor, add some chopped chilies, either fresh, dried, or canned, to the wet ingredients.

Makes 12 servings

2 cups yellow cornmeal (12 ounces)
2 teaspoons baking powder
½ teaspoon baking soda
¼ teaspoon salt
1¼ cups buttermilk
1 1-pound can salt-free (or regular) cream-style corn
3 egg whites
¼ cup honey
2 tablespoons canola oil
1 cup shredded reduced-fat Cheddar cheese (4 ounces)

Preheat oven to 400°. Spray a 10-inch cast-iron skillet with nonstick cooking spray. In a large bowl, combine cornmeal, baking powder, baking soda, and salt. Mix well. In another bowl, combine buttermilk, corn, egg whites, honey, and oil. Beat with a fork or wire whisk until blended. Stir in cheese. Add to dry mixture, stirring until all ingredients are moistened.

Heat skillet in oven for 3 minutes. Remove from oven and immediately pour in batter. Bake 30 to 35 minutes, until a toothpick inserted in the center of the bread comes out clean. Cut into wedges and serve hot.

Per Serving: Calories 181, Total Fat 4.1g, Cholesterol 3mg, Sodium 287mg, Total Carbohydrate 30g Fiber 2g, Protein 6.3g

Beer Bread

This bread is so quick and easy, you'll make it time and again. It tastes wonderful and the texture is divine! What more could you ask for?

Makes 12 servings

1¼ cups all-purpose flour
1 cup whole wheat flour
2 tablespoons sugar
2¼ teaspoons baking powder
½ teaspoon salt
1 12-ounce can light beer, at room temperature

Preheat oven to 375°. Spray a 4 x 8-inch loaf pan with nonstick cooking spray. In a large bowl, combine both types of flour, sugar, baking powder, and salt. Mix well. Add beer. Stir until foam subsides and all ingredients are moistened. Pour batter into prepared pan.

Bake 45 to 50 minutes, until a toothpick inserted in the center of the bread comes out clean. Cool in pan on a wire rack for 5 minutes, then turn out onto rack to finish cooling. For a delicious variation that tastes like rye bread, add ⅛ teaspoon garlic powder and 1 teaspoon caraway seeds to the dry ingredients.

Per Serving: Calories 94, Total Fat 0.3g, Cholesterol 0mg, Sodium 189mg, Total Carbohydrate 19.9g, Fiber 1.6g, Protein 2.8g

Scones

A popular English treat, these pie-shaped rolls taste great with strawberry jam. Served warm with a cup of tea, they're such a friendly treat.

Makes 8 scones

¾ cup all-purpose flour
¾ cup whole wheat flour
1½ teaspoons baking powder
¼ teaspoon salt
1 tablespoon sugar
2 tablespoons plus 2 teaspoons margarine
¼ cup raisins
½ cup skim milk
2 teaspoons vinegar
2 egg whites
1 teaspoon grated fresh lemon peel

Preheat oven to 400°. Spray a baking sheet with nonstick cooking spray. In a large bowl, combine both types of flour, baking powder, salt, and sugar. Mix well. Add margarine. Mix with a fork or pastry blender until mixture resembles coarse crumbs. Stir in raisins. Place milk in a small bowl. Add vinegar and let stand 1 minute. Add egg whites and lemon peel. Beat with a fork or wire whisk until blended. Add to dry mixture, mixing until all ingredients are moistened.

Turn dough out onto prepared baking sheet. Flatten dough into an 8-inch circle, wetting your hands lightly to prevent sticking. With a sharp knife, score the dough, marking 8 pie-shaped wedges. Bake 15 minutes, until bottom of bread is lightly browned. Transfer to a wire rack and serve warm for best flavor.

Each Scone Provides: Calories 150, Total Fat 4g, Cholesterol 0mg, Sodium 230mg, Total Carbohydrate 23.8g, Fiber 1.8g, Protein 4.1g

Quick Onion Biscuits

Turn refrigerator biscuits into hot onion rolls with just 2 extra ingredients.

Makes 5 biscuits

2½ teaspoons margarine, melted
2½ teaspoons minced onion flakes
1 5-ounce package refrigerator biscuits

Preheat oven to 450°. Combine margarine and onion flakes in a small bowl or custard cup. Place biscuits on a nonstick baking sheet. With your finger, make a large dent in the center of each biscuit. Divide the margarine mixture evenly and fill the dents in the biscuits. Bake 8 to 10 minutes, until biscuits are golden. Remove from pan right away and serve hot.

Each Biscuit Provides: Calories 116, Total Fat 5.9g, Cholesterol 0mg, Sodium 324mg, Total Carbohydrate 13.7g, Fiber 0.1g, Protein 2.1g

Sweet Potato "Ruffins"

Unique and delicious, these bumpy, crusty rolls are a cross between a roll and a muffin. I enjoy them all year long, and they always make an appearance at my holiday tables.

Makes 12 muffins

1½ cups whole wheat flour
¾ cup all-purpose flour
2 teaspoons baking powder
1 teaspoon baking soda
3 tablespoons dried chives
1 teaspoon dried basil
½ teaspoon dried thyme
2 egg whites
1 teaspoon grated fresh lemon peel
1 cup plain nonfat yogurt
2 tablespoons canola oil
12 ounces finely shredded sweet potato, unpeeled (1½ cups packed)

Preheat oven to 400°. Spray 12 muffin cups with nonstick cooking spray. In a large bowl, combine both types of flour, baking powder, baking soda, and herbs. Mix well. In another bowl, combine remaining ingredients except sweet potato. Mix well. Stir in sweet potato. Add to dry mixture, mixing until all ingredients are moistened. Divide dough evenly into prepared muffin cups. Bake 15 to 18 minutes, until a toothpick inserted in the center of a muffin comes out clean. Remove muffins to a wire rack and serve warm for best flavor.

Each Muffin Provides:Calories 143, Total Fat 2.7g, Cholesterol 0mg, Sodium 227mg, Total Carbohydrate 24.7g, Fiber 3g, Protein 5g

Yogurt Biscuits

Try 'em while they're hot! Topped with jam or made into little sandwiches, you'll love the moist texture of these delectable biscuits.

Makes 6 biscuits

½ cup plus 2 tablespoons all-purpose flour
½ cup whole-wheat flour
1½ teaspoons baking powder
¼ teaspoon baking soda
1 teaspoon sugar
¼ teaspoon salt
2 tablespoons margarine
½ cup plain nonfat yogurt
½ teaspoon skim milk

Preheat oven to 425°. Have a nonstick baking sheet ready. In a large bowl, combine both types of flour, baking powder, baking soda, sugar, and salt. Add margarine. Using a fork or pastry blender, mix until mixture resembles coarse crumbs. Add yogurt, mixing until all ingredients are moistened. Add a little skim milk if necessary (about a tablespoon at a time) to form a soft dough.

Place dough on a lightly floured surface and knead gently to form a ball. Place dough on baking sheet and roll or pat into a rectangle, about ½-inch thick. With a sharp knife, cut the dough, forming 6 even biscuits, but do not separate them. With your finger, "paint" the top of the biscuits with the milk. Bake 10 to 12 minutes, until biscuits are golden. Remove to a wire rack and serve warm for best flavor.

Each Biscuit Provides: Calories 132, Total Fat 4.1g, Cholesterol 0mg, Sodium 332mg, Total Carbohydrate 19.8g, Fiber 1.6g, Protein 4g

Cheese Pinwheels

Biscuits rolled with cheese make pretty pinwheels that add a spark to any meal.

Makes 9 servings (2 pinwheels each serving)

1 recipe Yogurt Biscuits (see above)
3 ounces shredded reduced-fat Cheddar cheese (¾ cup)

Prepare dough for Yogurt Biscuits as directed. Preheat oven to 425°. Have a nonstick baking sheet ready. Place dough on a lightly floured surface and roll or pat into a rectangle about ¼-inch thick. Sprinkle evenly with cheese. Starting with 1 long side, roll dough tightly into a log. Cut into 18 even slices. Place slices on baking sheet. Bake 12 minutes, until lightly browned. Remove pinwheels to a wire rack and serve warm for best flavor.

Per Serving: Calories 104, Total Fat 3.4g, Cholesterol 2mg, Sodium 279mg, Total Carbohydrate 13.3g, Fiber 1g, Protein 4.9g

Jelly Muffins

These tender, egg-free muffins have a surprise burst of flavor in the center. I prefer the taste of raspberry or blackberry jam, but any flavor will work.

Makes 12 muffins

Topping:
2½ teaspoons sugar
¼ teaspoon ground cinnamon

Muffins:
1¼ cups all-purpose flour
1 cup whole wheat flour
1½ teaspoons baking powder
1 teaspoon baking soda
¾ teaspoon ground cinnamon
2 cups skim milk
⅓ cup honey
2 tablespoons canola oil
1½ teaspoons vanilla extract
½ teaspoon almond extract
¼ cup fruit-only raspberry or blackberry spread

Preheat oven to 400°. Spray 12 muffin cups with nonstick cooking spray. Combine topping ingredients in a small bowl and set aside. In a large bowl, combine both types of flour, baking powder, baking soda, and cinnamon. Mix well. In another bowl, combine milk, honey, oil, and extracts. Beat with a fork or wire whisk until blended. Add to dry mixture. Mix until all ingredients are moistened. (Batter will be loose.)

Divide mixture evenly into prepared muffin cups. Place a teaspoon of the jam on the top center of each muffin. Sprinkle evenly with topping. Bake 18 to 20 minutes, until a toothpick near the center of each muffin (not in the jam) comes out clean. Remove muffins to a rack and serve warm for best flavor.

Each Muffin Provides: Calories 166, Total Fat 2.7g, Cholesterol 1mg, Sodium 187mg, Total Carbohydrate 31.5g, Fiber 1.7g, Protein 4.1g

Cinnamon Yogurt Muffins

Mmm...a hot cup of tea and a warm, moist cinnamon-flavored muffin. What better way to enrich a friendship?

Makes 12 muffins

Topping:
2 teaspoons sugar
¼ teaspoon ground cinnamon
⅛ teaspoon ground nutmeg

Muffins:
1¼ cups whole wheat flour
1 cup all-purpose flour
1½ teaspoons baking powder
1½ teaspoons baking soda
2¼ teaspoons ground cinnamon
¼ teaspoon ground nutmeg
2 egg whites
1½ cups vanilla nonfat yogurt
¼ cup plus 2 tablespoons sugar
2 tablespoons canola oil
2 teaspoons vanilla extract

Preheat oven to 400°. Spray 12 muffin cups with nonstick cooking spray. In a small bowl or custard cup, combine topping ingredients. Set aside. In a large bowl, combine both types of flour, baking powder, baking soda, cinnamon, and nutmeg. Mix well. In another bowl, combine remaining ingredients. Beat with a fork or wire whisk until blended. Add to dry mixture, mixing until all ingredients are moistened.

Divide mixture evenly into prepared muffin cups. Sprinkle evenly with topping. Bake 15 minutes, until a toothpick inserted in the center of a muffin comes out clean. Remove muffins to a wire rack and serve warm for best flavor.

Each Muffin Provides: Calories 156, Total Fat 2.6g, Cholesterol 1mg, Sodium 244mg, Total Carbohydrate 28.7g, Fiber 2g, Protein 4.5g

Maple Bran Muffins

Serving these muffins warm, right out of the oven, really accentuates the sweet, maple flavor. You won't believe that a muffin so low in fat and high in fiber can taste so good.

Makes 12 muffins

¾ cup all-purpose flour
¾ cup whole-wheat flour
1½ cups bran (3 ounces) (This is wheat bran, not bran cereal, and it's found in the cereal section of most large grocery stores.)
2 teaspoons baking powder
1 teaspoon baking soda
½ teaspoon ground cinnamon
½ cup raisins
1½ cups skim milk
¼ cup plus 2 tablespoons maple syrup
2 tablespoons canola oil
2 tablespoons firmly packed brown sugar
2 egg whites
1¼ teaspoons maple extract
1 teaspoon vanilla extract

Preheat oven to 400°. Spray 12 muffin cups with nonstick cooking spray. In a large bowl, combine both types of flour, bran, baking powder, baking soda, and cinnamon. Mix well. Stir in raisins. In another bowl, combine remaining ingredients. Beat with a fork or wire whisk until blended. Add to dry mixture, mixing until all ingredients are moistened.

Divide mixture evenly into prepared muffin cups. Bake 15 minutes, until a toothpick inserted in the center of a muffin comes out clean. Remove muffins to a wire rack and serve warm for best flavor.

Each Muffin Provides: Calories 172, Total Fat 2.9g, Cholesterol 0mg, Sodium 212mg, Total Carbohydrate 32.1g, Fiber 4.5g, Protein 4.6g

Pumpkin Apple Muffins

Moist, tender, and filled with fruit and spices, these muffins will grace your holiday table or please your family all year long.

Makes 12 muffins

1¼ cups all-purpose flour
1 cup whole wheat flour
2 teaspoons baking powder
½ teaspoon baking soda
1 teaspoon ground cinnamon
½ teaspoon ground nutmeg
¼ teaspoon ground cloves
¼ teaspoon ground ginger
¼ cup plus 2 tablespoons raisins
2 egg whites
2 tablespoons canola oil
½ cup sugar
½ cup orange juice
1 teaspoon vanilla extract
1 cup canned pumpkin
2 small apples, unpeeled, coarsely shredded (1 cup)

Preheat oven to 400°. Spray 12 muffin cups with nonstick cooking spray. In a large bowl, combine both types of flour, baking powder, baking soda, and spices. Mix well. Stir in raisins. In another bowl, combine egg whites, oil, sugar, orange juice, and vanilla. Beat with a fork or wire whisk until blended. Add pumpkin and apples and whisk until blended. Add to dry mixture, mixing until all ingredients are moistened.

Divide mixture evenly into prepared muffin cups. Bake 15 to 18 minutes, until a toothpick inserted in the center of a muffin comes out clean. Remove muffins to a wire rack and serve warm for best flavor.

Each Muffin Provides: Calories 176, Total Fat 2.7g, Cholesterol 0mg, Sodium 142mg, Total Carbohydrate 34.3g, Fiber 2.7g, Protein 3.6g

Banana Date-Nut Muffins

The sweetness of the bananas, teamed up with chewy dates and crunchy nuts, makes a special combination. For the sweetest muffins, make sure the bananas are super-ripe.

Makes 12 muffins

1¼ cups whole wheat flour
1 cup all-purpose flour
1½ teaspoons baking powder
1 teaspoon baking soda
4 dates, chopped (1½ ounces)
2 tablespoons chopped walnuts (½ ounce)
2 egg whites
¾ cup skim milk
⅓ cup firmly packed brown sugar
2 tablespoons canola oil
2 teaspoons vanilla extract
2 medium, very ripe bananas, mashed (1 cup)

Preheat oven to 400°. Spray 12 muffin cups with nonstick cooking spray. In a large bowl, combine both types of flour, baking powder, and baking soda. Mix well. Stir in dates and nuts. In another bowl, combine egg whites, milk, brown sugar, oil, and vanilla. Beat with a fork or wire whisk until blended. Whisk in bananas. Add to dry mixture, mixing until all ingredients are moistened.

Divide mixture evenly into prepared muffin cups. Bake 15 to 18 minutes, until a toothpick inserted in the center of a muffin comes out clean. Remove muffins to a wire rack and serve warm for best flavor.

Each Muffin Provides: Calories 173, Total Fat 3.5g, Cholesterol 0mg, Sodium 185mg, Total Carbohydrate 31.2g, Fiber 2.7g, Protein 4.3g

Zucchini Muffins

Everyone's favorite made light, these delicious muffins are an ideal way to take advantage of the abundant garden zucchini. The muffins freeze well, so you can make lots.

Makes 12 muffins

1¼ cups all-purpose flour
1 cup whole wheat flour
1½ teaspoons baking powder
1 teaspoon baking soda
1½ teaspoons ground cinnamon
¾ teaspoon ground nutmeg
¼ cup plus 2 tablespoons raisins
2 egg whites
½ cup skim milk
½ cup sugar
2 tablespoons canola oil
1 teaspoon vanilla extract
½ teaspoon lemon extract
1½ cups zucchini (packed), unpeeled, finely shredded

Preheat oven to 400°. Spray 12 muffin cups with nonstick cooking spray. In a large bowl, combine both types of flour, baking powder, baking soda, and spices. Mix well. Stir in raisins. In another bowl, combine all ingredients except zucchini. Beat with a fork or wire whisk until blended. Stir in zucchini. Add to dry mixture, mixing until all ingredients are moistened.

Divide mixture evenly into prepared muffin cups. Bake 15 to 18 minutes, until a toothpick inserted in the center of a muffin comes out clean. Remove muffins to a wire rack and serve warm for best flavor.

Each Muffin Provides: Calories 162, Total Fat 2.7g, Cholesterol 0mg, Sodium 179mg, Total Carbohydrate 31g, Fiber 2.1g, Protein 3.8g

Cheddar 'n' Onion Muffins

A perfect accompaniment to a bowl of thick soup or stew, these muffins are best when served hot, right out of the oven.

Makes 12 muffins

1½ cups all-purpose flour
¾ cup whole wheat flour
1½ teaspoons baking powder
1½ teaspoons baking soda
1 tablespoon plus 1 teaspoon dried chives
2 teaspoons onion powder
⅛ teaspoon salt
2 egg whites
2 tablespoons canola oil
2 tablespoons grated onion
1½ cups plain nonfat yogurt
4 ounces shredded reduced-fat Cheddar cheese (1 cup)

Preheat oven to 400°. Spray 12 muffin cups with nonstick cooking spray. In a large bowl, combine both types of flour, baking powder, baking soda, chives, onion powder, and salt. Mix well. In another bowl, combine all ingredients except Cheddar cheese. Beat with a fork or wire whisk until blended. Stir in cheese. Add to dry mixture, mixing until all ingredients are moistened.

Divide mixture evenly into prepared muffin cups. Bake 15 to 18 minutes, until tops of muffins are light brown and a toothpick inserted in the center of a muffin comes out clean. Remove muffins to a wire rack and serve right away for best flavor.

Each Muffin Provides: Calories 139, Total Fat 3.4g, Cholesterol 2mg, Sodium 332mg, Total Carbohydrate 20.6g, Fiber 1.3g, Protein 7.2g

Savory Herbed Muffins

The mellow herbs create an aroma and flavor that spells h-o-m-e. A basket of these golden muffins, with their bumpy, crusty appearance, will definitely grace any table.

Makes 12 muffins

1½ cups all-purpose flour
¾ cup whole wheat flour
1½ teaspoons baking soda
1 teaspoon baking powder
2 packets low-sodium instant chicken- or vegetable-flavored broth mix
2 tablespoons minced onion flakes
¼ teaspoon dill weed
2 tablespoons canola oil
2 egg whites
1 tablespoon plus 1 teaspoon honey
1½ cups plain nonfat yogurt

Preheat oven to 400°. Spray 12 muffin cups with nonstick cooking spray. In a large bowl, combine both types of flour, baking soda, baking powder, broth mix, onion flakes, and dill. Mix well. In another bowl, combine remaining ingredients. Beat with a fork or wire whisk until blended. Add to dry mixture, mixing until all ingredients are moistened.

Divide mixture into prepared muffin cups. Bake 15 to 18 minutes, until tops of muffins are golden and a toothpick inserted in the center of a muffin comes out clean. Remove to a wire rack and serve warm for best flavor.

Each Muffin Provides: Calories 135, Total Fat 2.7g, Cholesterol 0mg, Sodium 233mg, Total Carbohydrate 23.2g, Fiber 1.5g, Protein 5.1g

Notes:

Fruits

Fruits are sweet, natural gifts from Mother Nature. Their versatility is endless, whether used as appetizers, entrées, desserts, or as in-between-meals snacks. Most fruits are low in fat and high in carbohydrates, supplying our bodies with necessary vitamins, minerals, and fiber.

In preparing fruit recipes, always choose varieties of fruits that are naturally sweet. The sweeter the fruit, the less sugar you will need to use. Also, for added nutrition, leave the skin on whenever possible.

So, enjoy exploring the many culinary possibilities I've created here for you, and browse through my other sections, too, to find fruits uniquely combined with unusual ingredients and as an added bonus in many of my cakes and pies.

Company Fruit Compote

One of my quick and easy favorites, I adapted this recipe from one that I used to make with lots of butter. The delightful combination of extracts helps to create a unique and delicious flavor.

Makes 4 servings

½ cup canned, sliced peaches (packed in juice), drained (Reserve 2 tablespoons of the juice.)
12 large frozen dark, sweet cherries (unsweetened)
½ cup canned, sliced pears (packed in juice), drained (Reserve 2 tablespoons of the juice.)
½ cup canned pineapple chunks (packed in juice), drained (Reserve 2 tablespoons of the juice.)
2 tablespoons firmly packed brown sugar
¼ teaspoon ground cinnamon
½ teaspoon vanilla extract
¼ teaspoon maple extract
¼ teaspoon lemon extract
1 tablespoon plus 1 teaspoon cornstarch

Preheat oven to 350°. Spray a 1-quart casserole with nonstick cooking spray. Combine fruits in a large bowl. Sprinkle with brown sugar and cinnamon. Mix well. Place in prepared casserole. In a small bowl, combine reserved fruit juices, extracts, and cornstarch. Stir to dissolve cornstarch. Pour mixture over fruit. Bake, uncovered, 15 to 20 minutes, until hot and bubbly. Serve warm for best flavor.

Per Serving: Calories 99, Total Fat 0.1g, Cholesterol 0mg, Sodium 5mg, Total Carbohydrate 24g, Dietary Fiber 1.5g, Protein 0.6g

Fruit Salad in a Watermelon Basket

Always a crowd pleaser, this elegant dish is really easy to prepare. My fruits are just a suggestion. Feel free to fill the watermelon with whatever fresh fruits are available. My amounts are also a suggestion, and they will vary according to the size of the watermelon.

Makes 16 servings

1 medium watermelon
2 cups watermelon balls
1 cup cantaloupe balls
1 cup honeydew melon balls
1 cup strawberries, halved
1 cup blueberries
2 medium peaches, peeled, pitted, cut into chunks
24 large seedless red grapes
¼ medium, ripe pineapple, pared, cut into chunks
3 tablespoons orange juice
1 tablespoon lime juice (preferably fresh)
2 tablespoons confectioners' sugar
½ teaspoon rum extract

To prepare basket, cut the watermelon in half lengthwise. Using a melon ball scoop, remove the pulp. Measure 2 cups of watermelon balls, reserving remaining watermelon balls for another use. Using a sharp knife, scallop the edges of the watermelon. Slice a very thin piece off the bottom of the melon to keep it from tipping over. Chill prepared watermelon basket. Also chill watermelon balls and remaining fruits, keeping them all separate. Just before serving, combine all fruits in a large bowl. Combine orange juice, lime juice, sugar, and rum extract. Pour over fruit and mix well. Spoon fruit into watermelon basket.

Per Serving: Calories 49, Total Fat 0.2g, Cholesterol 0mg, Sodium 3mg, Total Carbohydrate 11.1g, Dietary Fiber 1.2g, Protein 0.7g

Tropical Fruits with Apricot-Rum Sauce

These fruits are only a suggestion. The unique sauce can be served over any combination of fruits. It's great with peaches, melons, apricots, berries, etc. It's also good over low-fat vanilla ice cream and makes a delicious shortcake with angel food cake and any ripe, fresh fruit.

Makes 6 servings

Apricot-Rum Sauce:
1 cup apricot nectar
1 tablespoon cornstarch
2 teaspoons honey
1 teaspoon lime juice (or lemon juice)
½ teaspoon rum extract
1/16 teaspoon ground allspice

Fruits:
1 small mango, cut into chunks (A medium papaya can be substituted, if desired.)
1 medium, ripe banana, sliced
¼ medium, ripe pineapple, pared and cut into chunks

Combine all sauce ingredients in a small saucepan. Mix well to dissolve cornstarch. Cook over medium heat, stirring constantly, until mixture comes to a boil. Continue to cook, stirring, 1 to 2 minutes. Spoon into a bowl and chill thoroughly. At serving time: Combine fruit and divide evenly into 6 individual serving bowls. Stir chilled sauce, divide evenly, and spoon over fruit.

Per Serving: Calories 113, Total Fat 0.4g, Cholesterol 0mg, Sodium 3mg, Total Carbohydrate 26.5g, Dietary Fiber 2.1g, Protein 0.8g

Fruit Yogurt

Making your own fruit yogurt means lots more fruit and lots less sugar than most commercial varieties. Choose fruits that are packed in juice, and the possibilities are endless.

Makes 1 serving

¾ cup plain nonfat Greek yogurt
2 teaspoons sugar
½ teaspoon vanilla extract
⅛ teaspoon any other extract, such as orange, lemon, coconut, rum, or almond
¼ cup canned sliced pears, *or* sliced peaches, *or* crushed pineapple, *or* blueberries

In a small bowl, combine yogurt, sugar, and extracts. Stir in fruit. Enjoy!

Per Serving: Calories 169, Total Fat 0.3g, Cholesterol 3mg, Sodium 143mg, Total Carbohydrate 30.7g, Dietary Fiber 1g, Protein 10.7g

Quick Peach Melba

Now you can enjoy a slimmed-down version of this classic dessert in no time.

Makes 2 servings

¼ cup part-skim ricotta cheese
2 tablespoons nonfat vanilla yogurt
2 teaspoons sugar
1 teaspoon vanilla extract
⅛ teaspoon almond extract
1 medium, very ripe peach, peeled, cut in half, center pit removed *or* 2 canned peach halves (packed in juice), drained
4 teaspoons fruit-only raspberry spread

In a small bowl, combine the ricotta cheese, yogurt, sugar, and extracts. Mix well. Place a peach half, cut-side up, in each of two small serving bowls. Fill peaches with cheese mixture. Top with raspberry spread. Serve right away. (If you want to save for a later serving, refrigerate the peaches and cheese mixture separately and assemble just before serving.)

Per Serving: Calories 121, Total Fat 2.4g, Cholesterol 10mg, Sodium 46mg, Total Carbohydrate 20.3g, Dietary Fiber 1g, Protein 4.4g

Red, White, and Blueberry Parfaits

This colorful, patriotic dessert is perfect for that Fourth of July picnic. Fresh summer berries are always delicious.

Makes 4 servings

1 cup strawberries, sliced
½ cup blueberries
2 tablespoons sugar
½ cup part-skim ricotta cheese
½ cup vanilla nonfat yogurt
½ teaspoon vanilla extract
⅛ teaspoon almond extract
⅛ teaspoon orange extract

Place strawberries and blueberries each in a separate small bowl. Toss each with 1 teaspoon of the sugar. In another bowl, combine ricotta cheese with remaining sugar, yogurt, and extracts. Mix well. In each of 4 parfait glasses, place 2 tablespoons of the strawberries. Top each with 2 tablespoons of the ricotta mixture. Divide blueberries evenly over the parfaits. Divide remaining ricotta mixture over blueberries. Top with remaining strawberries. Serve right away or chill for up to several hours before serving.

Per Serving: Calories 113, Total Fat 2.6g, Cholesterol 11mg, Sodium 56mg, Total Carbohydrate 17.2g, Dietary Fiber 1.4g, Protein 5g

Pears Belle Helene

This is just a fancy way of saying "Chocolate-Topped Pears and Cheese." However you say it, it's quick, easy, and delicious.

Makes 4 servings

Pears:
1 cup part-skim ricotta cheese
1 tablespoon plus 1 teaspoon sugar
1½ teaspoons vanilla extract
4 canned pear halves (packed in juice), drained

Chocolate Topping:
1 tablespoon plus 1 teaspoon sugar
1 tablespoon cocoa (unsweetened)
2 teaspoons cornstarch
½ cup evaporated skim milk
½ teaspoon vanilla extract

In a small bowl, combine ricotta cheese, sugar, and vanilla. Mix well. Place a pear half, cut-side up, in each of 4 small serving bowls. Fill pears with cheese mixture.

Prepare topping: In a small saucepan, combine sugar, cocoa, and cornstarch. Slowly stir in evaporated milk, mixing well. Cook over medium-low heat, stirring constantly, until sauce thickens. Remove from heat and stir in vanilla. Spoon over pears. Serve right away. (If you wish, you can make the cheese filling ahead and refrigerate until you are ready to assemble the dessert.)

Per Serving: Calories 177, Total Fat 5.2g, Cholesterol 20mg, Sodium 116mg, Total Carbohydrate 22.5g, Dietary Fiber 1.4g, Protein 9.9g

Baked Pears

Bartlett pears work well for this crispy, spiced version of a fall fruit favorite. They can he served warm or cold and are delicious topped with a dollop of vanilla nonfat yogurt.

Makes 4 servings

2 large pears, peeled, cored, cut in half lengthwise
½ cup water
2 teaspoons lemon juice
2 teaspoons honey
3 tablespoons graham cracker crumbs
¼ teaspoon ground cinnamon
2 teaspoons reduced-calorie margarine

Preheat oven to 350°. Place the pears, cut-side down, in an 8-inch square baking pan. Pour water around pears. Drizzle pears with lemon juice and honey. Cover and bake 45 minutes, or until pears are tender. Uncover. Combine graham cracker crumbs and cinnamon. Sprinkle evenly over the pears. Dot with margarine. Return to the oven and bake, uncovered, 10 minutes more.

Per Serving: Calories 93, Total Fat 1.4g, Cholesterol 0mg, Sodium 39mg, Total Carbohydrate 19.1g, Dietary Fiber 2.2g, Protein 0.6g

Brandy and Nut-Filled Pears

Serve this elegant dish warm or at room temperature and, to make it extra special, top it with vanilla nonfat yogurt.

Makes 4 servings

Pears:

2 tablespoons firmly packed brown sugar
¼ cup water
1 teaspoon lemon juice
2 large pears, peeled, cut in half lengthwise

Filling:

2 tablespoons finely chopped walnuts (½ ounce)
1 tablespoon firmly packed brown sugar
1 tablespoon plain nonfat yogurt
¼ teaspoon vanilla extract
½ teaspoon brandy extract

Preheat oven to 350°. Combine brown sugar, water, and lemon juice in an 8-inch-square baking pan. Mix until brown sugar is dissolved. Cut a thin slice off the bottom of each pear half so it will not roll around when served. Scoop out the seeds, making a small "cup" in each pear half. Place the pears, scooped-side down, in the baking pan. Baste with the liquid. Cover tightly and bake 45 minutes, or until pears are tender. (Length of cooking time will vary according to the variety and ripeness of the pears.)

When pears are tender, place them, scooped-side up, in either 1 serving bowl or in 4 individual serving bowls. Spoon liquid from pan over pears. Let cool 10 minutes. Combine filling ingredients in a small bowl or custard cup. Mix well. Spoon into pear cavities. Serve right away or let cool to lukewarm to serve. Refrigerate leftovers and serve cold or reheat in a microwave.

Per Serving: Calories 125, Total Fat 2.5g, Cholesterol 0mg, Sodium 6mg, Total Carbohydrate 24g, Dietary Fiber 2.2g, Protein 1.4g

Apricot-Almond Cranberry Sauce

Why open a can of cranberry sauce when you can make your own so easily? And this one is really special. It's laced with the flavors of apricot and almond and is tart and delicious, as cranberries should be. (If you don't like it as tart, you can add a little extra sugar.)

Makes 9 servings (⅓ cup each serving)

1 cup sugar
1 cup water
3 cups cranberries
⅓ cup fruit-only apricot spread
½ teaspoon almond extract

Combine sugar and water in a small saucepan. Bring to a boil over medium heat. Continue to boil, without stirring, 5 minutes. Stir in cranberries and cook, stirring occasionally, until cranberries burst and mixture comes to a full boil. Continue to boil 5 minutes. Remove from heat and stir in apricot spread and almond extract. Cool slightly, then chill.

Per Serving: Calories 132, Total Fat 0.1g, Cholesterol 0mg, Sodium 0mg, Total Carbohydrate 32.7g, Dietary Fiber 1.5g, Protein 0.1g

Chewy Fruit Squares

Made with pure fruit juice, here's a treat you can encourage the kids to eat.

Makes 4 squares

3 envelopes unflavored gelatin
1 cup water
½ cup frozen orange juice concentrate, thawed

Sprinkle gelatin over water in a medium saucepan. Let soften a few minutes. Heat over low heat, stirring frequently, until gelatin is completely dissolved. Remove from heat. Stir in orange juice. Pour mixture into a 4 x 8-inch loaf pan. Chill several hours. Cut into squares to serve. As a variation, substitute grape juice concentrate for the orange juice.

Each Square Provides:Calories 79, Total Fat 0.1g, Cholesterol 0mg, Sodium 14mg, Total Carbohydrate 18.4g, Dietary Fiber 0.3g, Protein 1.2g

Baked Pineapple Tapioca

Serve this delicious dish warm or cold, topped with vanilla or lemon nonfat yogurt. It's soothing and delicious.

Makes 4 servings

2 cups canned crushed pineapple (packed in juice), drained (Reserve juice.)
¾ cup hot water
3 tablespoons sugar
2 tablespoons plus 2 teaspoons quick-cooking tapioca
¼ teaspoon lemon extract
Dash ground cinnamon

Preheat oven to 325°. Spray a 1-quart casserole with nonstick cooking spray. Add additional water to pineapple juice, if necessary, to equal ½ cup. Add to prepared casserole, along with remaining ingredients. Mix well. Let stand 10 minutes. Bake, uncovered, 40 minutes, or until tapioca granules are clear. Serve warm or cold.

Per Serving: Calories 154, Total Fat 0.1g, Cholesterol 0mg, Sodium 45mg, Total Carbohydrate 37.7g, Dietary Fiber 1g, Protein 0.5g

Sautéed Pineapple

This elegant dish makes a great appetizer as well as a luscious dessert.

Makes 4 servings

2 teaspoons margarine
½ of a medium, ripe pineapple, sliced crosswise into 1-inch slices, skin removed
1 tablespoon plus 1 teaspoon sugar (You may need more or less, depending on the ripeness of the pineapple.)
½ teaspoon ground cinnamon

Melt margarine in a large nonstick skillet over medium-high heat. Add pineapple. Cook, turning pineapple frequently, until lightly browned on both sides. Combine sugar and cinnamon, mixing well. Place pineapple on serving plate and sprinkle with sugar mixture. Serve hot.

Per Serving: Calories 96, Total Fat 2.4g, Cholesterol 0mg, Sodium 23mg, Total Carbohydrate 18.4g, Dietary Fiber 1.6g, Protein 0.4g

Baked Pineapple with Creamy Coconut Sauce

Baking really brings out the flavor of fresh pineapple. Served warm, this easy, refreshing dish makes a great appetizer or dessert.

Makes 8 servings

Coconut Sauce:
1⅓ cups low-fat (1%) cottage cheese
¼ cup firmly packed brown sugar
3 tablespoons skim milk
1½ teaspoons vanilla extract
¾ teaspoon coconut extract

Pineapple:
1 medium ripe pineapple
4 teaspoons firmly packed brown sugar
Ground cinnamon

To prepare sauce: In a blender, combine all sauce ingredients. Blend until smooth. Spoon into a bowl and chill several hours, or overnight.

To prepare pineapple: Preheat oven to 375°. Remove and discard top of pineapple. Cut pineapple lengthwise into quarters. Remove and discard center core. Cut each quarter into chunks, but leave the chunks resting in place in the shells. Sprinkle brown sugar along the top ledge of each quarter. (It will run down during cooking.) Sprinkle liberally with cinnamon. Wrap each quarter tightly in aluminum foil. Bake 1 hour. Carefully unwrap pineapple, and sprinkle with additional cinnamon. Serve hot and top each serving with 3 tablespoons of the sauce.

Per Serving: Calories 126, Total Fat 0.9g, Cholesterol 2mg, Sodium 161mg, Total Carbohydrate 24.4g, Dietary Fiber 1.4g, Protein 5.3g

Pineapple-Grapefruit Combo

Tart and tangy, yet so refreshing, this combination is a perfect marriage of flavors. Serve it as an appetizer, a dessert, or a delicious addition to breakfast.

Makes 4 servings

¼ medium ripe pineapple, cut into bit-sized pieces, skin removed *or* 1 cup canned pineapple tidbits (packed in juice), drained
1 medium grapefruit, peeled and sectioned, then cut into bit-sized pieces, white membrane discarded
½ cup vanilla nonfat yogurt
2 tablespoons confectioners' sugar
1 teaspoon vanilla extract

Combine all ingredients, mixing well. Serve right away.

Per Serving: Calories 97, Total Fat 0.1g, Cholesterol 1mg, Sodium 18mg, Total Carbohydrate 22.2g, Dietary Fiber 1.1g, Protein 1.9g

Broiled Grapefruit Delight

Indeed, this dish is a delight. Hot and bubbly, this makes a wonderful and welcome morning treat.

Makes 4 servings

2 medium, pink grapefruits, cut in half crosswise
2 teaspoons margarine, melted
1 teaspoon rum extract
1 tablespoon firmly packed brown sugar

Preheat broiler. Place grapefruit on a broiler pan, cut-side up. Combine margarine and rum extract and spread evenly over grapefruit. Sprinkle evenly with brown sugar. Broil 6 inches from heat about 5 minutes, until grapefruit is hot and bubbly and edges just begin to brown. Serve hot.

Per Serving: Calories 54, Total Fat 2g, Cholesterol 0mg, Sodium 23mg, Total Carbohydrate 8.6g, Dietary Fiber 0.7g, Protein 0.4g

Orange Fruit Cups

These bright and cheery fruit cups can easily be varied by filling them with different fruits. Let your imagination and taste buds guide you.

Makes 4 servings

2 small oranges, cut in half crosswise
½ cup blueberries, fresh or frozen (unsweetened)
½ cup canned crushed pineapple (packed in juice), drained
1 teaspoon confectioners' sugar

Carefully cut out orange pulp, using a small, sharp knife. Leave the shells intact. Remove and discard white membranes. (For a fancy touch, you can scallop the edges of the orange halves with a sharp knife.) In a small bowl, combine orange sections with blueberries and pineapple. Chill at least 1 hour. Cover orange shells and chill them separately. To serve, pile fruit mixture into orange shells. (If necessary, slice a very thin slice off the bottom of each orange half to keep it from tipping over.) Sprinkle with confectioners' sugar and serve right away.

Per Serving: Calories 68, Total Fat 0.2g, Cholesterol 0mg, Sodium 2mg, Total Carbohydrate 15.8g, Dietary Fiber 2.9g, Protein 0.8g

Bananas New Orleans

One of my most popular dishes, this one can easily be prepared for dessert while the coffee is brewing. It's delicious by itself, or it really makes a statement when served over vanilla low-fat ice cream.

Makes 4 servings

1 teaspoon margarine
½ cup orange juice
2 tablespoons firmly packed brown sugar
½ teaspoon rum extract
½ teaspoon vanilla butternut flavor*
2 medium, ripe bananas, cut in half lengthwise, then each piece cut in half crosswise (Choose bananas that are ripe, yet firm.)
Ground cinnamon

Melt margarine in a medium nonstick skillet over medium heat. Stir in orange juice, brown sugar, and extracts. Add bananas. Cook 2 to 3 minutes, then turn bananas carefully and cook another 1 to 2 minutes. Sprinkle with cinnamon. Place 2 banana pieces in each of 4 individual serving bowls. Spoon sauce over bananas. Serve right away.

**Often called "vanilla butter and nut flavor," it is found with the extracts in many large grocery stores. If you cannot locate this flavor, use ½ teaspoon vanilla extract plus ½ teaspoon butter-flavor extract in its place.*

Per Serving: Calories 108, Total Fat 1.3g, Cholesterol 0mg, Sodium 15mg, Total Carbohydrate 23.2g, Dietary Fiber 1.5g, Protein 0.8g

Baked Banana Crumble

Baked until crisp on the outside, bananas are still wonderfully moist and tender on the inside.

Makes 4 servings

2 medium, ripe bananas, sliced in half lengthwise
1 teaspoon lemon juice
3 tablespoons graham cracker crumbs
1 tablespoon plus 1 teaspoon firmly packed brown sugar
½ teaspoon ground cinnamon
2 teaspoons reduced-calorie margarine

Preheat oven to 400°. Spray a shallow baking pan with nonstick cooking spray. Place banana halves in the prepared pan. Using your finger, "paint" them with lemon juice. In a small bowl, combine graham cracker crumbs, brown sugar, and cinnamon. Sprinkle evenly over bananas. Dot with margarine. Bake 10 minutes, or until bananas are lightly browned. Serve right away.

Per Serving: Calories 100, Total Fat 1.4g, Cholesterol 0mg, Sodium 42mg, Total Carbohydrate 20.9g, Dietary Fiber 1.7g, Protein 0.9g

Banana Toast

This is an unbelievable eggless version of French toast that you're sure to love. Drizzled with maple syrup, it tastes absolutely decadent! (Be sure to use a nonstick skillet for this recipe, as it gets very sticky.)

Makes 2 servings

1 medium, very ripe banana
¼ cup skim milk
2 teaspoons sugar
½ teaspoon vanilla extract
2 slices whole wheat bread (1-ounce slices)
2 teaspoons reduced-calorie margarine
Ground cinnamon

In a blender, combine banana, milk, sugar, and vanilla. Blend until smooth. Place bread in a shallow pan. Pour banana mixture over bread. Turn bread several times, until it has absorbed most of the banana mixture. Melt *half* of the margarine in a large nonstick skillet over medium-low heat. Carefully place bread in skillet, using a spatula. Drizzle any remaining banana mixture over bread. Brown toast on both sides, then turn carefully, adding remaining margarine. Sprinkle with cinnamon and serve.

Per Serving: Calories 172, Total Fat 3.1g, Cholesterol 0mg, Sodium 196mg, Total Carbohydrate 32.3g, Dietary Fiber 3.5g, Protein 4.3g

Russian Prune Pudding

I modernized this old-fashioned dessert by using jarred baby food instead of cooking and mashing the prunes the way it is done in the more traditional version. This airy pudding is usually served warm and provides a light ending to any meal.

Makes 6 servings

3 tablespoons sugar
1/16 teaspoon ground cinnamon
2 egg whites
1 teaspoon vanilla extract
2 4-ounce jars baby food prunes

Preheat oven to 300°. Have a 1-quart baking dish ready. (Do not oil it.) In a small bowl or custard cup, combine sugar and cinnamon. Mix well. Place egg whites in a medium, deep bowl. Beat on high speed of an electric mixer until stiff. Beat in sugar and cinnamon mixture a few teaspoons at a time, beating well after each addition. Beat in vanilla. Gently, but thoroughly, fold prunes into egg whites. Spoon into pan, smoothing top of pudding with the back of a spoon. Bake 40 minutes. Serve warm for best flavor. (Refrigerate leftovers and serve cold.)

Per Serving: Calories 66, Total Fat 0g, Cholesterol 0mg, Sodium 22mg, Total Carbohydrate 15.5g, Dietary Fiber 1.1g, Protein 1.1g

Rhubarb and Pineapple

This irresistible mixture is delicious by itself or it can be served as a sauce and spooned over angel food cake or low-fat ice cream.

Makes 8 servings (⅓ cup each serving)

1 1-pound bag frozen rhubarb, thawed partially (or 3 cups of fresh rhubarb, chopped, discarding leaves)
1 8-ounce can crushed pineapple (packed in juice), drained (Reserve juice.)
½ cup firmly packed brown sugar
1 tablespoon granulated sugar
½ teaspoon lemon extract
2 tablespoons cornstarch

In a medium saucepan, combine the rhubarb, pineapple, both sugars, and lemon extract. Place cornstarch in a small bowl or custard cup. Add 3 tablespoons of the reserved pineapple juice and stir to dissolve cornstarch. Set aside. Add remaining pineapple juice to saucepan. Bring mixture to a boil over medium heat, stirring occasionally. Reduce heat to medium-low, cover, and simmer 10 minutes, until rhubarb begins to fall apart. Stir in cornstarch mixture. When mixture returns to a boil, cook, stirring constantly, 2 minutes, until mixture is thick and bubbly. Serve warm or cold.

Per Serving: Calories 99, Total Fat 0.1g, Cholesterol 0mg, Sodium 6mg, Total Carbohydrate 24.2g, Dietary Fiber 1.2g, Protein 0.4g

Sautéed Maple Peaches

Fresh or frozen peaches will work in this delicious hot dish. It makes a great dessert, either by itself or topped with vanilla nonfat yogurt, and it is also a delectable addition to your morning oatmeal.

Makes 4 servings

2 teaspoons margarine
½ cup orange juice
1 tablespoon plus 1 teaspoon firmly packed brown sugar
½ teaspoon maple extract
¼ teaspoon ground cinnamon
4 medium, ripe peaches, peeled, sliced ¼ -inch thick (If using frozen peaches, choose the unsweetened ones and thaw first)

Melt margarine in a large nonstick skillet over medium heat. Stir in orange juice, brown sugar, maple extract, and cinnamon. Add peaches. Cook, turning peaches frequently, until tender, about 5 minutes. Serve warm.

Per Serving: Calories 97, Total Fat 2.1g, Cholesterol 0mg, Sodium 24mg, Total Carbohydrate 18.5g, Dietary Fiber 2.2g, Protein 0.9g

Snowcapped Peaches

Peach halves, filled with raspberry jam and topped with meringue, make a truly elegant finale to any meal. And, best of all, they contain no fat at all.

Makes 4 servings

8 canned peach halves (packed in juice), drained
2 tablespoons plus 2 teaspoons fruit-only raspberry spread
2 egg whites
¼ teaspoon cream of tartar
2 tablespoons sugar

Preheat oven to 350°. Have a shallow nonstick baking pan ready. Drain peaches well on towels. Place, cut-side up, in prepared pan. If necessary, slice a very thin sliver off the bottom of each peach to keep them from rolling around. Spoon 1 teaspoon of jam into the center of each peach. In a small, deep bowl, beat egg whites on high speed with an electric mixer until soft peaks form. Add cream of tartar and beat until stiff. Beat in sugar. Spread the meringue evenly over the peaches, covering the fruit spread. Bake 10 to 15 minutes, or until meringue is golden. Serve right away.

Per Serving: Calories 99, Total Fat 0g, Cholesterol 0mg, Sodium 28mg, Total Carbohydrate 22.6g, Dietary Fiber 1.1g, Protein 2.1g

Sautéed Apples

Any variety of apples will work in this easy dish; however, the length of cooking time may vary. It tastes best when the apples are cooked until just tender, so be careful not to let them get mushy.

Makes 4 servings

2 teaspoons margarine
4 small, sweet apples, unpeeled, cored, and cut into rings ¼-inch thick
2 tablespoons firmly packed brown sugar
1 teaspoon vanilla extract
½ teaspoon ground cinnamon
¼ teaspoon ground nutmeg

Melt margarine in a large nonstick skillet over medium heat. Add apples. Cook, stirring and turning apples frequently, until tender, about 10 minutes. Add small amounts of water if necessary, to prevent sticking. Sprinkle apples with remaining ingredients. Toss to melt the sugar and coat the apples evenly. Serve warm.

Per Serving: Calories 119, Total Fat 2.4g, Cholesterol 0mg, Sodium 25mg, Total Carbohydrate 24.4g, Dietary Fiber 3.3g, Protein 0.2g

Baked Apple Alaska

Baked apples are taken one step further in this unusual presentation. Frosted with meringue, they look and taste luscious.

Makes 4 servings

4 small sweet apples, peeled, cored, and cut in half lengthwise (Macintosh, Rome, or Jonathan are good choices for this dish.)
2 tablespoons firmly packed brown sugar
¼ teaspoon ground cinnamon

Meringue:
2 egg whites
¼ teaspoon cream of tartar
2 tablespoons sugar

Preheat oven to 350°. Place apples, cut-side down, in a shallow baking pan. Sprinkle evenly with brown sugar and cinnamon. Pour water around apples to a depth of ½ inch. Cover and bake 30 minutes, or until apples are tender. (Length of cooking time will depend on variety and ripeness of apples.) Let apples cool. (Or you can chill them and complete the dessert at a later time.)

Just before serving: Preheat oven to 350°. In a small, deep bowl, beat egg whites on high speed with an electric mixer until soft peaks form. Add cream of tartar and beat until stiff. Beat in sugar. Place apples, cut-side down, on a nonstick cookie sheet. Frost with meringue. Bake 10 to 15 minutes, or until meringue is golden. Serve right away.

Per Serving: Calories 131, Total Fat 0.4g, Cholesterol 0mg, Sodium 28mg, Total Carbohydrate 30.1g, Dietary Fiber 2.3g, Protein 1.8g

Quick and Creamy Applesauce Dessert

Toast a slice of angel food cake or fat-free pound cake and top it with this delicious applesauce combo for a quick and easy dessert.

Makes 2 servings

1 cup applesauce (unsweetened)
¾ cup vanilla nonfat yogurt
1 tablespoon sugar
½ teaspoon vanilla extract
½ teaspoon apple pie spice *or* ¼ teaspoon *each* ground cinnamon and nutmeg and a pinch of ground cloves

Combine all ingredients in a small bowl. Mix thoroughly. Serve right away or chill for a later serving.

Per Serving: Calories 147, Total Fat 0.2g, Cholesterol 2mg, Sodium 52mg, Total Carbohydrate 32.5g, Dietary Fiber 1.8g, Protein 3.7g

Applesauce Raisin Supreme

Whipped topping folded into applesauce makes it creamy and smooth.

Makes 6 servings

2 cups applesauce (unsweetened)
¼ cup raisins
1 tablespoon confectioners' sugar
½ teaspoon grated fresh orange peel
½ teaspoon vanilla extract
1 cup reduced-fat frozen whipped topping, thawed
Ground cinnamon

In a medium bowl, combine applesauce, raisins, sugar, orange peel, and vanilla. Mix well. Fold in whipped topping. Spoon mixture into a shallow bowl. Chill at least 1 hour. Just before serving, fold mixture again gently and sprinkle with cinnamon.

Per Serving: Calories 107, Total Fat 3g, Cholesterol 0mg, Sodium 3mg, Total Carbohydrate 19.8g, Dietary Fiber 1.3g, Protein 0.3g

Desserts

You've heard it said before, but now you can truly have your cake and eat it, too. In this section, I've created a special grouping of luscious desserts in which the taste has been heightened, while the calories and fat have been lightened.

My secret? Substituting high-fat ingredients with their low-fat counterparts. Try this:

IN PLACE OF:	**USE:**
whole milk	skim milk
sour cream	nonfat yogurt or nonfat Greek yogurt
cream	evaporated skim milk
baking chocolate	cocoa
whole eggs	egg whites or egg substitute
sugar	*half* the amount called for
chopped nuts	*half* the amount called for
coconut	*a quarter* of the amount called for
cream cheese	fat-free cream cheese
cottage cheese	low-fat (1%) cottage cheese
ricotta cheese	part-skim or fat-free ricotta cheese
pie with double crust	pie with one crust
vegetable oil in cakes and muffins	replace at least half with applesauce or yogurt icing sprinkling of sugar and cinnamon

Add fiber to cakes by replacing half of the flour with whole wheat flour and using wheat germ as a topping for cakes and also as a substitute for ground nuts. Fruit also adds fiber in addition to adding flavor, moistness, and important vitamins. Now you can embrace lean and luscious.

And don't forget my favorite fat-free addition: extracts. Vanilla adds a sweet, rich flavor to desserts, tricking your taste buds into thinking foods are sweeter than they really are. Other extracts can also add delectable flavors without adding unnecessary calories and fat.

My dessert cart is overflowing with puddings, molds, frozen desserts, cakes, pies, cobblers, crisps, cookies, and candies. Yes, desserts can be both lean and luscious.

Enjoy! Enjoy! Enjoy!

Floating Islands

Picture a mound of lemon-flavored pudding floating on a bed of blueberries. Now indulge!

Makes 4 servings

1 cup water
1 envelope unflavored gelatin
1 cup lemon nonfat yogurt
2 tablespoons sugar
1 teaspoon vanilla extract
¼ teaspoon lemon extract
¼ teaspoon almond extract
2 tablespoons orange juice
2 cups frozen blueberries (unsweetened), thawed, undrained

Place water in a small saucepan. Sprinkle gelatin over water and let soften a few minutes. Heat, stirring frequently, over low heat, until gelatin is completely dissolved. Remove from heat. In a blender, combine yogurt, sugar, and extracts. Add gelatin mixture and blend until smooth. Pour mixture into 4 custard cups. Chill until firm. Add orange juice to blueberries and chill until serving time.

To serve, place ½ cup blueberries in each of 4 serving bowls. Unmold a pudding into the center of each. Spoon a few berries over the top of each pudding. Spoon any remaining liquid over the puddings. Note: To unmold, dip each cup in a bowl of hot water for 10 seconds, carefully run a knife around the edge, and invert.

Per Serving: Calories 122, Total Fat 0.5g, Cholesterol 0mg, Sodium 44mg, Total Carbohydrate 25.2g, Dietary Fiber 2.1g, Protein 4.2g

Piña Colada Fluff

This fluffy dessert contains all of the flavors of the tropics. It works best if the pineapple is cold, so place it in the refrigerator at least an hour before making the pudding.

Makes 4 servings

¾ cup water
1 envelope unflavored gelatin
⅔ cup nonfat dry milk
2 tablespoons sugar
1 teaspoon vanilla extract
½ teaspoon coconut extract
¼ teaspoon rum extract
1 cup canned crushed pineapple (packed in juice), drained
7 large ice cubes

Place water in a small saucepan. Sprinkle gelatin over water and let soften a few minutes. Heat over low heat, stirring frequently, until gelatin is completely dissolved. Remove from heat.

In a blender, combine dry milk, sugar, extracts, and pineapple. Add gelatin mixture. Turn blender on and carefully add ice cubes, one at a time, while blending. Blend 1 minute, or until ice is gone. Pudding may be divided into 4 serving bowls and eaten right away or, if a slightly firmer texture is desired, chilled for at least 15 minutes before serving.

Per Serving: Calories 143, Total Fat 0.2g, Cholesterol 4mg, Sodium 111mg, Total Carbohydrate 26.5g, Dietary Fiber 0.5g, Protein 9g

Mocha Fluff

Light as a feather, this fluffy pudding is an ideal quick dessert or after-school snack. To make Chocolate Fluff, simply eliminate the coffee.

Makes 4 servings

¾ cup water
1 envelope unflavored gelatin
⅔ cup nonfat dry milk
3 tablespoons sugar
1 tablespoon plus 1 teaspoon cocoa (unsweetened)
1½ teaspoons vanilla extract
¼ teaspoon rum or almond extract
1½ teaspoons instant coffee granules (regular or decaffeinated)
7 large ice cubes

Place water in a small saucepan. Sprinkle gelatin over water and let soften a few minutes. Heat over low heat, stirring frequently, until gelatin is completely dissolved. Remove from heat.

In a blender, combine dry milk, sugar, cocoa, extracts, and coffee granules. Add gelatin mixture. Turn blender on and carefully add ice cubes, one at a time, while blending. Blend 1 minute, or until ice is gone. Pudding may be divided into 4 serving bowls and eaten right away or, if a slightly firmer texture is desired, chilled for at least 15 minutes before serving.

Per Serving: Calories 123, Total Fat 0.4g, Cholesterol 4mg, Sodium 110mg, Total Carbohydrate 21g, Dietary Fiber 0.6g, Protein 9g

Creamy Chocolate Pudding

By adding your favorite extract to this creamy pudding, you can create chocolate-almond, chocolate-rum, chocolate-coconut, or any other combination you can imagine.

Makes 2 servings

½ cup water
1 envelope unflavored gelatin
1 cup evaporated skim milk
2 tablespoons cocoa (unsweetened)
1 teaspoon vanilla extract
¼ teaspoon any other extract (optional)
2 tablespoons plus 1½ teaspoons sugar

Place water in a small saucepan. Sprinkle gelatin over water and let soften a few minutes. Heat over low heat, stirring frequently, until gelatin is completely dissolved.

In a blender, combine remaining ingredients. Add gelatin mixture. Blend until smooth. Pour pudding into a bowl and chill until set, about 20 minutes. Just before serving, beat chilled pudding on the high speed of an electric mixer until creamy.

Per Serving: Calories 197, Total Fat 1g, Cholesterol 4mg, Sodium 155mg, Total Carbohydrate 33.3g, Dietary Fiber 1.8g, Protein 13.8g

Banana Bavarian

The riper the bananas, the sweeter this easy pudding will be.

Makes 4 servings

½ cup water
2 envelopes unflavored gelatin
2 cups evaporated skim milk
2 medium, very ripe bananas
2 tablespoons sugar
⅛ teaspoon ground cinnamon
Pinch ground nutmeg
1 teaspoon vanilla extract
¼ teaspoon banana extract

Place water in a small saucepan. Sprinkle gelatin over water and let soften a few minutes. Heat over low heat, stirring frequently, until gelatin is completely dissolved.

In a blender, combine remaining ingredients. Add gelatin mixture. Blend until smooth. Pour into 4 individual serving bowls and chill until set.

Per Serving: Calories 194, Total Fat 0.6g, Cholesterol 4mg, Sodium 155mg, Total Carbohydrate 34.2g, Dietary Fiber 1.4g, Protein 13.3g

Vanilla Tapioca Pudding

The wonderful texture of the tapioca adds a special old-time note to this popular dessert.

Makes 4 servings

2 cups skim milk
2 tablespoons sugar
3 tablespoons quick-cooking tapioca
1 teaspoon vanilla extract

Place milk and sugar in a small saucepan. Sprinkle tapioca over milk and let it stand to soften for 5 minutes. Cook over medium heat, stirring constantly, until mixture comes to a boil. Boil, stirring, 2 minutes. Remove from heat and stir in vanilla. Divide mixture into 4 custard cups. Chill.

Per Serving: Calories 108, Total Fat 0.2g, Cholesterol 2mg, Sodium 114mg, Total Carbohydrate 22.2g, Dietary Fiber 0g, Protein 4.2g

Orange Tapioca Pudding

Fruit juices cooked with tapioca make wonderful puddings. This one makes a great dessert or after-school snack.

Makes 4 servings

2 cups orange juice
3 tablespoons quick-cooking tapioca
1 tablespoon plus 1 teaspoon firmly packed brown sugar
¼ teaspoon lemon extract
1/16 teaspoon ground cinnamon

Combine all ingredients except cinnamon in a small saucepan. Mix and let stand 5 minutes. Bring mixture to a boil over medium heat, stirring frequently. Remove from heat and stir in cinnamon. Cool mixture in pan 20 minutes, then stir and spoon into 4 custard cups. Chill.

Per Serving: Calories 114, Total Fat 0.3g, Cholesterol 0mg, Sodium 54mg, Total Carbohydrate 26.8g, Dietary Fiber 0.2g, Protein 1g

Creamy Rice and Raisin Pudding

Unlike most rice puddings, which are made with eggs, this one is made with cornstarch. The result is a creamy, rich pudding with just a trace of fat and lots of flavor. The servings are generous, and this dessert doubles as a filling, nutritious breakfast.

Makes 4 servings

2 cups skim milk
2 tablespoons sugar
1 tablespoon cornstarch
2 cups cooked brown (or white) rice
2 teaspoons vanilla extract
¼ teaspoon ground cinnamon
¼ cup raisins
Ground nutmeg

In a medium saucepan, combine milk, sugar, and cornstarch. Stir to dissolve cornstarch. Add rice. Heat over medium heat, stirring constantly, until mixture comes to a boil. Continue to cook and stir 1 minute. Remove from heat and stir in vanilla, cinnamon, and raisins. Spoon mixture into a shallow bowl. Sprinkle with nutmeg. Chill.

Per Serving: Calories 218, Total Fat 1g, Cholesterol 2mg, Sodium 65mg, Total Carbohydrate 45.4g, Dietary Fiber 2.3g, Protein 6.8g

Grape Gelatin Dessert

As simple to prepare as the commercial product, but with real fruit juice and a lot less sugar, this tasty treat is fun for the kids to make. It's great all year round and is a refreshing, fat-free dessert or snack.

Makes 6 servings

2 cups grape juice
2 tablespoons sugar
1 envelope unflavored gelatin

Place grape juice and sugar in a small saucepan. Sprinkle with gelatin. Let soften a few minutes. Heat over low heat, stirring frequently, until gelatin is completely dissolved. Divide mixture evenly into 6 custard cups. Chill until firm.

Per Serving: Calories 74, Total Fat 0.1g, Cholesterol 0mg, Sodium 5mg, Total Carbohydrate 16.8g, Dietary Fiber 0.1g, Protein 1.5g

Grape Nuts Raisin Pudding

Incredibly thick and rich, this warm, satisfying, and quite unusual pudding doubles as a nutritious breakfast. What a nice way to start the day!

Makes 2 servings

1 cup water
⅓ cup Grape Nuts cereal (1½ ounces)
¼ cup raisins
2 tablespoons firmly packed brown sugar
1 tablespoon plus 1 teaspoon quick-cooking tapioca
1 teaspoon vanilla extract
¼ teaspoon maple extract
Ground cinnamon

Bring about 3 inches of water to a boil in the bottom of a double boiler over medium-high heat. Combine all ingredients *except* cinnamon in the top of the double boiler. Cook, stirring frequently, until mixture thickens slightly, about 5 minutes. Continue to cook, stirring constantly, until mixture is very thick, about 4 minutes more. Spoon into 2 serving bowls. Sprinkle with cinnamon. Serve right away.

Per Serving: Calories 230, Total Fat 0.5g, Cholesterol 0mg, Sodium 161mg, Total Carbohydrate 53.7g, Dietary Fiber 2.5g, Protein 2.7g

Pineapple Cheese Bread Pudding

This moist pudding tastes almost like cheesecake. Why not have it for breakfast? It's sweet and satisfying and much more nutritious than a doughnut.

Makes 8 servings

4 slices whole wheat bread (1-ounce slices), cut into cubes
1 cup canned crushed pineapple (packed in juice), drained slightly
2 cups skim milk
½ cup liquid egg substitute
½ cup part-skim ricotta cheese
3 tablespoons sugar
2 teaspoons vanilla extract
1 teaspoon lemon extract
½ teaspoon ground cinnamon

Preheat oven to 350°. Spray an 8-inch square baking pan with nonstick cooking spray. Place bread cubes in prepared pan. Spread pineapple evenly over the bread. In a blender, combine remaining ingredients. Blend until smooth. Pour mixture evenly over bread and pineapple. Let stand 10 minutes. Bake, uncovered, 35 to 40 minutes, until set. Serve warm or cold.

Per Serving: Calories 132, Total Fat 2.4g, Cholesterol 6mg, Sodium 154mg, Total Carbohydrate 20.2g, Dietary Fiber 1.3g, Protein 7.3g

Blueberry Bread 'n' Butter Pudding

Originally made with butter, this delectable, molded bread pudding can be served by itself or topped with vanilla nonfat yogurt. It's really an artistic creation.

Makes 4 servings

2 cups blueberries, fresh or frozen (unsweetened)
¼ cup plus 2 tablespoons water
3 tablespoons sugar
¼ teaspoon ground cinnamon
2 tablespoons plus 2 teaspoons reduced-calorie margarine
8 slices thin-sliced whole wheat bread (½-ounce slices)

Combine blueberries, water, sugar, and cinnamon in a small saucepan. Bring to a boil over medium heat. Reduce heat to medium-low and simmer 5 minutes. Remove from heat.

Spread margarine on both sides of each bread slice, using ½ teaspoon of margarine per side. Cut each slice of bread into 5 or 6 triangular-shaped pieces. Line the bottom of a 9-inch cake pan with *half* of the bread, arranging the pieces to fit like a jigsaw puzzle. Pour about ¾ of the berries evenly over the bread. Arrange remaining bread over berries and top evenly with remaining berries. Cover pan with plastic wrap and top with a dish or paper plate. Place weights, such as several 1-pound cans of food, on top of plate. Refrigerate overnight. To serve, loosen pudding with a spatula and unmold onto a serving platter.

Per Serving: Calories 183, Total Fat 4.4g, Cholesterol 0mg, Sodium 211mg, Total Carbohydrate 32.8g, Dietary Fiber 4.1g, Protein 3.2g

Tofu Rice Pudding

Look for silken tofu in small boxes in the produce section of health food stores and most large grocery stores. It adds a thickness and richness to puddings and pies.

Makes 4 servings

1 cup water
1 envelope unflavored gelatin
1 10-ounce package silken (or soft) tofu
¼ cup sugar
½ teaspoon ground cinnamon
1 teaspoon vanilla extract
⅛ teaspoon lemon extract
⅛ teaspoon almond extract
⅔ cup nonfat dry milk
1 cup cooked brown (or white) rice
¼ cup raisins
Ground cinnamon
Dash ground nutmeg

Place water in a small saucepan. Sprinkle gelatin over water and let soften a few minutes. Heat over low heat, stirring frequently, until gelatin is completely dissolved.

In a blender, combine gelatin mixture, tofu, sugar, cinnamon, extracts, and dry milk. Blend until smooth. Pour into a bowl and chill until firm, about 45 minutes. Beat chilled pudding on low speed of an electric mixer until smooth. Stir in rice and raisins. Spoon pudding into a serving bowl and sprinkle with cinnamon and a dash of nutmeg. Chill thoroughly.

Per Serving: Calories 256, Total Fat 2.5g, Cholesterol 4mg, Sodium 115mg, Total Carbohydrate 45g, Dietary Fiber 1.6g, Protein 13.5g

Tofu Chocolate Pudding

A delicious way to serve this creamy pudding is to top each serving with a dollop of raspberry jam.

Makes 4 servings

1 cup water
1 envelope unflavored gelatin
1 10-ounce package silken (or soft) tofu
⅔ cup nonfat dry milk
¼ cup confectioners' sugar
2 tablespoons cocoa (unsweetened)
1 teaspoon vanilla extract
⅛ teaspoon almond extract

Place water in a small saucepan. Sprinkle gelatin over water and let soften a few minutes. Heat over low heat, stirring frequently, until gelatin is completely dissolved.

In a blender, combine gelatin mixture with remaining ingredients. Blend until smooth. Chill thoroughly. Note: For a creamier texture, beat pudding on low speed of an electric mixer just before serving.

Per Serving: Calories 158, Total Fat 2.5g, Cholesterol 4mg, Sodium 115mg, Total Carbohydrate 21.6g, Dietary Fiber 1g, Protein 12.6g

Pineapple-Banana Cheese Pudding

The exotic island flavors of pineapple and banana are heightened by the addition of the rich-tasting coconut extract in this delectable pudding.

Makes 4 servings

¾ cup water
1 envelope unflavored gelatin
1⅓ cups low-fat (1%) cottage cheese
2 tablespoons sugar
1 teaspoon vanilla extract
½ teaspoon coconut extract
½ medium, very ripe banana
½ cup canned crushed pineapple (packed in juice), undrained

Place water in a small saucepan. Sprinkle gelatin over water and let soften a few minutes. Heat over low heat, stirring frequently, until gelatin is completely dissolved.

In a blender, combine gelatin mixture with remaining ingredients *except* pineapple. Blend until smooth. Stir in pineapple. Pour into 1 large bowl or 4 individual serving bowls. Chill until firm.

Per Serving: Calories 118, Total Fat 0.9g, Cholesterol 3mg, Sodium 309mg, Total Carbohydrate 16.5g, Dietary Fiber 0.5g, Protein 11g

Rum Raisin Pudding

So elegant, yet so easy, this rich pudding with its delectable combination of flavors can dress up any dinner party.

Makes 4 servings

¾ cup water
1 envelope unflavored gelatin
1 cup part-skim ricotta cheese
⅓ cup nonfat dry milk
3 tablespoons sugar
1 teaspoon vanilla extract
1 teaspoon rum extract
¼ cup raisins
Ground nutmeg

Place water in a small saucepan. Sprinkle gelatin over water and let soften a few minutes. Heat over low heat, stirring frequently, until gelatin is completely dissolved.

In a blender, combine gelatin mixture with remaining ingredients *except* raisins and nutmeg. Blend until smooth. Stir in raisins. Pour pudding into 1 large bowl or 4 individual serving bowls. Sprinkle with nutmeg. Chill until firm.

Per Serving: Calories 199, Total Fat 5g, Cholesterol 21mg, Sodium 135mg, Total Carbohydrate 26.1g, Dietary Fiber 0.4g, Protein 12.4g

Cottage Apple Pudding

What could taste better than apples laced with cinnamon and nutmeg and baked in a thick cheese custard? Served warm or cold, it's a real winner.

Makes 6 servings

6 small sweet apples, peeled, sliced very thin
¼ cup water
1 teaspoon ground cinnamon
½ teaspoon ground nutmeg
1⅓ cups low-fat (1%) cottage cheese
¾ cup liquid egg substitute
⅓ cup nonfat dry milk
¼ cup sugar
2 teaspoons vanilla extract
½ teaspoon almond extract

Place apples and water in a large nonstick skillet or saucepan. Sprinkle with half of the cinnamon and half of the nutmeg. Simmer over medium heat 10 minutes, or until apples are slightly tender. Remove from heat. Preheat oven to 350°. Spray an 8-inch square baking pan with nonstick cooking spray. In a blender, combine cottage cheese with remaining ingredients, including remaining cinnamon and nutmeg. Blend until smooth. Spread apples evenly in prepared pan. Pour cheese mixture over apples. Sprinkle lightly with additional cinnamon. Bake, uncovered, 25 to 30 minutes, or until set.

Per Serving: Calories 192, Total Fat 2.1g, Cholesterol 3mg, Sodium 296mg, Total Carbohydrate 30.8g, Dietary Fiber 2.4g, Protein 12.6g

Applesauce Cheese Pudding

This delicious blend of applesauce, cottage cheese, and spices makes a hearty and nutritious breakfast as well as a creamy dessert.

Makes 4 servings

⅔ cup low-fat (1%) cottage cheese
2 tablespoons sugar
1 teaspoon vanilla extract
½ teaspoon maple extract
½ teaspoon grated fresh orange peel
½ teaspoon ground cinnamon
⅛ teaspoon ground nutmeg
1 cup applesauce (unsweetened)
1 cup orange juice
2 tablespoons cornstarch

In a blender, combine cottage cheese, sugar, extracts, orange peel, cinnamon, and nutmeg. Blend until smooth. Spoon into a medium saucepan. Stir in applesauce. In a small bowl, combine orange juice and cornstarch. Stir to dissolve cornstarch. Add to saucepan, mixing well. Bring mixture to a boil over medium heat, stirring frequently. Continue to cook, stirring constantly, 2 minutes. Spoon into a shallow bowl. Chill thoroughly.

Per Serving: Calories 124, Total Fat 0.6g, Cholesterol 2mg, Sodium 155mg, Total Carbohydrate 24.5g, Dietary Fiber 1g, Protein 5.3g

Baked Custard

This old-time favorite can easily be varied with the addition of another extract. Try lemon, orange, almond, or coconut and enjoy the many delights of a real comfort food.

Makes 4 servings

½ cup liquid egg substitute
2 tablespoons sugar
2 cups skim milk
1 teaspoon vanilla extract
½ teaspoon another flavored extract (optional)
Ground nutmeg

Preheat oven to 350°. Spray 4 custard cups with nonstick cooking spray. In a medium bowl, combine egg substitute and sugar. Add milk slowly, stirring constantly. Stir in vanilla. (Add optional extract, if desired.) Pour mixture into prepared cups. Sprinkle with nutmeg. Place cups in a shallow baking pan. Pour enough hot water in the larger pan to come halfway up the sides of the cups. Bake 30 to 40 minutes, until a knife inserted near the center comes out clean. Cool slightly, then chill.

Per Serving: Calories 93, Total Fat 1.2g, Cholesterol 2mg, Sodium 119mg, Total Carbohydrate 12.4g, Dietary Fiber 0g, Protein 8g

Pineapple Bavarian Cream

Cool and creamy, this refreshing mold is usually served as a dessert. However, I've also made individual molds and served them on a bed of lettuce for a delicious light lunch.

Makes 4 servings

½ cup water
1 cup canned crushed pineapple (packed in juice), drained (Reserve juice.)
1 envelope unflavored gelatin
1⅓ cups low-fat (1%) cottage cheese
2 tablespoons sugar
1 teaspoon vanilla extract
¼ teaspoon lemon extract

In a small saucepan, combine water and ¼ cup of the pineapple juice. Sprinkle with gelatin and let soften a few minutes. Heat over low heat, stirring frequently, until gelatin is completely dissolved.

In a blender, combine gelatin mixture, cottage cheese, sugar, and extracts. Blend until smooth. Pour into a bowl and chill until slightly set, about 15 minutes. Stir in pineapple. Place mixture in a 3-cup mold, or divide into 4 individual molds or parfait glasses. Chill until firm.

Per Serving: Calories 124, Total Fat 0.8g, Cholesterol 3mg, Sodium 310mg, Total Carbohydrate 18.1g, Dietary Fiber 0.5g, Protein 11.1g

Peaches 'n' Crème Mold

This delicious dessert makes great use of summer's fresh peaches. It has a nice, creamy texture and delicate flavor. Top each serving with a light sprinkling of cinnamon or freshly grated nutmeg.

Makes 6 servings

6 medium, very ripe peaches, peeled, pits removed, or 12 halves of canned, unsweetened peaches
⅓ cup sugar
2 cups water
2 envelopes unflavored gelatin
1½ cups vanilla nonfat yogurt
1 teaspoon vanilla extract
¼ teaspoon orange or lemon extract
⅛ teaspoon almond extract
Ground cinnamon or nutmeg

Slice 2 of the peaches into very thin slices. Sprinkle with 1 tablespoon of the sugar, mix, and set aside. Place 1 cup of the water in a small saucepan. Sprinkle gelatin over water and let it soften a few minutes. Heat over low heat, stirring frequently, until gelatin is completely dissolved. Remove from heat.

In a blender, combine yogurt and remaining unsliced peaches. Blend until smooth. Add gelatin mixture, remaining 1 cup of water, remaining sugar, and extracts. Blend until smooth. Stir in reserved sliced peaches. Pour mixture into a 9-cup mold and chill until firm. Unmold to serve. Top each serving with a little cinnamon or nutmeg. (If using nutmeg, try grating it fresh for the best flavor.)

Per Serving: Calories 135, Total Fat 0.1g, Cholesterol 2mg, Sodium 38mg, Total Carbohydrate 28.6g, Dietary Fiber 1.7g, Protein 4.9g

Tropical Fruit Mold

A delectable blend of flavors awaits you in this fruit-flavored dessert. It's refreshing on a hot summer day.

Makes 4 servings

¾ cup water
2 envelopes unflavored gelatin
¾ cup plain nonfat yogurt
1 cup strawberries, fresh or frozen (If frozen berries are used, there is no need to thaw them.)
½ cup canned crushed pineapple (packed in juice), drained (Reserve 2 tablespoons of juice.)
¼ cup sugar
1 teaspoon vanilla extract
¼ teaspoon *each* orange, lemon, and rum extracts

Place water in a small saucepan. Sprinkle gelatin over water and let soften a few minutes. Heat over low heat, stirring frequently, until gelatin is completely dissolved. Remove from heat. In a blender, combine yogurt, strawberries, pineapple, reserved pineapple juice, and sugar. Blend until fruit is in small pieces. Add gelatin mixture and extracts. Blend until smooth. Pour mixture into a 3-cup mold or a small bowl. Chill until firm. Unmold to serve.

Per Serving: Calories 120, Total Fat 0.2g, Cholesterol 1mg, Sodium 42mg, Total Carbohydrate 23.7g, Dietary Fiber 1.1g, Protein 5.9g

Mixed Fruit Sherbet

This refreshing sherbet, with its delicious, fresh taste, makes a perfect, light ending to any meal.

Makes 4 servings

1½ cups lemon nonfat yogurt
½ cup orange juice
1 cup strawberries, fresh or frozen
1 cup canned crushed pineapple (packed in juice), drained
1 tablespoon plus 1 teaspoon honey
1 tablespoon plus 1 teaspoon sugar

In a blender or food processor, combine all ingredients. Blend until smooth. Pour mixture into a 7 x 11-inch glass baking dish. Freeze 1 hour, until partially frozen. While mixture is chilling, place a large bowl in the refrigerator to chill. Place partially frozen sherbet into chilled bowl. Beat on low speed of an electric mixer 30 seconds. Place mixture in a 1-quart container. Cover tightly. Freeze until serving time.

Per Serving: Calories 172, Total Fat 0.2g, Cholesterol 0mg, Sodium 61mg, Total Carbohydrate 38.4g, Dietary Fiber 1.5g, Protein 4.2g

Strawberry Ice Cream in a Flash

There's just a trace of fat in a frosty, cold dish of this easy, ice cream-type dessert. Just throw a few ingredients in the blender and enjoy.

Makes 2 servings

⅓ cup nonfat dry milk
2 tablespoons sugar
½ cup ice water
½ teaspoon vanilla extract
2 cups frozen strawberries (unsweetened), still frozen

In a blender, combine dry milk, sugar, water, vanilla, and 1 cup of the strawberries. Blend just until berries are chopped into small pieces. Add remaining berries. Blend until smooth. Spoon into 2 serving bowls. Serve right away.

Per Serving: Calories 209, Total Fat 0.4g, Cholesterol 4mg, Sodium 111mg, Total Carbohydrate 43.2g, Dietary Fiber 4.6g, Protein 8.2g

Orange Dreamsicle Freeze

Reminiscent of the frozen confection I enjoyed as a kid, this frozen dessert will be loved by all. Not only will they adore it, but they'll be eating a nutritious dessert as well. And you don't need an ice cream machine or any fancy equipment to make it.

Makes 4 servings

½ cup frozen orange juice concentrate, thawed
1 cup skim milk
¼ cup ice water
⅓ cup nonfat dry milk
1 tablespoon lemon juice
3 tablespoons sugar

In a large bowl, mix orange juice concentrate with skim milk. Set aside. In a medium bowl, beat water and dry milk on the medium speed of an electric mixer for 2 minutes. Beat on high speed until soft peaks form. Add lemon juice and continue beating on high speed until stiff. Gradually beat in sugar. Fold fluffy mixture into orange mixture gently but thoroughly.

Pour mixture into a 7 x 11-inch pan and place in the freezer for 1 hour, or until firm but not solid. Spoon mixture into a bowl and beat on low speed of an electric mixer until smooth. Return mixture to pan. Cover and freeze until firm. Let stand at room temperature for 10 minutes before serving.

Per Serving: Calories 155, Total Fat 0.3g, Cholesterol 3mg, Sodium 87mg, Total Carbohydrate 31.5g, Dietary Fiber 0.3g, Protein 6.5g

Tortoni

A traditional Italian dessert that is usually made with whipped cream, this version is just as refreshing as the original. And it's so creamy that you won't believe it isn't made with real cream.

Makes 4 servings

⅓ cup ice water
⅓ cup nonfat dry milk
2 tablespoons sugar
½ teaspoon almond extract
½ teaspoon rum extract
1 tablespoon graham cracker crumbs (one 2½ -inch square, crushed)

Place ice water and dry milk in a deep bowl. Beat on medium speed of an electric mixer for 2 minutes. Increase speed to high and continue to beat for 2 more minutes. Add sugar and beat 2 minutes on high speed, or until mixture is thick and forms soft peaks. Add extracts, beating well. Divide mixture evenly into 4 custard cups. Sprinkle with crumbs. Place cups in freezer until set, at least 1 hour. Let cups sit at room temperature for about 3 minutes before serving.

Per Serving: Calories 66, Total Fat 0.2g, Cholesterol 2mg, Sodium 62mg, Total Carbohydrate 12.4g, Dietary Fiber 0g, Protein 3.7g

Cherry-Berry Sorbet

Unbelievably easy and delicious, this practically fat-free dessert can be made in no time. Just keep frozen cherries in your freezer so they'll be handy when you crave something sweet and cold.

Makes 2 servings

2 cups frozen pitted dark sweet cherries (unsweetened), still frozen (12 ounces)
¼ cup water
1 tablespoon plus 1 teaspoon sugar
1 teaspoon strawberry extract
Few drops almond extract

In a blender, combine all ingredients. Blend just until smooth. (You will need to turn the blender on and off and rearrange the cherries several times in order for them all to blend.) Serve right away.

Per Serving: Calories 121, Total Fat 0.7g, Cholesterol 0mg, Sodium 2mg, Total Carbohydrate 26.8g, Dietary Fiber 2.7g, Protein 1.6g

Rum Fruit Cake

Instead of flour, this super-moist cake gets its luscious taste and texture from graham cracker crumbs. It's unusual and delicious.

Makes 6 servings

1 cup plus 2 tablespoons graham cracker crumbs
⅓ cup sugar
⅛ teaspoon each ground cinnamon, cloves, nutmeg, and allspice
1 teaspoon baking powder
2 egg whites
1 teaspoon rum extract
½ teaspoon grated fresh orange peel
1 1-pound can fruit cocktail (packed in juice), drained well (Reserve ¼ cup plus 2 tablespoons juice.)
3 tablespoons raisins

Preheat oven to 350°. Spray a 4 x 8-inch loaf pan with nonstick cooking spray. In a large bowl, combine graham cracker crumbs, sugar, spices, and baking powder. Mix well.

In a small bowl, combine egg whites, rum extract, orange peel, and reserved juice. Beat with a fork or wire whisk until blended. Stir in fruit cocktail and raisins. Add to dry mixture, mixing until all ingredients are moistened.

Spoon mixture into prepared pan. Smooth the top slightly with the back of a spoon. Bake 45 minutes, until cake is firm. Cool in pan on a wire rack.

Per Serving: Calories 170, Total Fat 1.6g, Cholesterol 0mg, Sodium 181mg, Total Carbohydrate 36.3g, Dietary Fiber 1.2g, Protein 2.4g

Surprise Apple Cake

The surprise? The wonderful texture and moistness comes from beans! Don't tell them it's good for them, and they'll never guess!

Makes 16 servings

¾ cup all-purpose flour
¾ cup whole wheat flour
2 teaspoons baking powder
1½ teaspoons ground cinnamon
½ teaspoon ground nutmeg
¼ teaspoon ground cloves
¼ teaspoon ground allspice
1 cup (6 ounces) canned pinto beans, rinsed and drained
½ cup applesauce, unsweetened
½ cup sugar
¼ cup canola oil
2 egg whites
2 teaspoons vanilla extract
1 small, sweet apple, unpeeled, diced into ¼-inch pieces
¼ cup raisins

Preheat oven to 350°. Spray a Bundt pan with nonstick cooking spray. In a large bowl, combine both types of flour, baking powder, and spices. Mix well.

In a blender, combine beans, applesauce, sugar, oil, egg whites, and vanilla. Blend until smooth. Add to dry ingredients along with apple and raisins. Mix until all ingredients are moistened.

Spoon mixture into prepared pan. Bake 35 to 40 minutes, until a toothpick inserted in the cake comes out clean. Cool in pan on a wire rack 5 minutes, then invert cake onto rack to finish cooling.

Per Serving: Calories 127, Total Fat 3.7g, Cholesterol 0mg, Sodium 82mg, Total Carbohydrate 20.8g, Dietary Fiber 1.9g, Protein 2.4g

Pumpkin-Graham Cake

It's hard to believe that a cake can be light and airy yet moist at the same time. This unusual cake is just that. It's a luscious taste treat.

Makes 8 servings

1 cup plus 2 tablespoons graham cracker crumbs (4½ ounces)
1 cup canned pumpkin
¾ cup liquid egg substitute
¼ cup honey
2 teaspoons vanilla extract
4 egg whites (Egg substitute will not work here.)
⅓ cup sugar

Preheat oven to 325°. Spray a 9-inch cake pan with nonstick cooking spray. Line the bottom of the pan with wax paper and spray again. In a large bowl, combine graham cracker crumbs, pumpkin, egg substitute, honey, and vanilla. Mix well.

Place egg whites in another large bowl. Beat on medium speed of an electric mixer until foamy, then beat on high speed until stiff. Gradually add sugar, beating well after each addition. Stir about one fourth of the egg whites into pumpkin mixture. Fold in remaining egg whites, gently yet thoroughly. Spoon batter into prepared pan and smooth the top.

Bake 55 minutes, until a toothpick inserted in the center of the cake comes out clean. Cool in pan on a wire rack for 10 minutes, then turn out onto rack to finish cooling. Remove wax paper. For a pretty effect, just before serving, place about ½ teaspoon of confectioners' sugar in a small strainer and shake evenly over cake.

Per Serving: Calories 174, Total Fat 2.5g, Cholesterol 0mg, Sodium 165mg, Total Carbohydrate 32.2g, Dietary Fiber 1.3g, Protein 5.8g

Banana Cake

Everyone's favorite, this delectable cake is perfect with a cup of coffee or tea. For a pretty presentation, dust the top of the cake lightly with confectioners' sugar just before serving.

Makes 18 servings

1¾ cups plus 2 tablespoons all-purpose flour
1½ cups whole wheat flour
2 teaspoons baking powder
1½ teaspoons baking soda
¾ cup sugar
½ cup skim milk
3 tablespoons canola oil
3 egg whites
1 tablespoon vanilla extract
¼ teaspoon banana extract (This is optional and adds flavor if the bananas are not very ripe and sweet.)
2¼ cups mashed, very ripe bananas (4½ medium bananas)

Preheat oven to 350°. Spray a 10-inch tube pan with nonstick cooking spray. In a large bowl, combine both types of flour, baking powder, and baking soda. Mix well. In another bowl, combine remaining ingredients *except* bananas. Beat with a fork or wire whisk until blended. Add bananas. Whisk again. Add to dry mixture, mixing until all ingredients are moistened.

Spoon batter into prepared pan. Smooth the top slightly with the back of a spoon. Bake 40 to 45 minutes, or until a toothpick inserted in the center of the cake comes out clean. Cool in pan on a wire rack for 5 minutes, then remove cake to rack. Serve warm for best flavor.

Per Serving: Calories 170, Total Fat 2.7g, Cholesterol 0mg, Sodium 157mg, Total Carbohydrate 32.8g, Dietary Fiber 2.2g, Protein 3.8g

Heavenly Chocolate Cake

Replacing part of the sugar with corn syrup adds moistness to this chocolatey cake. Yes, you can indulge in a heavenly dessert without a lot of fat.

Makes 8 servings

1 cup all-purpose flour
½ cup whole wheat flour
⅓ cup cocoa (unsweetened)
1 teaspoon baking powder
½ teaspoon baking soda
1 cup evaporated skim milk
¼ cup firmly packed brown sugar
¼ cup plus 2 tablespoons light corn syrup
1 tablespoon plus 1 teaspoon canola oil
3 egg whites
1 teaspoon vanilla extract
¼ teaspoon almond extract
2 tablespoons fruit-only raspberry spread (optional)
1 teaspoon confectioners' sugar (optional)

Preheat oven to 350°. Spray a 9-inch nonstick cake pan with nonstick cooking spray. In a large bowl, combine both types of flour, cocoa, baking powder, and baking soda. Mix well. In another bowl, combine remaining ingredients except optional ingredients. Beat with a fork or wire whisk until blended. Add to dry mixture. Mix until all ingredients are moistened.

Spoon into prepared pan. Bake 20 to 25 minutes, until a toothpick inserted in the center of the cake comes out clean. Cool 5 minutes in pan on a wire rack, then invert onto rack to finish cooling.

If desired, cut cooled cake in half horizontally and spread raspberry spread over bottom half. Replace top. Just before serving, sprinkle with confectioners' sugar.

Per Serving: Calories 232, Total Fat 3.1g, Cholesterol 1mg, Sodium 202mg, Total Carbohydrate 44.4g, Dietary Fiber 2.5g, Protein 6.9g

Chocolate Zucchini Spice Cake

Similar to brownies, this luscious cake is moist and tender and very rich-tasting. The versatile squash reigns again!

Makes 16 servings

¾ cup whole wheat flour
¾ cup all-purpose flour
3 tablespoons cocoa (unsweetened)
1 teaspoon baking powder
½ teaspoon baking soda
1 teaspoon ground cinnamon
¼ teaspoon ground nutmeg
⅛ teaspoon ground allspice
⅔ cup sugar
⅓ cup skim milk
2 tablespoons canola oil
2 egg whites
1 teaspoon vanilla extract
½ teaspoon grated fresh orange peel
1 cup (packed) finely shredded zucchini, unpeeled

Preheat oven to 350°. Spray an 8-inch square baking pan with nonstick cooking spray. In a large bowl, combine both types of flour, cocoa, baking powder, baking soda, and spices. Mix well.

In another bowl, combine remaining ingredients except zucchini. Beat with a fork or wire whisk until blended. Stir in zucchini. Add to dry mixture, mixing until all ingredients are moistened. Spoon into prepared pan.

Bake 30 minutes, until a toothpick inserted in the center of the cake comes out clean. Cool in pan on a wire rack. Cut into squares to serve.

Per Serving: Calories 99, Total Fat 2g, Cholesterol 0mg, Sodium 71mg, Total Carbohydrate 18g, Dietary Fiber 1.4g, Protein 2.3g

Tropical Pineapple Banana Cake

With its tender chunks of pineapple and banana, the flavor is reminiscent of the tropics.

Makes 8 servings

Cake:
¾ cup whole wheat flour
¾ cup all-purpose flour
1½ teaspoons baking powder
¼ teaspoon baking soda
½ teaspoon ground cinnamon
1 cup skim milk
1 tablespoon vinegar
⅔ cup sugar
2 egg whites
2 tablespoons canola oil
1 teaspoon vanilla extract
½ teaspoon lemon extract
1 8-ounce can crushed pineapple (packed in juice), drained very well
1 medium, ripe banana, diced into ½-inch pieces

Topping:
2 teaspoons sugar
¼ teaspoon ground cinnamon

Preheat oven to 350°. Spray a 9-inch nonstick cake pan with nonstick cooking spray. In a large bowl, combine both types of flour, baking powder, baking soda, and cinnamon. Mix well. Combine milk and vinegar in a medium bowl. Let stand a few minutes. Add sugar, egg whites, oil, and extracts. Beat with a fork or wire whisk until blended. Gently stir in pineapple and banana. Add to dry mixture, stirring until all ingredients are moistened. Spoon into prepared pan. For topping, combine sugar and cinnamon and sprinkle evenly over top of cake.

Bake 35 minutes, until a toothpick inserted in the center of the cake comes out clean. Cool 10 minutes in pan on a wire rack, then either serve warm right from the pan, or remove cake to rack (topping-side up) to finish cooling.

Per Serving: Calories 233, Total Fat 3.9g, Cholesterol 0mg, Sodium 136mg, Total Carbohydrate 44.8g, Dietary Fiber 2.3g, Protein 4.7g

Carrot Cake

Unlike most carrot cakes that get their moistness from lots of oil, this one owes its wonderful, moist texture to applesauce.

Makes 8 servings

Cake:
¾ cup whole wheat flour
¾ cup all-purpose flour
1½ teaspoons baking powder
1½ teaspoons ground cinnamon
¼ teaspoon ground nutmeg
⅛ teaspoon ground allspice
¼ cup raisins
1 cup applesauce (unsweetened)
2 egg whites
½ cup firmly packed brown sugar
2 tablespoons plus 2 teaspoons canola oil
1 teaspoon vanilla extract
1 cup finely shredded carrots
1 8-ounce can crushed pineapple (packed in juice), drained well

Topping:
¼ cup plus 1 tablespoon tub-style fat-free cream cheese
1 teaspoon vanilla extract
1 tablespoon plus 1 teaspoon confectioners' sugar

Preheat oven to 350°. Spray an 8-inch square baking pan with nonstick cooking spray. In a large bowl, combine both types of flour, baking powder, and spices. Mix well and stir in raisins. In another bowl, combine applesauce, egg whites, brown sugar, oil, and vanilla. Beat with a fork or wire whisk until blended. Stir in carrots and pineapple. Add to dry mixture, mixing until all ingredients are moistened. Place in prepared pan.

Bake 40 to 45 minutes, until a toothpick inserted in the center of the cake comes out clean. Cool in pan on a wire rack.

Combine topping ingredients in a small bowl. Mix well. Refrigerate until needed. Just before serving, spread topping on cake. Refrigerate leftover cake.

Per Serving: Calories 252, Total Fat 4.8g, Cholesterol 1mg, Sodium 143mg, Total Carbohydrate 46.6g, Dietary Fiber 3.2g, Protein 5.4g

Apple Pudding Cake

Lots of chopped apples fill this super-moist cake.

Makes 8 servings

Cake:
4 small sweet apples, peeled, chopped into ¼-inch pieces
1 cup liquid egg substitute
1 cup part-skim ricotta cheese
¾ cup all-purpose flour
⅔ cup nonfat dry milk
⅓ cup sugar
1 teaspoon baking powder
½ teaspoon baking soda
2 teaspoons vanilla extract
1 teaspoon ground cinnamon

Topping:
1 tablespoon sugar
¼ teaspoon ground cinnamon

Preheat oven to 350°. Spray an 8-inch square baking pan with nonstick cooking spray. Place apples in a large bowl. In a blender, combine remaining cake ingredients. Blend until smooth. Spoon over apples and stir gently. Spoon mixture into prepared pan. Combine topping ingredients and sprinkle evenly over cake.

Bake 50 to 55 minutes, until cake is firm and nicely browned. Remove pan to a wire rack. Serve warm for best flavor. Refrigerate leftovers and reheat or serve cold.

Per Serving: Calories 223, Total Fat 3.8g, Cholesterol 12mg, Sodium 272mg, Total Carbohydrate 34.7g, Dietary Fiber 1.6g, Protein 12.2g

Peach Kuchen

This is an easy version of an old-time favorite. It's low in fat, but it sure is high in flavor.

Makes 8 servings

Cake:
4 slices whole wheat bread (1-ounce slices), crumbled
⅔ cup nonfat dry milk
2 tablespoons sugar
2 tablespoons plus 2 teaspoons reduced-calorie margarine
1 teaspoon baking powder
½ teaspoon ground cinnamon
1½ teaspoons vanilla extract
1 1-pound can sliced peaches (packed in juice), drained

Topping:
1 cup liquid egg substitute
1 cup vanilla nonfat yogurt
½ teaspoon almond extract
2 tablespoons sugar

Preheat oven to 350°. Spray a 7 x 11-inch baking pan with nonstick cooking spray. In a large bowl, combine bread, dry milk, sugar, margarine, baking powder, cinnamon, and vanilla. Mix with a fork until mixture is in the form of coarse crumbs. Press crumbs firmly into prepared pan.

Bake 10 minutes. Slice peaches in half lengthwise and arrange them on crust. Combine topping ingredients in a medium bowl. Beat with a fork or wire whisk until blended. Pour over peaches. Bake 30 minutes, until topping is set. Cool slightly. Cut into squares and serve lukewarm.

Per Serving: Calories 186, Total Fat 3.1g, Cholesterol 3mg, Sodium 278mg, Total Carbohydrate 29g, Dietary Fiber 1.8g, Protein 10.4g

Cinnamon Orange Coffee Cake

Orange juice concentrate gives this delicious cake a rich flavor and moist texture. It's delicious served warm and tastes great alongside a scoop of vanilla nonfat ice cream or frozen yogurt.

Makes 8 servings

Cake:
1 cup all-purpose flour
½ cup whole wheat flour
1½ teaspoons baking powder
¼ teaspoon baking soda
1 teaspoon ground cinnamon
2 egg whites
½ cup sugar
¼ cup plus 2 tablespoons frozen orange juice concentrate, thawed
⅔ cup skim milk
2 tablespoons canola oil
1 teaspoon vanilla extract
½ teaspoon orange extract

Topping:
2 tablespoons frozen orange juice concentrate, thawed
1 teaspoon sugar
¼ teaspoon ground cinnamon

Preheat oven to 350°. Spray a 9-inch nonstick cake pan with nonstick cooking spray. In a large bowl, combine both types of flour, baking powder, baking soda, and cinnamon. Mix well. In another bowl, combine remaining cake ingredients. Beat with a fork or wire whisk until blended. Add to dry mixture, mixing until all ingredients are moistened. Place mixture in prepared pan.

Bake 30 minutes, until a toothpick inserted in the center of the cake comes out clean. Place pan on a wire rack. For topping, spread orange juice concentrate evenly over hot cake. Combine sugar and cinnamon and sprinkle evenly over cake.

Per Serving: Calories 206, Total Fat 3.7g, Cholesterol 0mg, Sodium 130mg, Total Carbohydrate 38.8g, Dietary Fiber 1.6g, Protein 4.5g

Apricot Coffee Cake

The delicate flavor of the apricots is highlighted by the flavors of almond and orange in this delicious cake. Served warm along with a cup of coffee or tea, it makes a perfect dessert or snack.

Makes 8 servings

Cake:
1 cup all-purpose flour
½ cup whole wheat flour
1½ teaspoons baking powder
½ teaspoon baking soda
1 1-pound can apricots (packed in juice), drained (Reserve juice.)
2 egg whites
⅓ cup sugar
2 tablespoons canola oil
1½ teaspoons vanilla extract
1 teaspoon almond extract
¼ teaspoon orange extract

Topping:
2 teaspoons sugar
¼ teaspoon ground cinnamon

Preheat oven to 350°. Spray a 9-inch nonstick cake pan with nonstick cooking spray. In a large bowl, combine both types of flour, baking powder, and baking soda. Mix well.

Place drained apricots in a blender. Blend until smooth. Pour into a measuring cup and add reserved liquid, if necessary, to equal 1 cup. Place in a small bowl. Add remaining cake ingredients. Beat with a fork or wire whisk until blended. Add to dry ingredients, mixing until all ingredients are moistened. Beat with a spoon for 30 seconds. Spoon mixture into prepared pan. Combine sugar and cinnamon and sprinkle evenly over cake.

Bake 30 minutes, until a toothpick inserted in the center of the cake comes out clean. Place pan on a wire rack. Serve cake warm for best flavor.

Per Serving: Calories 185, Total Fat 3.7g, Cholesterol 0mg, Sodium 161mg, Total Carbohydrate 34.1g, Dietary Fiber 2.2g, Protein 3.8g

Cinnamon Streusel Coffee Cake

So good with coffee or tea, this tender cake is at its best when served warm. For a special treat, serve it alongside a scoop of vanilla nonfat frozen yogurt.

Makes 8 servings

Cake:
1 cup all-purpose flour
½ cup whole wheat flour
2 teaspoons baking powder
1 teaspoon baking soda
2 egg whites
1 cup vanilla nonfat yogurt
⅓ cup firmly packed brown sugar
1 tablespoon plus 1 teaspoon canola oil
1 tablespoon vanilla extract

Topping:
1 tablespoon firmly packed brown sugar
1 tablespoon wheat germ
½ teaspoon ground cinnamon

Preheat oven to 350°. Spray an 8-inch square baking pan with nonstick cooking spray. In a large bowl, combine both types of flour, baking powder, and baking soda. Mix well. In another bowl, combine remaining cake ingredients. Beat with a fork or wire whisk until blended. Add to dry mixture, mixing until all ingredients are moistened. Spoon into prepared pan.

In a small bowl or custard cup, combine topping ingredients, mixing well. Sprinkle evenly over cake.

Bake 25 to 30 minutes, until a toothpick inserted in the center of the cake comes out clean. Place pan on a wire rack and spray the top of the hot cake lightly with nonstick cooking spray. Serve warm for best flavor.

Per Serving: Calories 175, Total Fat 2.6g, Cholesterol 1mg, Sodium 282mg, Total Carbohydrate 33.1g, Dietary Fiber 1.5g, Protein 4.8g

Pumpkin Log

This elegant dessert makes a perfect ending for any special meal. What a treat!
Makes 8 servings

Cake:
¾ cup all-purpose flour
1 teaspoon baking powder
2 teaspoons ground cinnamon
½ teaspoon ground nutmeg
⅛ teaspoon *each* ground allspice and ground ginger
¾ cup liquid egg substitute
⅓ cup sugar
¼ cup water
1 tablespoon plus 1 teaspoon canola oil
1 teaspoon vanilla extract
½ cup canned pumpkin

Filling:
1¼ cups part-skim ricotta cheese
2 tablespoons sugar
2 teaspoons vanilla extract
¼ teaspoon rum extract

Preheat oven to 375°. Spray a 10 x 15-inch nonstick jelly roll pan with nonstick cooking spray. Into a small bowl, sift flour, baking powder, and spices. In another bowl, beat egg substitute on medium speed of an electric mixer for 2 minutes. Reduce speed to low and beat in sugar, water, oil, and vanilla. Add pumpkin and beat until blended. Gradually add dry mixture, beating well after each addition. Spread batter evenly in prepared pan.

Bake 10 minutes. Let cake cool in pan 3 minutes, then loosen sides with a spatula. Run the spatula under the sides of the cake, loosening the entire cake. Turn cake out onto a towel. Roll the cake and the towel into a log, starting with one short side. Cool completely. In a medium bowl, combine all filling ingredients, mixing well.

Gently unroll cooled cake. Spread filling evenly over cake. Roll up carefully. Chill thoroughly.

Per Serving: Calories 188, Total Fat 6.2g, Cholesterol 12mg, Sodium 136mg, Total Carbohydrate 24.6g, Dietary Fiber 1g, Protein 8.6g

Honey Sweet Sticky Buns

Yes, you can indulge in this sticky treat! And, with refrigerator biscuits nothing could be easier.

Makes 10 servings

3 tablespoons plus 1 teaspoon soft, tub-style (not diet) margarine, melted
2 tablespoons firmly packed brown sugar
1 tablespoon honey
¼ cup plus 1 tablespoon raisins
1 10-ounce package refrigerator biscuits (10 biscuits)

Preheat oven to 350°. Combine margarine, brown sugar, and honey in the bottom of a 9-inch pie pan. Mix well and spread mixture evenly in pan. Sprinkle with raisins. Arrange biscuits evenly in pan. Press them down slightly with the palm of your hand. Bake 20 minutes, until biscuits are lightly browned. Remove from oven and let stand 1 minute, then invert onto a serving plate. Serve warm.

Per Serving: Calories 162, Total Fat 8.3g, Cholesterol 0mg, Sodium 320mg, Total Carbohydrate 19.9g, Dietary Fiber 0.7g, Protein 1.9g

Almond Oatmeal Breakfast Bars

These quick, easy bars make a great dessert or a unique and nutritious breakfast-on-the-go. Imagine having your cereal, milk, and fruit all rolled into one delicious bar.

Makes 8 servings

1 cup rolled oats, uncooked (3 ounces)
⅔ cup nonfat dry milk
½ teaspoon baking powder
½ teaspoon baking soda
½ teaspoon ground cinnamon
¼ teaspoon ground nutmeg
Dash ground allspice
¼ cup raisins
1 cup applesauce (unsweetened)
3 tablespoons sugar
1 teaspoon vanilla extract
¾ teaspoon almond extract

Preheat oven to 350°. Spray an 8-inch square baking pan with nonstick cooking spray. In a large bowl, combine oats, dry milk, baking powder, baking soda, and spices. Mix well. Stir in raisins. In a small bowl, combine remaining ingredients, mixing well. Add to dry mixture, mixing until all ingredients are moistened. Spoon into prepared pan. Smooth the top with the back of a spoon. Bake 30 minutes, until lightly browned. Cool in pan on a wire rack. Cut into bars.

Per Serving: Calories 129, Total Fat 0.8g, Cholesterol 2mg, Sodium 158mg, Total Carbohydrate 24.8g, Dietary Fiber 1.8g, Protein 5.6g

Pink Bean "Pumpkin" Pie

This delectable pie is so unusual that you'll just have to try it to believe it. Close your eyes, and you'll think it's pumpkin pie! (Thanks for this one, Bubbie!)

Makes 8 servings

Crust:
½ cup all-purpose flour
¼ cup whole wheat flour
¼ teaspoon baking powder
2 tablespoons plus 2 teaspoons margarine
3 tablespoons plus 2 teaspoons ice water

Filling:
1 19-ounce can pinto beans, rinsed and drained (This will yield approximately 12 ounces of beans.)
1½ cups evaporated skim milk
½ cup liquid egg substitute
½ cup sugar
1¼ teaspoons ground cinnamon
½ teaspoon ground nutmeg
½ teaspoon ground cloves
⅛ teaspoon ground ginger

Preheat oven to 400°. Have a 9-inch pie pan ready. In a medium bowl, combine both types of flour and baking powder, mixing well. Add margarine. Mix with a fork or pastry blender until mixture resembles coarse crumbs. Add water. Mix with a fork until all ingredients are moistened. Work dough into a ball, using your hands. (Add a little more flour if dough is sticky, or a little more water if dough is too dry.)

Roll dough between 2 sheets of wax paper into an 11-inch circle. Remove top sheet of wax paper and invert crust into prepared pan. Fit crust into pan, leaving an overhang. Carefully remove remaining wax paper. Bend edges of crust under and flute dough with your fingers or a fork. Prick the bottom and sides of crust about 30 times with a fork.

Bake 10 minutes. Remove from oven. Reduce oven to 375°. In a blender, combine all filling ingredients. Blend until smooth. Pour mixture into crust. Bake 30 minutes, until set. Cool slightly, the chill.

Per Serving: Calories 214, Total Fat 4.9g, Cholesterol 2mg, Sodium 262mg, Total Carbohydrate 33.7g, Dietary Fiber 2.9g, Protein 8.9g

Chocolate Tofu Cheese Pie

Tofu adds just the right creamy texture to this luscious, rich pie. No one will ever guess what's in it!

Makes 8 servings

Crust:
1 tablespoon plus 1½ teaspoons margarine, melted
1 tablespoon plus 1½ teaspoons honey
¾ cup graham cracker crumbs

Filling:
1½ envelopes unflavored gelatin
1½ cups water
9 ounces soft or medium tofu, sliced and drained well between layers of towels
1 cup nonfat dry milk
¾ cup part-skim ricotta cheese
⅓ cup sugar
2 tablespoons cocoa (unsweetened)
1 teaspoon vanilla extract
1 teaspoon almond extract
¼ teaspoon rum extract

Preheat oven to 350°. Combine margarine and honey in a 9-inch pie pan. Add graham cracker crumbs and mix until crumbs are moistened. Press crumbs into bottom and sides of pan to form a crust. Bake 5 minutes. Cool completely.

In a small saucepan, sprinkle gelatin over water and let soften a few minutes. Heat over low heat, stirring frequently, until gelatin is completely dissolved. In a blender, combine gelatin mixture with remaining ingredients. Blend until smooth. Pour mixture into cooled crust. Chill until firm.

Per Serving: Calories 212, Total Fat 5.9g, Cholesterol 10mg, Sodium 187mg, Total Carbohydrate 28.3g, Dietary Fiber 0.6g, Protein 11.4g

Banana Tofu Cream Pie

Adding banana extract to this pie really deepens the rich flavor. And the riper the bananas, the sweeter this delectable pie will be.

Makes 8 servings

Crust:
1 tablespoon plus 1½ teaspoons margarine, melted
1 tablespoon plus 1½ teaspoons honey
¾ cup graham cracker crumbs

Filling:
9 ounces soft or medium tofu, sliced and drained well between layers of towels
¾ cup liquid egg substitute
1½ medium, ripe bananas, cut into chunks
1 cup low-fat (1%) cottage cheese
⅓ cup sugar
1 tablespoon all-purpose flour
1 teaspoon vanilla extract
1 teaspoon banana extract
Ground nutmeg

Preheat oven to 350°. Combine margarine and honey in a 9-inch pie pan. Add graham cracker crumbs and mix until crumbs are moistened. Press crumbs into bottom and sides of pan to form a crust. Bake 5 minutes.

In a blender, combine all filling ingredients except nutmeg. Blend until smooth. Pour into crust. Sprinkle very lightly with nutmeg, preferably freshly ground. Bake 30 to 35 minutes, until set. Cool slightly, then chill.

Per Serving: Calories 181, Total Fat 5g, Cholesterol 1mg, Sodium 232mg, Total Carbohydrate 25.3g, Dietary Fiber 0.7g, Protein 8.6g

Orange Sponge Pie

My version of a Pennsylvania Dutch dessert, this fluffy pie is light-tasting and delicious.

Makes 8 servings

Crust:
1 tablespoon plus 1½ teaspoons margarine, melted
1 tablespoon plus 1½ teaspoons honey
¾ cup graham cracker crumbs
¼ teaspoon ground cinnamon

Filling:
½ cup sugar
⅔ cup nonfat dry milk
½ cup liquid egg substitute
½ cup frozen orange juice concentrate, thawed
⅓ cup water
2 tablespoons all-purpose flour
1 teaspoon grated fresh orange peel
1 teaspoon vanilla extract
½ teaspoon orange extract
3 egg whites (Egg substitute will not work here.)

Preheat oven to 350°. Combine margarine and honey in a 9-inch pie pan. Add graham cracker crumbs and cinnamon; mix until crumbs are moistened. Press crumbs into bottom and sides of pan to form a crust. Bake 5 minutes. Let crust cool.

In a large bowl, combine half of the sugar with remaining ingredients except egg whites. Beat on low speed of an electric mixer until combined. Then beat on medium speed 1 minute.

In another bowl, using clean, dry beaters, beat egg whites until stiff. Gradually add remaining sugar, beating well after each addition. Fold into orange mixture gently but thoroughly. Pour mixture into prepared crust. Bake 25 minutes, until set and lightly browned. Cool on a wire rack for 10 minutes, then chill.

Per Serving: Calories 206, Total Fat 3.5g, Cholesterol 2mg, Sodium 175mg, Total Carbohydrate 35.8g, Dietary Fiber 0.4g, Protein 7.8g

Marbled Cheese Pie

This easy pie is lovely to look at and delightful to eat.

Makes 8 servings

Crust:
1 tablespoon plus 1½ teaspoons margarine, melted
1 tablespoon plus 1½ teaspoons honey
¾ cup graham cracker crumbs

Filling:
2 envelopes unflavored gelatin
½ cup water
2 cups part-skim ricotta cheese
1 cup evaporated skim milk
1½ teaspoons vanilla extract
½ cup sugar
¼ teaspoon rum extract
2 tablespoons cocoa (unsweetened)
¼ teaspoon almond extract

Preheat oven to 350°. Combine margarine and honey in a 9-inch pie pan. Add graham cracker crumbs; mix until crumbs are moistened. Press crumbs into bottom and sides of pan to form a crust. Bake 5 minutes. Let crust cool completely.

Sprinkle gelatin over water in a small saucepan. Let soften a few minutes. Heat over low heat, stirring frequently, until gelatin is completely dissolved. In a blender, combine gelatin mixture, ricotta cheese, milk, vanilla, and half of the sugar. Blend until smooth. Pour half of the mixture into a bowl and stir in rum extract. To remaining mixture, add remaining sugar, cocoa, and almond extract. Blend until combined. Pour into a second bowl.

Chill both mixtures 5 to 10 minutes, until slightly thickened. Using 2 large serving spoons, drop mixture alternately into cooled crust. Marble the top with a knife in a crisscross pattern. Chill until firm.

Per Serving: Calories 237, Total Fat 8.1g, Cholesterol 20mg, Sodium 190mg, Total Carbohydrate 29.4g, Dietary Fiber 0.6g, Protein 11.7g

Pineapple Cheese Pie

Light and delicate, this easy pie makes a refreshing, light-tasting dessert.

Makes 8 servings

Crust:
1 tablespoon plus 1½ teaspoons margarine, melted
1 tablespoon plus 1½ teaspoons honey
¾ cup graham cracker crumbs

Filling:
1½ envelopes unflavored gelatin
½ cup water
1⅓ cups low-fat (1%) cottage cheese
1 cup cold orange juice
⅔ cup nonfat dry milk
¼ cup sugar
2 teaspoons vanilla extract
¼ teaspoon lemon extract

Topping:
1 cup canned crushed pineapple (packed in juice), drained (Reserve ¼ cup of the juice.)
1 tablespoon sugar
2 teaspoons cornstarch
2 tablespoons water

Preheat oven to 350°. Combine margarine and honey in a 9-inch pie pan. Add graham cracker crumbs; mix until crumbs are moistened. Press crumbs into bottom and sides of pan to form a crust. Bake 5 minutes. Let crust cool completely.

Sprinkle gelatin over water in a small saucepan. Let soften a few minutes. Heat over low heat until gelatin is completely dissolved, stirring frequently. In a blender, combine gelatin mixture with remaining filling ingredients. Blend until smooth. Pour into cooled crust. Chill until firm.

In a small saucepan, combine pineapple, reserved juice, and sugar. Stir cornstarch into water in a small bowl and add to pineapple mixture. Cook over medium heat, stirring constantly, until mixture comes to a boil. Boil 1 minute, stirring. Spread evenly over cold pie. Chill.

Per Serving: Calories 200, Total Fat 3.5g, Cholesterol 4mg, Sodium 283mg, Total Carbohydrate 32g, Dietary Fiber 0.5g, Protein 10.2g

Almond Buttermilk Pie

Buttermilk gives the flavor of this quick, no-crust pie a tangy surprise.

Makes 8 servings

1½ cups buttermilk
1 cup liquid egg substitute
½ cup sugar
¼ cup plus 2 tablespoons all-purpose flour
¼ cup tub-style diet margarine
2 tablespoons plus 2 teaspoons nonfat dry milk
2 teaspoons baking powder
2 teaspoons vanilla extract
1 teaspoon almond extract

Preheat oven to 350°. Spray a 9-inch pie pan with nonstick cooking spray. In a blender, combine all ingredients. Blend on low speed until all ingredients are moistened. Blend on high speed for 1 minute. Pour mixture into prepared pan. Let stand for 5 minutes. Bake 35 minutes, or until pie is set and lightly browned. Cool 10 minutes, then chill.

Per Serving: Calories 145, Total Fat 3.6g, Cholesterol 2mg, Sodium 253mg, Total Carbohydrate 21.1g, Dietary Fiber 0.2g, Protein 6.8g

Fresh Orange Pie

Fresh oranges make a cool, refreshing filling for this scrumptious pie. Any variety of orange can be used, but navel oranges definitely get my vote!

Makes 8 servings

Crust:
1 tablespoon plus 1½ teaspoons margarine, melted
1 tablespoon plus 1½ teaspoons honey
¾ cup graham cracker crumbs
¼ teaspoon ground cinnamon
¼ teaspoon grated fresh orange peel

Filling:
2 tablespoons plus 2 teaspoons cornstarch
1½ cups orange juice
¼ cup sugar
1 tablespoon lemon juice
¼ teaspoon orange extract
2½ cups fresh orange sections, drained, white membranes discarded

Preheat oven to 350°. Combine margarine and honey in a 9-inch pie pan. Add graham cracker crumbs, cinnamon, and orange peel; mix until crumbs are moistened. Press crumbs into bottom and sides of pan to form a crust. Bake 5 minutes. Let crust cool completely.

Dissolve cornstarch in a small amount of the orange juice in a small saucepan. Add remaining orange juice, sugar, lemon juice, and orange extract. Bring mixture to a boil over medium heat, stirring constantly. Boil 1 minute, stirring. Remove from heat and stir in orange sections. Pour into crust. Chill.

Per Serving: Calories 154, Total Fat 3.1g, Cholesterol 0mg, Sodium 74mg, Total Carbohydrate 30.1g, Dietary Fiber 1.8g, Protein 1.5g

Chocolate Cheese Dream Pie

Two kinds of cheese blend in a delicious pie!

Makes 8 servings

Crust:
1 tablespoon plus 1½ teaspoons margarine, melted
1 tablespoon plus 1½ teaspoons honey
¾ cup graham cracker crumbs

Filling:
2 envelopes unflavored gelatin
1½ cups water
⅔ cup nonfat dry milk
⅔ cup low-fat (1%) cottage cheese
½ cup part-skim ricotta cheese
⅓ cup sugar
2 tablespoons plus 2 teaspoons cocoa (unsweetened)
2 teaspoons vanilla extract
1 teaspoon rum or almond extract
1 teaspoon chocolate extract
12 medium ice cubes

Preheat oven to 350°. Combine margarine and honey into a 9-inch pie pan. Add the graham cracker crumbs; mix until crumbs are moistened. Press crumbs into bottom and sides of pan to form a crust. Bake 5 minutes. Let crust cool completely.

Sprinkle gelatin over water in a small saucepan. Let soften a few minutes. Heat over low heat, stirring frequently, until gelatin is completely dissolved. In a blender, combine gelatin mixture with remaining ingredients except ice cubes. Blend until smooth. While continuing to blend, carefully add ice cubes, two at a time. Blend until mixture thickens. (You may need more or less ice cubes, depending on their size.) Spoon into cooled crust, discarding any remaining bits of ice. Chill.

Per Serving: Calories 182, Total Fat 4.6g, Cholesterol 8mg, Sodium 225mg, Total Carbohydrate 25.1g, Dietary Fiber 0.8g, Protein 10g

Strawberry Cream Pie

This luscious pie chills quickly thanks to the frozen strawberries, making it a great last-minute dessert.

Makes 8 servings

Crust:
1 tablespoon plus 1½ teaspoons margarine, melted
1 tablespoon plus 1½ teaspoons honey
¾ cup graham cracker crumbs

Filling:
1½ envelopes unflavored gelatin
¾ cup water
1½ cups part-skim ricotta cheese
¼ cup sugar
1½ teaspoons vanilla extract
¾ teaspoon strawberry extract
3 cups frozen strawberries, unsweetened (Do not thaw.)

Preheat oven to 350°. Combine margarine and honey in a 9-inch pie pan. Add graham cracker crumbs; mix until crumbs are moistened. Press crumbs into bottom and sides of pan to form a crust. Bake 5 minutes. Let crust cool completely.

Sprinkle gelatin over water in a small saucepan. Let soften a few minutes. Heat over low heat, stirring frequently, until gelatin is completely dissolved. In a blender, combine gelatin mixture with remaining filling ingredients *except* strawberries. Blend until smooth. Add strawberries. Blend, stopping blender to stir frequently, until berries are pureed and mixture is smooth. Spoon into crust. Chill.

Per Serving: Calories 192, Total Fat 6.6g, Cholesterol 14mg, Sodium 136mg, Total Carbohydrate 25.6g, Dietary Fiber 1.9g, Protein 7.3g

Strawberry-Topped Cheese Pie

This luscious, creamy pie is so pretty when fresh strawberries are in season. For another variation, you can also use blueberries, raspberries, or a combination of all three.

Makes 8 servings

Crust:
1 tablespoon plus 1½ teaspoons margarine, melted
1 tablespoon plus 1½ teaspoons honey
¾ cup graham cracker crumbs
¼ teaspoon ground cinnamon

Filling:
2 cups part-skim ricotta cheese
1 cup liquid egg substitute
½ cup sugar
1 tablespoon all-purpose flour
2 teaspoons vanilla extract

Topping:
1 cup orange juice
1 tablespoon plus 1 teaspoon cornstarch
1 tablespoon sugar
1 teaspoon strawberry extract
Few drops red food color (optional)
2 cups fresh strawberries, cut in half lengthwise

Preheat oven to 350°. Combine margarine and honey in a 9-inch pie pan. Add graham cracker crumbs and cinnamon; mix until crumbs are moistened. Press crumbs into bottom and sides of pan to form a crust. Bake 5 minutes. Increase oven temperature to 375°.

In a blender, combine all filling ingredients. Blend until smooth. Pour filling into crust. Bake 25 to 30 minutes, until filling is set.

In a small saucepan, combine orange juice, cornstarch, and sugar, stirring to dissolve cornstarch. Cook over medium heat, stirring constantly, until mixture comes to a boil. Continue to cook, stirring, for 1 minute. Remove from heat and stir in extract. Add food color if desired. Arrange strawberries over top of pie. Spoon glaze evenly over berries. Chill.

Per Serving: Calories 267, Total Fat 9g, Cholesterol 19mg, Sodium 206mg, Total Carbohydrate 34.7g, Dietary Fiber 1.2g, Protein 11.8g

Coconut Custard Cheese Pie

"Rich and delicious" is the only way to describe this heavenly pie!

Makes 8 servings

Crust:
1 tablespoon plus 1½ teaspoons margarine, melted
1 tablespoon plus 1½ teaspoons honey
¾ cup graham cracker crumbs

Filling:
2 cups part-skim ricotta cheese
1 cup liquid egg substitute
½ cup sugar
1 tablespoon all-purpose flour
2 teaspoons vanilla extract
1 teaspoon coconut extract
1 tablespoon shredded coconut (unsweetened)

Preheat oven to 350°. Combine margarine and honey in a 9-inch pie pan. Add graham cracker crumbs; mix until crumbs are moistened. Press crumbs into bottom and sides of pan to form a crust. Bake 5 minutes. Increase oven temperature to 375°.

In a blender, combine all filling ingredients except coconut. Blend until smooth. Stir in coconut. Pour filling into crust. Bake 25 to 30 minutes, until filling is set. Cool slightly, then chill.

Per Serving: Calories 241, Total Fat 9.9g, Cholesterol 19mg, Sodium 207mg, Total Carbohydrate 26.4g, Dietary Fiber 0.5g, Protein 11.5g

Apple Custard Squares

Served warm or cold, this is one of the tastiest fruit puddings. Using unpeeled apples adds more fiber to the dish, so unless the apple skins are especially tough, there's no need to peel them.

Makes 8 servings

⅓ cup Grape Nuts cereal, crushed (1½ ounces)
1 tablespoon plus 1 teaspoon margarine, melted
1 cup liquid egg substitute
1⅓ cups nonfat dry milk
3 tablespoons sugar
2 teaspoons vanilla extract
½ teaspoon ground cinnamon
⅛ teaspoon ground nutmeg
4 small, sweet apples (such as Golden Delicious), unpeeled, coarsely shredded

Preheat oven to 350°. Combine cereal and margarine in an 8-inch-square baking pan. Mix until cereal is moistened. Press crumbs lightly in bottom of pan, forming a thin crust. Bake 8 minutes.

In a large bowl, combine egg substitute, dry milk, sugar, vanilla, cinnamon, and nutmeg. Mix with a fork or wire whisk until blended. Stir in apples. Spoon mixture over baked crust. Gently press apples down into custard. Sprinkle with additional cinnamon. Bake 25 minutes, or until custard is set. Serve warm or cold.

Per Serving: Calories 188, Total Fat 3.3g, Cholesterol 4mg, Sodium 213mg, Total Carbohydrate 28g, Dietary Fiber 2g, Protein 11.6g

Cinnamon Raisin Cheese Squares

Guaranteed to be a hit, this rich dessert gets its flavor and moistness from two sweet, fruity ingredients—applesauce and orange juice concentrate. That's why it tastes so luscious yet is so low in fat.

Makes 8 servings

Crust:
2 tablespoons honey
2 teaspoons margarine, melted
⅔ cup Grape Nuts cereal (3 ounces)
¼ teaspoon ground cinnamon

Filling:
1⅔ cups low-fat (1%) cottage cheese
¾ cup liquid egg substitute
1 cup applesauce (unsweetened)
¼ cup sugar
2 tablespoons frozen orange juice concentrate, thawed
3 tablespoons all-purpose flour
½ teaspoon ground cinnamon
¼ teaspoon ground nutmeg
1½ teaspoons vanilla extract
¼ cup plus 2 tablespoons raisins

Preheat oven to 325°. In an 8-inch square baking pan, combine honey, margarine, Grape Nuts, and cinnamon. Mix until cereal is moistened. Press firmly in bottom of pan. Bake 10 minutes.

In a blender, combine all filling ingredients except raisins. Blend until smooth. Stir in raisins. Pour over crust. Bake, uncovered, 40 minutes, or until set. Cool slightly, then chill.

Per Serving: Calories 198, Total Fat 2.4g, Cholesterol 2mg, Sodium 303mg, Total Carbohydrate 33.6g, Dietary Fiber 1.7g, Protein 10.4g

Apple Crisp

Few can resist my apple crisp. The milk baked right into the topping adds a delectable flavor. This is a comfort food they'll love.

Makes 6 servings

Apples:
6 small, sweet apples, peeled, cored, and very thinly sliced
1 cup water
3 tablespoons sugar
2 teaspoons lemon juice
1 teaspoon vanilla extract
1 teaspoon ground cinnamon
⅛ teaspoon ground nutmeg
2 teaspoons cornstarch dissolved in 1 tablespoon water

Topping:
1 cup nonfat dry milk
1 cup Grape Nuts cereal (4½ ounces)
3 tablespoons sugar
1 teaspoon ground cinnamon
Dash ground nutmeg
3 tablespoons reduced-calorie margarine
2 tablespoons water

Preheat oven to 375°. Spray a 9-inch pie pan with nonstick cooking spray. Place apples in a large saucepan. Add water, sugar, lemon juice, vanilla, cinnamon, and nutmeg. Toss to combine. Bring to a boil over medium heat, stirring occasionally. Add cornstarch mixture. Cook, stirring constantly, until mixture has thickened and apples are slightly tender, about 5 minutes. Spoon apples into prepared pan.

In a medium bowl, combine all topping ingredients except water. Mix with a fork until milk and margarine are evenly distributed. Add water and mix well. Sprinkle topping evenly over apples. Bake, uncovered, 20 minutes, or until lightly browned. For best flavor, serve warm.

Per Serving: Calories 281, Total Fat 3.1g, Cholesterol 4mg, Sodium 265mg, Total Carbohydrate 54.1g, Dietary Fiber 3.9g, Protein 9.3g

Pineapple-Cranberry Crisp

This easy, colorful crisp is sweet yet tart with a deep, fruity flavor that's accented and brought to life by the almond extract.

Makes 8 servings

Fruit:
1 1-pound can whole-berry cranberry sauce
1 1-pound can pineapple tidbits (packed in juice), drained (Reserve 2 tablespoons of the juice.)
1 tablespoon sugar
½ teaspoon almond extract

Topping:
¾ cup rolled oats, uncooked (2¼ ounces)
3 tablespoons all-purpose flour
2 tablespoons sugar
½ teaspoon ground cinnamon
2 tablespoons canola oil

Preheat oven to 350°. Spray a 9-inch pie pan with nonstick cooking spray. In a large bowl, combine cranberry sauce, pineapple, sugar, and almond extract. Mix well. Place in prepared pan.

In another bowl, combine oats, flour, sugar, and cinnamon. Mix well. Add oil and reserved pineapple juice, mixing until all ingredients are moistened. Sprinkle evenly over cranberry mixture. Bake 30 minutes, or until lightly browned. Serve warm or cold.

Per Serving: Calories 216, Total Fat 4g, Cholesterol 0mg, Sodium 17mg, Total Carbohydrate 43.1g, Dietary Fiber 2.1g, Protein 1.8g

Blueberry Cobbler

You can use fresh or frozen berries for this popular favorite. If using frozen, be sure to buy the unsweetened ones and thaw them before using.

Makes 4 servings

2 cups blueberries
3 tablespoons sugar
2 teaspoons cornstarch
½ cup all-purpose flour
¼ cup whole wheat flour
1 teaspoon baking powder
1 tablespoon plus 1 teaspoon margarine
⅓ cup skim milk

Preheat oven to 375°. Spray a 1-quart baking dish with nonstick cooking spray. Place blueberries in a bowl. Add sugar and cornstarch and toss to coat berries. Place berries in prepared baking pan.

In a medium bowl, combine both types of flour and baking powder. Mix well. Add margarine. Mix with a fork or pastry blender until mixture resembles coarse crumbs. Stir in milk. Drop batter in 4 equal mounds onto blueberries. Bake 25 to 30 minutes, until lightly browned. Serve warm for best flavor.

Per Serving: Calories 210, Total Fat 4.3g, Cholesterol 0mg, Sodium 149mg, Total Carbohydrate 39.4g, Dietary Fiber 3.3g, Protein 3.8g

Cinnamon Roll-Ups

These rolled-up, cinnamon-filled pastries are finger-licking good!

Makes 8 servings (3 pastries each serving)

Pastry:
¾ cup all-purpose flour
⅓ cup low-fat (1%) cottage cheese
2 tablespoons sugar
2 tablespoons plus 2 teaspoons reduced-calorie margarine
1 teaspoon vanilla extract

Topping:
1 tablespoon plus 1 teaspoon sugar
½ teaspoon ground cinnamon

Preheat oven to 375°. Have a nonstick baking sheet ready. In a medium bowl, combine flour, cottage cheese, sugar, margarine, and vanilla. Mix with a fork until all ingredients are moistened. With your hands, work dough into a ball. Place dough on a lightly floured surface and roll into an 8 x 12-inch rectangle. Combine sugar and cinnamon for topping and sprinkle 1 tablespoon of the mixture evenly over the dough.

Starting with one long side, roll dough up tightly like a jelly roll. Using a sharp knife, cut dough crosswise into 24 slices, each ½-inch wide. Place rolls on baking sheet, cut-side down. Sprinkle rolls with remaining topping mixture. Bake 15 minutes, or until bottoms of rolls are lightly browned. Remove to a wire rack to cool. Serve warm or at room temperature.

Per Serving: Calories 82, Total Fat 1.5g, Cholesterol 0mg, Sodium 64mg, Total Carbohydrate 14.5g, Dietary Fiber 0.4g, Protein 2.4g

Pastry Crisps

Nice and crispy-crunchy, these cookies make a wonderful snack or accompaniment to any fruit dessert.

Makes 8 servings (about 5 crisps each serving)

Pastry:
1 cup plus 2 tablespoons all-purpose flour
Pinch salt
¼ teaspoon baking powder
¼ teaspoon baking soda
½ cup quick cooking oats, uncooked (1½ ounces)
3 tablespoons sugar
¼ cup margarine, melted
¼ cup plain nonfat yogurt

Topping:
1 tablespoon plus 1 teaspoon sugar
1 teaspoon ground cinnamon

Preheat oven to 400°. Have a nonstick baking sheet ready. Into a medium bowl, sift flour, salt, baking powder, and baking soda. Stir in oats and sugar. Add margarine and yogurt. Stir until well blended. Knead dough a few times until it holds together.

Roll dough between 2 sheets of wax paper into a rectangle ⅛-inch thick. Carefully remove top sheet of wax paper. Combine topping ingredients and sprinkle evenly over dough.

Cut dough into 1 x 3-inch strips and place on baking sheet. Bake 8 minutes, until golden. Remove crisps to a wire rack to cool.

Per Serving: Calories 165, Total Fat 6.2g, Cholesterol 0mg, Sodium 160mg, Total Carbohydrate 24.4g, Dietary Fiber 1.2g, Protein 3.1g

Shortbread Cookies

This is my delicious version of a traditional butter cookie. The butter flavor extract adds the butter flavor without all of the fat.

Makes 8 servings (3 cookies each serving)

¾ cup all-purpose flour
½ teaspoon baking powder
¼ cup reduced-calorie margarine
2 tablespoons sugar
2 teaspoons butter flavor extract

Preheat oven to 375°. Have a nonstick baking sheet ready. In a small bowl, combine flour and baking powder. Mix well. Add remaining ingredients and blend well with a fork to form a dough.

Work dough into a ball with your hands. Divide dough into 24 pieces and roll each into a ball. Place on baking sheet. Flatten each cookie to ¼-inch, using the bottom of a glass. Bake 10 minutes, until bottoms of cookies are lightly browned. Remove cookies to a wire rack to cool.

Per Serving: Calories 74, Total Fat 2.3g, Cholesterol 0mg, Sodium 68mg, Total Carbohydrate 12.1g, Dietary Fiber 0.3g, Protein 1.2g

Orange Cookies

For another delicious variation, these cookies can be made with lemon extract and grated lemon peel.

Makes 8 servings (3 cookies each serving)

¾ cup all-purpose flour
½ teaspoon baking powder
¼ cup reduced-calorie margarine
2 tablespoons sugar
1 teaspoon orange extract
½ teaspoon grated fresh orange peel

Preheat oven to 375°. Have a nonstick baking sheet ready. In a small bowl, combine the flour and baking powder. Mix well. Add remaining ingredients and blend well with a fork to form a dough.

Work dough into a ball with your hands. Divide dough into 24 pieces and roll each into a ball. Place on baking sheet. Flatten each cookie to ¼-inch using a fork, and make a crisscross pattern. Bake 10 minutes, until bottoms of cookies are lightly browned. Remove cookies to a wire rack to cool.

Per Serving: Calories 74, Total Fat 2.3g, Cholesterol 0mg, Sodium 68mg, Total Carbohydrate 12.1g, Dietary Fiber 0.3g, Protein 1.2g

Oatmeal Raisin Drops

An easy favorite without the fat of most oatmeal cookies, these chewy cookies are delicious warm. If you prefer crunchy cookies, freeze them and enjoy them right from the freezer.

Makes 6 servings (4 cookies each serving)

½ cup plus 1 tablespoon all-purpose flour
¾ cup rolled oats, uncooked (2¼ ounces)
½ teaspoon baking powder
½ teaspoon baking soda
¼ teaspoon ground cinnamon
⅓ cup firmly packed brown sugar
1 tablespoon margarine
¼ cup plus 2 tablespoons raisins
1 egg white
2 tablespoons apple juice
½ teaspoon vanilla extract

Preheat oven to 375°. Have a nonstick baking sheet ready. In a medium bowl, combine flour, oats, baking powder, baking soda, cinnamon, and brown sugar. Add margarine. Mix well with a fork until mixture is crumbly and margarine is completely incorporated into the crumbs. Stir in raisins. Add remaining ingredients, stirring until all ingredients are moistened.

Drop mixture by rounded teaspoonfuls onto baking sheet. Bake 10 to 12 minutes, until bottoms of cookies are lightly browned. Remove cookies to a wire rack to cool.

Per Serving: Calories 185, Total Fat 2.6g, Cholesterol 0mg, Sodium 171mg, Total Carbohydrate 36.6g, Dietary Fiber 1.9g, Protein 3.6g

Banana Drop Cookies

These soft, moist cookies are almost like little bites of banana cake.

Makes 4 servings (3 cookies each serving)

¼ cup rolled oats, uncooked (¾ ounce)
3 tablespoons all-purpose flour
¼ teaspoon baking powder
¼ teaspoon baking soda
½ medium, very ripe banana, mashed
1 tablespoon sugar
½ teaspoon vanilla extract
¼ teaspoon banana extract

Preheat oven to 375°. Have a nonstick baking sheet ready. In a small bowl, combine oats, flour, baking powder, and baking soda. Mix well. Add remaining ingredients and stir until blended. Drop mixture by rounded teaspoonfuls onto baking sheet. Bake 8 to 10 minutes, until bottoms of cookies are lightly browned.

Remove cookies to a wire rack to cool.

Per Serving: Calories 69, Total Fat 0.5g, Cholesterol 0mg, Sodium 102mg, Total Carbohydrate 14.5g, Dietary Fiber 1g, Protein 1.5g

Apple Chews

These soft, chewy cookies can be made so quickly. They're perfect for a snack and go so well with a cup of hot coffee or tea.

Makes 4 servings (5 cookies each serving)

¼ cup plus 2 tablespoons graham cracker crumbs
⅔ cup nonfat dry milk
1 tablespoon plus 1 teaspoon sugar
½ teaspoon baking powder
¼ teaspoon ground cinnamon
1 small, sweet apple, unpeeled, coarsely shredded
1 egg white
1 teaspoon vanilla extract

Preheat oven to 350°. Have a nonstick baking sheet ready. In a small bowl, combine graham cracker crumbs, dry milk, sugar, baking powder, and cinnamon. Mix well. Add remaining ingredients, mixing with a fork until well blended.

Drop mixture by rounded teaspoonfuls onto baking sheet. Bake 15 minutes, until bottoms of cookies are lightly browned. Remove cookies to a wire rack to cool.

Per Serving: Calories 145, Total Fat 1.1g, Cholesterol 4mg, Sodium 212mg, Total Carbohydrate 25.2g, Dietary Fiber 1.1g, Protein 8.7g

Chocolate-Raisin Peanut Butter Bars

These scrumptious candy bars are easy enough for children to make.

Makes 8 servings

⅔ cup nonfat dry milk
¼ cup water
2 tablespoons peanut butter (Choose one without added sugar or fat.)
1 tablespoon plus 2 teaspoons sugar
2 teaspoons cocoa (unsweetened)
1½ ounces non-sugarcoated breakfast cereal, such as corn or oat flakes, crushed slightly (1 cup)
2 tablespoons raisins

Have an ungreased 4 x 8-inch loaf pan ready. In a small bowl, combine dry milk, water, peanut butter, sugar, and cocoa. Mix well. Add cereal and raisins. Mix until cereal is coated with peanut butter mixture. Press mixture into bottom of pan. Place in freezer for at least 1 hour. Cut into 8 bars. Refrigerate leftovers.

Per Serving: Calories 103, Total Fat 2.3g, Cholesterol 2mg, Sodium 130mg, Total Carbohydrate 15.3g, Dietary Fiber 0.5g, Protein 5.1g

Marzipan

The almond extract makes this fat-free candy taste a lot like the real stuff.

Makes 4 candies

⅓ cup nonfat dry milk
1 tablespoon plus 1 teaspoon sugar
1½ teaspoons water
¼ teaspoon almond extract
¼ teaspoon vanilla extract
2 drops food color, any color (optional)

In a small bowl, combine all ingredients. Mix until all ingredients are moistened. Divide mixture evenly and shape into 4 balls. Place on a wax paper-lined plate. Cover and chill. Serve cold.

Each Candy Provides: Calories 53, Total Fat 0.1g, Cholesterol 2mg, Sodium 54mg, Total Carbohydrate 9.3g, Dietary Fiber 0g, Protein 3.6g

Rum Balls

These delightful morsels are a wonderful holiday treat. No one will believe they're so low in fat!

Makes 6 candies

⅓ cup nonfat dry milk
3 tablespoons graham cracker crumbs
2 tablespoons sugar
2 teaspoons cocoa (unsweetened)
½ teaspoon vanilla extract
¼ teaspoon rum extract
2¾ teaspoons water

In a small bowl, combine dry milk, graham cracker crumbs, sugar, and cocoa. Mix well. Add remaining ingredients. Mix until all ingredients are moistened. Divide mixture evenly and shape into 6 balls. Place on a plate. Cover and chill. Serve cold. For different taste treats, in place of the rum extract try ¼ teaspoon almond extract or ⅛ teaspoon peppermint extract.

Each Candy Provides: Calories 54, Total Fat 0.5g, Cholesterol 1mg, Sodium 52mg, Total Carbohydrate 10g, Dietary Fiber 0.3g, Protein 2.7g

Coconut Bon Bons

Normally, foods made with coconut are extremely high in fat. These candies, made with nonfat milk, are a delicious exception.

Makes 4 candies

⅓ cup nonfat dry milk
1 tablespoon plus 1 teaspoon sugar
2 teaspoons shredded coconut (unsweetened)
½ teaspoon coconut extract
¼ teaspoon vanilla extract
1½ teaspoons water

In a small bowl, combine all ingredients. Mix until all ingredients are moistened. Divide mixture evenly and shape into 4 balls. Place on a wax paper-lined plate. Cover and chill. Serve cold.

Each Candy Provides: Calories 67, Total Fat 1.5g, Cholesterol 2mg, Sodium 55mg, Total Carbohydrate 9.8g, Dietary Fiber 0.3g, Protein 3.7g

Notes:

Sauces and Toppings

Sauces can enhance even the simplest of foods. But all too often, these tasty additions add lots of unwanted calories and fat. Not so if you follow a few easy rules:

- Use low-sodium broth or reduced-sodium soy sauce as a base for sauces and marinades.
- Add spices to salt-free tomato sauce to create fat-free sauces for chicken and fish.
- Combine nonfat yogurt with herbs and spoon over cooked vegetables.
- Use nonfat yogurt in place of sour cream to top baked potatoes.
- Top angel food cake and pancakes with fruit toppings.
- Combine nonfat yogurt with fruit to make creamy sauces to top desserts.
- Use evaporated skim milk to replace cream in cream sauces.

Honey Mustard Sauce

Use this delicious sauce to top sliced chicken or turkey, served either hot or cold, and either plain or on a sandwich.

Makes ¾ cup

½ cup prepared yellow mustard
¼ cup honey
2 teaspoons reduced-sodium soy sauce

Combine all ingredients in a small bowl, mixing well. Serve right away or chill for later servings.

Each Tablespoon Provides: Calories 25, Total Fat 0g, Cholesterol 0mg, Sodium 150mg, Total Carbohydrate 5.9g, Dietary Fiber 0g, Protein 0.4g

Chili Orange Barbecue Sauce

This is a perfect sauce to brush on chicken or meat while broiling or grilling.

Makes ½ cup

¼ cup plus 2 tablespoons bottled chili sauce
2 tablespoons frozen orange juice concentrate, thawed
2 teaspoons vegetable oil

Combine all ingredients in a small bowl. Mix well.

Each Tablespoon Provides: Calories 29, Total Fat 1.1g, Cholesterol 0mg, Sodium 173mg, Total Carbohydrate 4.7g, Dietary Fiber 0g, Protein 0.1g

Apricot Brandy Sauce

Delicious on sliced chicken or turkey, this sauce can turn leftovers into an elegant meal.

Makes ¾ cup

½ cup water
2 teaspoons cornstarch
¼ cup fruit-only apricot spread
1 packet low-sodium instant chicken-flavored broth mix
1½ teaspoons brandy extract

Place water in a small saucepan. Add cornstarch, stirring until dissolved. Add remaining ingredients. Bring mixture to a boil over medium-low heat, stirring frequently. Continue to cook, stirring constantly, 2 minutes more. Serve hot.

Each Tablespoon Provides: Calories 16, Total Fat 0g, Cholesterol 0mg, Sodium 0mg, Total Carbohydrate 3.9g, Dietary Fiber 0g, Protein 0g

Orange "Butter"

Spread a little on baked sweet potatoes or on French toast or regular toast. It adds a wonderful flavor boost.

Makes ¼ cup

¼ cup reduced-calorie margarine
1½ teaspoons grated fresh orange peel
¾ teaspoon orange extract

Combine all ingredients in a small bowl or custard cup. Mix well. Serve right away or chill and use for later servings.

Each Tablespoon Provides: Calories 41, Total Fat 4.4g, Cholesterol 0mg, Sodium 90mg, Total Carbohydrate 0.2g, Dietary Fiber 0.1g, Protein 0g

Baked Potato Topper

Turn a baked potato into an elegant dish without adding fat. This simple mixture also doubles as a salad dressing, and the herbs can be varied to accommodate everyone's taste.

Makes 4 servings (¼ cup each serving)

1 cup plain nonfat yogurt or nonfat Greek yogurt
½ teaspoon dill weed
¼ teaspoon salt
⅛ teaspoon pepper
2 teaspoons imitation bacon bits
2 teaspoons dried chives

In a small bowl, combine yogurt, dill, salt, and pepper. Mix well. Chill. To serve, spoon ¼ cup of the yogurt on a baked potato. Sprinkle each potato with ½ teaspoon of the bacon bits and ½ teaspoon of the chives.

Per Serving: Calories 39, Total Fat 0.5g, Cholesterol 1mg, Sodium 216mg, Total Carbohydrate 4.9g, Dietary Fiber 0g, Protein 3.7g

Whipped Topping

Creamy, smooth, and glossy, here's an almost fat-free topping that you can make yourself. And you can flavor it any way you like by adding a few drops of your favorite extract. Try coconut, lemon, almond...

Makes 4 servings (¼ cup each serving)

½ teaspoon unflavored gelatin
¼ cup water
⅔ cup nonfat dry milk
2 tablespoons sugar
¾ teaspoon vanilla extract
Few drops any other extract (optional)
¼ cup ice water

Chill a medium bowl and the beaters from an electric mixer in the freezer for at least 30 minutes. Sprinkle gelatin over ¼ cup of water in a small saucepan. Heat over low heat until gelatin is completely dissolved. Remove bowl from freezer and place it in a large bowl of ice cubes.

In the chilled bowl, place dry milk, sugar, vanilla, optional extract, and ice water. Beat on low speed with electric mixer, gradually adding gelatin mixture. Increase speed to high and beat until soft peaks form. Chill in a covered container 10 to 15 minutes before serving.

Note: Topping will keep well in the refrigerator for 1 to 2 days.

Per Serving: Calories 97, Total Fat 0.2g, Cholesterol 4mg, Sodium 108mg, Total Carbohydrate 16.7g, Dietary Fiber 0g, Protein 7.4g

Raspberry Melba Sauce

A gourmet's delight, this versatile sauce can be served hot or cold over fruit, angel food cake, or vanilla low-fat frozen yogurt.

Makes 8 servings (2 tablespoons each serving)

1 10-ounce package frozen raspberries, in light syrup
3 tablespoons sugar
3 tablespoons water
1 tablespoon plus 1 teaspoon cornstarch*

In a small saucepan, combine raspberries, sugar, and 2 tablespoons of the water. Bring to a boil over medium heat. In a small bowl or custard cup, combine remaining water with cornstarch, stirring to dissolve cornstarch. Add to berries. Continue to cook, stirring constantly, 1 minute. Pour mixture through a strainer into a small bowl. Discard seeds. Serve sauce hot or cold.

*If you are going to serve this sauce cold, use only 1 tablespoon of cornstarch.

Per Serving: Calories 63, Total Fat 0.1g, Cholesterol 0mg, Sodium 0mg, Total Carbohydrate 15.2g, Dietary Fiber 1.6g, Protein 0.2g

Strawberry Yogurt Sauce

Great over fresh berries or fruit salad, this sauce can turn a simple fruit dish into a fancy dessert.

Makes 8 servings (¼ cup each serving)

1 cup vanilla nonfat yogurt or nonfat Greek yogurt
1 cup fresh or frozen (unsweetened) strawberries (If using frozen strawberries, thaw and drain them well.)
1 tablespoon sugar
1 teaspoon vanilla extract

In a blender, combine *half* of the yogurt with remaining ingredients. Blend until smooth. Stir in remaining yogurt. Chill thoroughly.

Per Serving: Calories 34, Total Fat 0.1g, Cholesterol 1mg, Sodium 17mg, Total Carbohydrate 7g, Dietary Fiber 0.4g, Protein 1.3g

Double Strawberry Sauce

You get a double dose of berries in this delectable, sweet sauce. Use it to top French toast, pancakes, fruit salad, low-fat ice cream, or angel food cake. It's so versatile.

Makes 4 servings (¼ cup each serving)

1 cup frozen strawberries (unsweetened), thawed and drained (Measure while still frozen.)
1 tablespoon fruit-only strawberry spread

Combine berries and fruit spread in a small bowl and mix well. Use right away or chill for later servings.

Per Serving: Calories 32, Total Fat 0.1g, Cholesterol 0mg, Sodium 1mg, Total Carbohydrate 7.5g, Dietary Fiber 1.2g, Protein 0.2g

Cinnamon Yogurt Sauce

Here's an easy mix to spoon over baked apples or cooked winter squash.

Makes 4 servings (¼ cup each serving)

1 cup vanilla nonfat yogurt
1 tablespoon firmly packed brown sugar
1 teaspoon ground cinnamon
1 teaspoon vanilla extract

In a small bowl, combine all ingredients, mixing well. Chill thoroughly.

Per Serving: Calories 57, Total Fat 0g, Cholesterol 2mg, Sodium 34mg, Total Carbohydrate 11.9g, Dietary Fiber 0.3g, Protein 2.3g

Hot Fudge Sauce

A practically fat-free hot fudge sauce? Fantastic! Spoon over low-fat ice cream or use as a luscious fondue for dipping fresh fruit.

Makes 8 servings (2 tablespoons each serving)

2 tablespoons cocoa (unsweetened)
1 tablespoon plus 1 teaspoon cornstarch
3 tablespoons sugar
1 cup evaporated skim milk
1 teaspoon vanilla extract

In a small saucepan, combine cocoa, cornstarch, and sugar. Mix well, pressing out all lumps with the back of a spoon. Gradually stir in evaporated milk, mixing until cornstarch and cocoa are dissolved. Bring to a boil over medium-low heat, stirring constantly. Continue to cook, stirring, 1 minute. Remove from heat and stir in vanilla. Serve hot.

Per Serving: Calories 55, Total Fat 0.3g, Cholesterol 1mg, Sodium 37mg, Total Carbohydrate 10.3g, Dietary Fiber 0.4g, Protein 2.7g

Chocolate Pineapple Sauce

Delicious, delicious, delicious! Serve over low-fat ice cream or on angel food cake and you've created an elegant dessert.

Makes 8 servings (2 tablespoons each serving)

⅔ cup nonfat dry milk
1 tablespoon plus 1 teaspoon cocoa (unsweetened)
1 tablespoon plus 1 teaspoon sugar
½ cup canned crushed pineapple (packed in juice), drained
(Reserve 2 tablespoons of the juice.)
1 teaspoon vanilla extract

In a small bowl, combine dry milk and cocoa. Mix well, pressing out any lumps with the back of a spoon. Add remaining ingredients and mix well. Chill several hours.

Per Serving: Calories 58, Total Fat 0.2g, Cholesterol 2mg, Sodium 54mg, Total Carbohydrate 10.2g, Dietary Fiber 0.4g, Protein 3.9g

Lemon Sauce

This delicate sauce is great to spoon over bread pudding, rice pudding, or noodle pudding.

Makes 1 cup

1 cup water
2 tablespoons plus 2 teaspoons sugar
1 tablespoon plus 1½ teaspoons lemon juice
1 tablespoon plus 1 teaspoon cornstarch
2 drops yellow food color

Combine all ingredients in a small saucepan. Stir until cornstarch is dissolved. Cook over medium heat, stirring constantly, until mixture comes to a boil. Continue to cook, stirring, 1 to 2 minutes. Serve hot.

Each Tablespoon Provides: Calories 11, Total Fat 0g, Cholesterol 0mg, Sodium 0mg, Total Carbohydrate 2.7g, Dietary Fiber 0g, Protein 0g

Index

C

J

Q

R

Z